MANAGEMENT, WORK AND ORGANISATIONS

Series editors: **Gibson Burrell**, Warwick Business School
Mick Marchington, Manchester School of Management, UMIST
Paul Thompson, Department of Human Resource Managment, University of Edinburgh

This series of new textbooks covers the areas of human resource management, employee relations, organisational behaviour and related business and management fields. Each text has been specially commissioned to be written by leading experts in a clear and accessible way. An important feature of the series is the international orientation. The titles will contain serious and challenging material, be analytical rather than prescriptive and be particularly suitable for use by students with no prior specialist knowledge.

The series is relevant for many business and management courses, including MBA and post-experience courses, specialist masters and postgraduate diplomas, professional courses and final-year undergraduate and related courses. The books will become essential reading at business and management schools worldwide.

Published

Paul Blyton and Peter Turnbull **The Dynamics of Employee Relations** (2nd edn)
J. Martin Corbett **Critical Cases in Organisational Behaviour**
Sue Ledwith and Fiona Colgan (eds) **Women in Organisations**
Karen Legge **Human Resource Management**
Stephen Procter and Frank Mueller (eds) **Teamworking**
Michael Rowlinson **Organisations and Institutions**
Harry Scarbrough (ed.) **The Management of Expertise**
Adrian Wilkinson, Mick Marchington, Tom Redman and Ed Snape
     Managing with Total Quality Management
Diana Winstanley and Jean Woodall (eds) **Ethical Issues in Contemporary Human Resource Management**

Forthcoming

Pippa Carter and Norman Jackson **Critical Issues in Organisational Behaviour**
Irena Grugulis **Training and Development**
Marek Korczynski **Human Resource Management in the Service Sector**
John Purcell and Peter Boxall **Managing People for Business Performance**
Helen Rainbird (ed.) **Training in the Workplace**
Jill Rubery and Damian Grimshaw **Employment Policy and Practice**
Hugh Scullion and Len Holden **International Human Resource Mangement**

Series Standing Order
If you would like to receive future titles in this series as they are published, you can make use of our standing order facility. To place a standing order please contact your bookseller or, in case of difficulty, write to us at the address below with your name and address and the name of the series. Please state with which title you wish to begin your standing order. (If you live outside the United Kingdom we may not have the rights for your area, in which case we will forward your order to the publisher concerned.)

Customer Services Department, Macmillan Distribution Ltd
Houndmills, Basingstoke, Hampshire RG21 6XS, England

D0413528

Other books by the authors include:

Core Personnel and Development
M. Marchington and A. Wilkinson

Managing Managers
E. Snape, T. Redman and G. Bamber

Making Quality Critical
A. Wilkinson and H. Willmott

Managing the Team
M. Marchington

Changing Patterns of Employee Relations
M. Marchington and P. Parker

MANAGING WITH TOTAL QUALITY MANAGEMENT

Theory and Practice

Adrian Wilkinson
Tom Redman
Ed Snape
and
Mick Marchington

MACMILLAN
Business

First published 1998 by
MACMILLAN PRESS LTD
Houndmills, Basingstoke, Hampshire RG21 6XS
and London
Companies and representatives
throughout the world

ISBN 0–333–62006–2 hardcover
ISBN 0–333–62007–0 paperback

A catalogue record for this book is available
from the British Library.

This book is printed on paper suitable for recycling and
made from fully managed and sustained forest sources.

10   9   8   7   6   5   4
07   06   05   04   03   02   01

Editing and origination by
Aardvark Editorial, Suffolk

Printed in China

Contents

List of Figures and Tables		vi
Acknowledgements		vii
1	Introduction	1
2	What Do We Mean by 'Quality' and 'TQM'?	7
3	The Origins and Development of TQM	17
4	TQM, Organisational Change and Human Resource Management	34
5	TQM in Practice	60
6	Citizens as Customers: the Politics of Quality in Local Government	88
7	Making TQM Work in a Tough Environment: British Steel Teesside Works	109
8	Fads and Fixes – Waving Goodbye to Quality in Financial Services?	125
9	Re-imaging Customer Service: the Management of Quality in Food Retailing	142
10	Pay, Rewards and Recognition: Managing Quality in a Small Firm	160
11	Conclusions: Whither TQM?	176
References		189
Index		207

List of Tables and Figures

Tables

3.1	Quality circles and TQM compared	25
4.1	From control to commitment: workforce strategies	38–40
4.2	TQM and the management of performance: two competing views	45
4.3	Employee involvement and TQM: contrasting perspectives	50
5.1	What two features of your product or service are most crucial for competitive success? Evidence from the 1990 Workplace Industrial Relations Survey	61
5.2	UK studies: summary	65
5.3	London Business School findings	66
5.4	What factors have led to recent changes in quality management in your organisation?	72
5.5	How is quality improvement measured in the organisation?	74
5.6	How would you rate the overall success of your quality management programme to date?	75
5.7	What effect has quality management had on each of the following?	76
5.8	To what extent has lack of commitment from the following groups been a difficulty in the implementation of quality management?	81
5.9	Difficulties faced by organisations in the improvement of quality	83
8.1	The building society movement and the 'new' building societies	127
8.2	Involving employees: the three phases of initiatives	131
8.3	National minimum service standards – branch achievements	135
8.4	Quality of service research – individual branch support	137
10.1	HR approach at Richer	169
10.2	Pay and customer service	171

Figures

4.1	The human resource management cycle	42
4.2	A model of commitment	48
4.3	The role of personnel in total quality management	53

Box 5.1	The PIMS research: relative perceived quality	62

Appendix 10.1	Customer questionnaire	174–5

Acknowledgements

This book draws on research projects undertaken over the last few years. We are grateful for funding and support from the Economic and Social Research Council, the Engineering and Physical Sciences Research Council, the Institute of Personnel and Development, the Employment Department, the Institute of Management and the European Foundation for Quality Management for their support during this period. Adrian Wilkinson is also grateful to Queensland University of Technology for appointing him as a Visiting Fellow at the Centre in Strategic Management.

We are grateful to the following publishers for allowing us to reproduce some material from our earlier published work: Industrial Relations Services, MCB University Press, Carfax Publications, Elsevier Press and the American Society of Quality Control. Various people, including Alan Tuckman and Ruth Holliday, have read parts of the manuscript and we thank them for their comments.

The authors and publishers wish to thank the following for permission to use copyright material: Harvard Business School Publishing for Table 1 from Walton, 'From Control to Commitment in the Workplace', *Harvard Business Review*, 63, pp. 77–84, March/April 1985; MCB University Press for Figure 2 from Oliver, 'Employee Commitment and Total Quality Control', *The International Journal of Quality and Reliability Management*, 7, No 1, pp. 21–9, 1990; John Wiley & Sons, Inc. for Figure 3.2 from Fombrun, Tichy and Devanna (eds.), *Strategic Human Resource Management*, 1984, p. 41.

Every effort has been made to trace all the copyright holders, but if any have been inadvertently overlooked, the publishers will be pleased to make the necessary arrangement at the first opportunity.

Ann Coldicott and Lisa Bourne helped in the word processing of the manuscript and Lisa Bourne also undertook the process of organising the authors. We would like to thank them for their efficiency. As usual, families make the major contribution and we thank them for their support. Finally, our thanks to the series editors, Paul Thompson and Gibson Burrell, and Stephen Rutt and Nicola Young at Macmillan for their patience.

To Jackie, Erin, Edwina, Rachel, Rosie, Lorrie, Jack and Lucy

CHAPTER 1

Introduction

Developments in product markets, technology and legislation have led employers to search for new strategies and structures. The saturation of mass markets, increasingly discerning and demanding customers, privatisation, deregulation and the rise of new competition, not least in East Asia, have combined to transform the competitive environment in recent years. In response, many companies are now focusing their products on niche markets, rather than selling standard mass produced goods. Product and service quality are high on the agenda for both private and public sector organisations, with quality certification and total quality management emerging as key concerns (Wilkinson, 1996). Some commentators interpret such developments as signalling the end of mass production and the rise of a new production paradigm based on 'flexible specialisation' (Piore and Sabel, 1984) or 'lean production' (Womack *et al.*, 1990). Under these conditions, enhanced product quality and greater responsiveness to customers are no longer merely options for management, but are essential if market share is to be retained, let alone developed. Peters and Waterman pointed to the importance of quality in *In Search of Excellence*:

> We usually think of principal barriers to entry as concrete and metal – the invest-ment cost of building the bellwether plant capacity addition. We have come to think, on the basis of the excellent companies data, however, that that's usually dead wrong. *The real barriers to entry are the 75-year investment in getting hundreds of thousands to live service, quality, and customer problem solving at IBM, or the 150-year invest-ment in quality at P&G.* These are the truly insuperable 'barriers to entry', based on people capital tied up in ironclad traditions of service, reliability and quality. (1982: 182)

The quest for quality is essentially a search for competitive advantage. According to Oakland, quality management is driven by the competitive environment and is universal in its appeal:

Whatever type of organisation you work in – a hospital, a university, a bank, an insurance company, local government, an airline, a factory – competition is rife: competition for customers, for students, for patients, for resources, for funds. There are very few people around in most types of organization who remain to be convinced that quality is the most important of the competitive weapons. If you doubt that, just look at the way some organisations, even whole industries in certain countries have used quality to take the heads off their competitors. (Oakland, 1993: 3)

Employers' concerns with quality are nothing new, but the notion that quality is the *key* to competitive advantage is quite a recent development. As Lillrank and Kano (1989) point out, in his seminal work on *Competitive Advantage,* Porter (1980) does not even include the word 'quality' in his subject index. Oakland argues that after the industrial revolution of the nineteenth century, and the computing revolution of the early 1980s, 'we are now, without doubt in the midst of the quality revolution' (1989: x).

Survey evidence points to the spread of quality management initiatives, including what has become known as Total Quality Management (TQM) (see, for example, Binney, 1992; Cruise O'Brien and Voss, 1992; Witcher and Whyte, 1992; Witcher, 1993). TQM is widely regarded as the major innovation in management practice of the late 1980s and 1990s, and has been hailed as a 'thought revolution' in management (Ishikawa, 1985: 1). By the early 1990s, quality management appeared to be more well developed in production industries than in services or the public sector, but even here new initiatives were being implemented (Wilkinson *et al.,* 1993).

Total Quality Management (TQM)

The central concern of this book is Total Quality Management (TQM). Arguably, this epitomises recent developments in quality management and represents the most coherent and advanced approach in the area of quality. We see TQM not in a narrow sense, for example ordering the principles and practice of quality management, but in relation to the organisational and environmental context in which it is located. This brings in considerations of organisational culture and structure, of employee relations and the balance of power between management and employees, and the role of human resource management (HRM). While there is debate about the exact nature of TQM, and while various definitions and approaches have been espoused, there are a number of common themes (see Chapter 2 for a more detailed discussion of the concept of quality and TQM).

First, quality can be defined as '**fitness for use**', including both quality of design (how a customer's requirements are translated into a set of specifica-tions) and conformance to the design (how an operation conforms to the specification of the design standard). Second, quality management emphasises not only the external customer but also the **internal customer**. Thus the concept of a quality chain is central, with every member of the organisation linked ultimately to the final customer via a series of internal customer – supplier relationships, each of which can be evaluated in quality terms. The chain can be broken at any point by one person or piece of equipment not meeting the requirements of the customer (internal or external), and this failure usually finds its way to the interface with external customers. Third, the aim of TQM is to have quality '**built in**' rather than inspected. Quality becomes the responsibility of all employees rather than of a specialist department. Associated with this is the notion that prevention rather than detection is the key with 'continuous improvement' as the ultimate goal (Juran, 1989) Fourth, rather than assuming that quality improvements necessarily lead to increased costs, TQM is held to actually result in cost savings by doing things '**right first time**'. Finally, management is charged with ultimate responsibility for quality because 85 per cent of failures are reckoned to be the fault of inadequate management systems.

TQM has evolved from its engineering origins and its primary association with tools and techniques. In the 1980s it was taken up as a general management philosophy concerned with the attainment of continuous improvement in all processes by all staff; hence the notion of 'totality'. For the most part, however, the principal contributions to the analysis of TQM have come from people in the Production and Operations Management area. Given these backgrounds, the leading gurus sought to develop seemingly objective means of gaining 'hard' information about processes of production and service delivery (for example, Wood, 1994).

Less consideration, however, has been given to the issue of winning employee commitment to the TQM philosophy of continuous improvement (Wilkinson, 1992). To a large extent this reflects a preoccupation with the so-called 'hard' production-oriented aspects of TQM and a relative neglect of human resource considerations which are often referred to as the 'soft' factors. These include issues relating to supervisory styles, compensation/payment systems, employee involvement and teamworking, employee responses, and the interactions between different managerial functions and organisational culture. There is a need for a more critical appraisal of TQM, considering much more explicitly the way in which employees perceive it in practice, and taking in questions of 'who gains what' from TQM.

TQM and HRM

Most writers on TQM (such as Crosby, 1979; Ishikawa, 1985) agree that its success is dependent on a people orientation, illustrated through initiatives such as teamworking, training and development, employee involvement (EI) and participation (Dale and Cooper, 1992). Apart from **assumptions** that these are essential to the success of TQM (for example, Juran, 1964; Deming, 1986;

Aubrey and Felkins, 1988), there is little discussion on how the people side of TQM should be developed. Both academic and business-led research tends to mirror this. Most work *asserts* the importance of human resource issues, but does not go beyond general references to a need for more training, enhanced motivation and changed cultures (Wilkinson, 1994). In other words, many of these writers, although formally recognising the importance of utilising human resources, largely ignore it in practice. However, there is clear evidence that TQM has often failed to fulfil its promise, and reports suggest this might be due to a lack of attention to such HRM issues (see, for example, Binney, 1992; Cruise O'Brien and Voss, 1992; Kearney, 1992; Miller, 1992; Wilkinson *et al.*, 1993).

It is important to appreciate that different versions of TQM *and* its implications for HRM are likely to be evident in different sectors. There is also the issue of 'fit' between TQM, business strategy, and the company's competitive situation. Quality gurus have tended to adopt a 'universalistic' approach to TQM, assuming that it is a fixed entity which can be applied to any company in any set of circumstances. Recent research, especially in the USA, has started to examine this assumption critically. Companies producing innovative products in a niche market are likely to adopt a different approach to TQM from mass producers in highly competitive markets. Similarly, companies which are struggling financially are likely to adopt a more cost-driven systems approach to TQM than those whose products are sold on the basis of high added value. Increasingly, the business strategy literature has debated the role that TQM can play in the organisational quest for competitive advantage, an issue to which we now turn.

TQM and competitive advantage

TQM has often been associated with so-called 'high road'/'differentiation' as opposed to 'low road'/'cost leadership' business strategies. High road companies compete on the basis of quality, variety and service, whilst low road companies compete on the basis of cost. Successful pursuit of either approach is said to yield high profits, in the case of differentiation through the ability to charge premium prices, under cost leadership because of lower-than-average costs whilst charging the market price (Porter, 1980, 1985).

Business strategy writers have often suggested that companies must make a definitive choice of strategy. Porter, for example, posits alternative strategic positions: differentiation, cost leadership and focus (Porter, 1980, 1985). To be successful, it is argued, an organisation must, with few exceptions, choose between these strategies. Firms with multiple goals are claimed to perform less well than firms with a single goal and such an approach is seen as a recipe for mediocrity. A hybrid strategy runs the risk of being 'stuck in the middle' and forces compromises in key strategic choices, resulting in sub-optimal performance. In part, this derives from the lack of strategic clarity and blurring of competitive advantage that follows from the adoption of multiple objectives. Of particular interest here is the claim that it is almost always necessary to choose between cost reduction and product differentiation/ quality strategies.

In fact, the quality management literature suggests that organisations do not necessarily face such a straight choice between high quality and low costs. The pre-TQM conception was of an either-or link between quality and cost, with a trade-off between the two, so that there was a clear choice between high quality and premium price on the one hand, and low costs on the other. However, the new orthodoxy of the TQM literature is that quality improvements may actually *reduce* costs due to lower failure rates, warranty costs, returned goods and costs of detection. One US study estimates that the typical factory spends between 20 and 50 per cent of its operating budget finding and fixing mistakes, with as many as a quarter of all employees occupied by rework (Eureka and Ryan, 1988). Oakland (1993) argues that such efforts merit the title of the 'hidden factory'. Estimates vary for the cost savings to be accrued from implementing TQM – from Oakland's (1993) rule of thumb of a third of operating costs, to as high as a half in the service sector (Atkinson, 1990).

Thus, whilst TQM has been associated with premium-price, differentiation strategies, rather than with cost leadership, it is by no means clear that quality is achieved only at the expense of higher costs. If this is correct, if higher quality can indeed be secured along with reduced costs, it implies that TQM is a necessity rather than a strategic option, since what would be the basis for competitive advantage in the absence of TQM? Indeed, whilst in the 1980s, many writers declared that quality management was the key to competitive advantage (Dale, 1994b), by the 1990s we are being told that quality is being replaced by flexibility and quick response, particularly as customers demand greater product choice (Deloitte and Touche, 1992). Some now argue that TQM is essentially an enabling strategy, which facilitates the search for competitive advantage through market strategies and technological innovation, once their competitive position is no longer hindered by poor quality products (Madu and Kuei, 1993). Furthermore, high quality organisations are argued to have the potential to adopt a wider variety of strategic options than those with low quality (Belohlav, 1993). According to this view, TQM is a necessary but no longer a sufficient condition for sustainable advantage.

Clearly, there is considerable debate about the contribution of quality and TQM to competitive advantage. Whether high quality is regarded as a necessary or a sufficient condition for success is an issue which will be explored further later; reality may well lie somewhere between these two views. It is highly likely that quality management's contribution to competitive advantage was talked up in the euphoria of its rapid adoption in Western economies in the late 1980s. Equally, its critics in the 1990s may be writing its obituaries too soon.

Outline of the book

'Quality' has been attributed to many types of management techniques and initiatives. Indeed the appeal of 'quality' is that it can be used to legitimise all sorts of measures and changes. The diverse and fluid meanings ascribed to quality initiatives, however, make it a seductive philosophy of management (Pfeffer and Coote, 1991) and an elusive topic of study. This partly explains why there are so many books that champion the cause of quality management or TQM (for example, Oakland, 1989, 1993; Bank, 1992; Drummond, 1992; Evans and Lindsay, 1993; Dale, 1994b), but comparatively few studies that examine it critically. Studies that begin to offer a more detached and reflective consideration of its claims have been the exception (Dawson and Palmer, 1994; Witcher, 1995; Kirkpatrick and Martinez-Lucio, 1995; Wilkinson and Willmott, 1995a, b; Webb, 1996). This book is intended to provide a more critical perspective for students, managers and other employees with an interest in the nature and effects of quality initiatives.

In short, our aim is to analyse the TQM concept, to account for its popularity, and to evaluate its effectiveness to date. To these ends, we review the large body of prescriptive, theoretical and empirical literature on TQM, summarise some of our own research on the topic, and present detailed case studies of quality management initiatives in UK organisations. The case studies, which are drawn from manufacturing and services and from the private and public sectors, form the core of the book. They present an evaluation of the rationales and effectiveness of TQM in those different organisations, and provide critical insights into the practice of quality management in a variety of contexts and over a period of time. Many TQM initiatives began in the late 1980s but, given the view that they take a long time to embed into the organisation, it seems appropriate to evaluate initiatives which have been ongoing for some time. Therefore it seems appropriate to look back at the last decade of quality management to analyse where the journey has taken us, and the issues and themes which have become apparent over time.

The structure of the book is as follows. In Chapter 2 we lay the basis for the remainder of the book by discussing the key concepts of 'quality' and 'total quality management' in detail. Chapter 3 traces the historical development of quality management, from the work of the early US quality 'gurus', through the application and development of their ideas in Japan, to the more recent quality management debates in the West. Chapter 4 then examines the organisational and HRM implications of quality management in detail, highlighting the central role of these, and also reviews the role of the personnel function. The book then moves on to consider the evidence on the implementation and effectiveness of quality management initiatives, firstly through a review of the existing empirical studies (Chapter 5) and then by presenting the case studies (Chapters 6 to 10). The concluding chapter then provides an overview of the findings and considers the way forward in light of recent innovations such as business process re-engineering.

CHAPTER 2

What do we Mean by 'Quality' and 'TQM'?

Introduction

In this chapter, we examine in detail our two central concepts: 'quality' and 'TQM'. The aim is to define these in as rigorous a way as possible, drawing on the practitioner and academic literature. As we shall see, the concepts are complex and the definitions are in themselves important. The danger is that TQM has been subjected to a somewhat premature evaluation by many writers, on the basis of incomplete definitions. For example, few studies aiming to evaluate its success have actually assessed the extent to which it has been implemented (Hackman and Wageman, 1995). In order to make a broader assessment we need first to rigorously define the concepts.

What is quality?

A simple question; but is there a simple answer? In fact, quality has proved to be a difficult concept to pin down. What is even more surprising is that despite the volume of writing on quality management, there has been only limited attention paid to defining exactly what is meant by the term 'quality'. This is important, not least because the lack of a clear definition makes it difficult to evaluate the effects of quality management on business outcomes (Reeves and Bednar, 1994). In part, at least, the neglect of defining quality stems from the difficulty in doing so. According to Garvin:

> Quality is an unusually slippery concept, easy to visualise and yet exasperatingly difficult to define. (1988: xi)

The word 'quality' normally conveys notions of nebulous factors that are not readily measured or tied down. Arguably, these vague but nonetheless positive associations make the appeal of 'quality' immediate and extensive. Who can be against quality? Quality conveys a positive connotation to whatever it is applied. Thus:

> Quality can be a compelling value in its own right. It is robust enough to pertain to products, innovations, service standards, and calibre of people… .Everyone at every level can do something about it and feel the satisfaction of having made a difference. Making products that work, or providing first class service is something we can identify with from our own experience. (Pascale, 1991: 248)

A wide variety of approaches to defining quality are evident. For example, quality has been defined as being about value (Feigenbaum, 1983); conformance to standards, specifications or requirements (for example, Crosby, 1979); fitness for use (Juran, 1989); quality as excellence (Peters and Waterman, 1982); meeting or exceeding and customer expectations (Parasuraman *et al.*, 1985) and more prosaically as 'delighting the customer' (Peters, 1989).

Each approach to defining quality has strengths in terms of generalisability, ease of measurement and utility. Thus, the 'quality as conformance to standards' approach is more relevant in a manufacturing environment than in a high-contact personal service industry and is of great value in emphasising efficiency and productivity. 'Quality as excellence' is seen as particularly valuable as a motivational device in the general call to arms in a quality management campaign. Employees, it is argued, can take pride in working for an organisation whose vision and mission statements emphasise being the best.

Each approach also has its weaknesses (Reeves and Bednar, 1994). Thus, a quality vision to 'conform to standards every time' is unlikely to be as effective as 'quality as excellence' in winning employee commitment to quality. 'Quality as excellence', however, is very difficult to measure or operationalise; 'quality as conformance' tends to have an internal focus and customers' views can thus be neglected; whilst 'quality as meeting customer expectations' is often plagued by complexity, difficulty and cost in measurement.

In terms of TQM, however, it is essential to appreciate that the quality gurus' conception of quality is meeting reliable and consistent standards in line with customer requirements; standards which may or may not be usually identified as exceptionally high but which nevertheless represent what customers say they want.

It is the latter which is at the heart of TQM, and which results in the notion of the customer-driven organisation. Quality is judged by the user rather than the producer. A variation on this theme is Juran's fitness for use: to take an extreme example, a useless product, such as a concrete parachute, could meet all the manufacturer's specifications and yet not be fit for use. Clearly, this definition may encompass the definitions referred to earlier, but the key points are that quality is not to be confused with 'excellence' or luxury, and that it is to be defined in terms of customer wants. This is the reasoning behind Crosby's view (1979) that quality is conformance to requirements, not elegance, or goodness or luxury or skinniness or weight. The Rolls Royce and the Mini, the Steinway and the Yamaha can all be 'quality' products.

Kordupleski *et al.* (1993) proposes that it would help in the understanding of quality if we differentiate between customer-perceived quality, which they term 'true quality' and business process quality, which they term 'internal quality'. This differentiation would then point up the internally focused nature of many quality management programme offerings and show the need for paying more attention to 'true quality', and hence a more outward looking role. Success in quality management is seen as deriving from linking up both aspects of quality. Further, there may be a danger of excessive internal focus in calling everyone a customer; this is something that is not unusual in typical TQM speak. Here the problem in regarding employees as internal customers is again that the 'real' customer, that is the one who pays for the service, can be overlooked.

What is TQM?

As with many new management approaches, theory development in TQM has taken a backseat to the prescriptive frameworks of management consultants and popular management writers. The development of TQM theory has, however, much to offer both the management academic as well as the practising manager. For example, for the manager a more soundly developed TQM theory base could start to explain why some TQM initiatives fail yet others succeed, and whether, and under what conditions TQM can lead to competitive advantage. For the academic community TQM provides a valuable test-bed for many key areas of management theory such as leadership, strategy, and employee involvement (Dean and Bowen, 1994). In this section we review the extant literature on TQM theory and in so doing attempt to provide a working definition of the concept.

TQM is not an approach or philosophy of management which is self-evident. Even Deming claimed that he did not know what the term meant (Boje, 1993). There are a number of reasons for this high level of ambiguity. First, as we have seen, there are definitional problems associated with the concept of quality itself. Second, the wide variety of activities, practices and techniques that are carried out under the rubric of TQM makes it difficult to maintain a clear conception of what the term means. For example Knutton (1994) claims that although the aims of introducing TQM are similar between organisations, it takes on a different guise in each adoption. In Chapter 4 we examine the survey evidence on the practice of TQM and discover that the label is often very loosely used. According to Dean and Bowen TQM 'has come to function as a sort of Rorschach test, to which peoples' reactions vary as a function of their own beliefs and experiences' (1994: 394).

Thus, the meaning of TQM has been attached to a multitude of diverse practices and often unrelated organisational change activities. However, as Wilkinson and Willmott (1995a: 7) note, 'far from being viewed as a difficulty for the coherence and credibility of quality management, this is embraced by some as its principal virtue':

> It sometimes seems unfortunate that there are so many different interpretations of quality. But by being amenable to wide and differing interpretations it remains appropriate in widely differing situations and circumstances. Thus it has a unifying effect in that all genuine aspirations to improve quality are known to be moving in the same direction. The total quality image is the sum of a set of attributes, each of which has its own quality criteria. (Dale and Plunkett, 1990: 346)

Bearing this in mind, what kinds of definitions have been suggested? One approach is to look at the TQM buzzwords. 'Zero defects' (Crosby), 'right first time' (Crosby), 'plan do check action' (Deming), 'fitness for use' (Juran); these and others are now prominent in the management vocabulary. This does not take us very far, however, because each one reflects the concerns of the partic- ular quality guru with which it is associated, without necessarily providing a coherent overview of TQM. This might not be too important if we accept Oakland's view that whilst gurus seem to 'present different solutions to the problems of quality management and control, in reality they are all talking the same "language" but they use different dialects' (1989: xi). Indeed, Hackman and Wageman's (1995) analysis of the convergent validity of the gurus' views on what constitutes TQM – that is, the extent to which the different versions of TQM share a common set of assumptions and prescriptions – finds that it passes such a test.

The Hackman and Wageman analysis also subjects TQM to a discriminant validity test, examining to what extent the TQM philosophy can be distin- guished from other organisational improvement strategies. Again TQM is found largely to pass such a test and be conceptually different from such change strategies as participative management, quality of working life (QWL), job- enrichment and job re-design programmes. We would argue, however, that it goes deeper than this; a distinction also needs to be made between TQM and other programmes such as 'quality control' and 'quality assurance' for a discrim- inant validity test to be fully satisfied.

Quality control is the control of quality both during an operational process and at the post-process stage. Its characteristics are containment and inspec- tion. Quality assurance is usually in the hands of a specialist department, and quality is seen as a business function in its own right. TQM includes the application of quality assurance to every company activity and is characterised by the application of good practice quality management principles, practices and techniques. TQM is often seen as a general business management philosophy, which is about the attainment of continuously improving customer satisfaction by quality-led company-wide management. This goes beyond the mere application of total quality ideas to the whole organisation and its management by any one business function, to being a new approach to corporate management itself. Quality becomes a way of life which permeates every part and aspect of the organisation (Wilkinson and Witcher, 1991: 44–5).

Dean and Bowen's (1994) review of the TQM literature suggests that its key principles are customer focus, continuous improvement and teamwork. Each of these principles is then implemented through a series of practices, such as collecting customer information and analysing processes, supported by the use of specific quality management techniques such as team-building and Pareto analysis. Raffio (1992) adds employee involvement and senior management commitment to these as the 'basic principles' of TQM, whilst Hart and Bogan (1992) identify TQM's distinctive features as a strong and pervasive customer orientation and an approach of managing quality for competitive advantage. Others emphasise TQM as culture change (Caudron, 1993). Powell (1995), combining the features promoted by Deming, Juran, Crosby and the American Baldrige Awards, comes up with twelve factors: committed leadership, adaption and communication of TQM, closer customer relationships, closer supplier relationships, benchmarking, increased training, open organisation, employee empowerment, zero-defects mentality, flexible manufacturing, process improvement and measurement. The problem with this approach is that it is something of an ideal type, and provides a template that few organisations could match.

The British Quality Association (BQA) offered three alternative definitions of TQM. The first focuses on the so called 'soft' qualitative characteristics, found in the work of US consultants such as Tom Peters and involving such themes as customer orientation, culture of excellence, removal of performance barriers, teamwork, training and employee participation. From this perspective, TQM is seen as consistent with open management styles, delegated responsibility and increased autonomy to staff. A typical definition in this vein would be that of Evans and Lindsay who see TQM as an 'integrative management concept for continuously improving the quality of goods and services delivered through the participation of all levels and functions' (1993: 28).

The second BQA definition emphasises the production aspects such as systematic measurement and control of work, setting standards of performance and using statistical procedures to assess quality. This is the 'hard' production/operations management type of view, which arguably involves less discretion for employees. A typical definition in this mode is that of Steingard and Fitzgibbons (1993) who define TQM as a 'set of techniques and procedures used to reduce or eliminate variation from a production process, or service delivery system in order to improve efficiency, reliability and quality'. The third definition is a mixture of 'hard' and 'soft', comprising three features: an obsession with quality; the need for a scientific approach; and the view that all employees are to be involved in this process (see Wilkinson *et al.*, 1992).

The leading UK proponents of TQM come from the operations management field and thus offer variants of the 'hard' or mixed approaches. Oakland defines TQM as 'a way of managing to improve the effectiveness, flexibility and competitiveness of the business as a whole' (1989: 2–3), meeting customer requirements both external and internal to the organisation. TQM is conceptualised in the form of a triangle, with the three points representing 'management commitment', 'statistical process control' and 'teamworking', and as a chain, indicating the interdependence of customer–supplier links throughout the organisation. The concept of a quality chain is central to Oakland's view of TQM. His concern is that the chain can be broken at any point by one person or piece of equipment not meeting the requirements on the way to the interface with external customers. By focusing on internal customer expectations all along the supply chain to the final customer in the market place, one is meant to build up an internal customer environment ('market-in' rather than 'product-out'). At the apex of Oakland's TQM model is senior management commitment. TQM proponents are united in agreement that a number of principles must be adopted, and be seen to be endorsed by top management. Senior management are the role models and must be seen actively to participate and promote by example quality ideas; they should also establish a quality infrastructure that seeks to ensure that quality and its organisation are built into the mainstream of planning and everyday activity of the organisation.

TQM has become the most celebrated form of quality management, in part because it is based on a common set of principles. Thus, whilst varying definitions and approaches are espoused, and whilst a single, clear definition of TQM has proved elusive, there are a number of basic principles underlying TQM as a generic approach to the management of organisations which draws from the work of Crosby (1979), Feigenbaum (1983), Ishikawa (1985), Deming (1986), and Juran (1989). As identified by Hill and Wilkinson (1995), these principles are:

1. *Customer orientation.* Quality means meeting customer requirements; customers are both external and internal, and the orientation of quality management is to satisfy customers. This customer orientation provides a common goal for all organisational activities and members, and incorporates both quality of design and conformance to quality specification.

    A customer's requirements must be translated into a design or set of specifications, so that the activities needed to produce the required product or service can be brought together. Thus, it is the customer's definition that is required, not one from an operations perspective. No matter how much production processes are improved and waste is eliminated, these are of little benefit unless the customer wishes to buy the product: a product cannot do more than it was designed to do.

Conformance to quality specification is simply how an operation or process *conforms to the specifications of the design standard.* This is where the traditional approach to quality has focused. Both design and conformance are important, and reliance on simply one aspect is inadequate. One could have the right quality of design, a product which customers wish to buy, but lose money because of poor conformance to quality specification. Alternatively, conformance to quality specification could be excellent, zero defects being achieved, but the product may not meet customer requirements.

2. *Process orientation.* The activities performed within an organisation can be broken down into basic tasks or processes (transformations of inputs into outputs). Basic processes are linked in series or 'quality chains' to form extended processes. The production process, for example, is modelled as an extended chain of interlinked basic processes. Quality management emphasises not only the external but also the internal customer, stemming from Ishikawa's view that the 'next process is our customer'. Organisations may be conceptualised as quality chains that cut across conventional internal boundaries such as functional specialisms (Oakland, 1993). Each process in the quality chain also has a customer, stretching back from the external customer through the various internal customers to the start of the series. In this way, TQM attempts to emphasise that all employees are ultimately involved in serving the final customer, so that quality matters at all stages, whilst teamwork and cooperation are essential. Thus the customer focus identified above is a means of unifying processes as well as determining the objective of organisational activities (Grant *et al.*, 1994).

3. <u>*Continuous improvement*</u>. Satisfying customer requirements involves the continuous improvement of products and processes. The most effective means of improvement is to use the people who do the job to identify and implement appropriate changes. There is an emphasis on 'kaizen', or 'improvement' (Imai, 1986). This means continuous improvement through incremental changes to the *status quo*. Kaizen involves both innovation and maintenance, and improvement through small steps, albeit often leading to radical breakthrough. However, the aim of involving all workers in continuous improvement in no way detracts from the view that management is ultimately responsible for designing the system. The role of the workforce is to assist in '… weeding out the last bugs from a product and process whilst giving workers an uplifting opportunity to use their brains and make a contribution to the improvement of their companies' (Lillrank and Kano, 1989: 29).

These principles are implemented in a specific manner and the mode of implementation is itself one defining feature of TQM. Implementation is by means of appropriate improvement tools, measurement systems, and management and organisational processes.

Improvement tools. These embrace statistical process control methods, to be used by all employees, process simplification and process re-engineering.

Measurement systems. Monitoring the cost of quality and customer satisfaction are novel metrics of TQM, and are supplementary to the more traditional measurement of defects or variation. Cost of quality is a financial measure of quality performance. Juran's view was that, to get to top management attention one had to speak the managerial language – hence the concept of the cost of quality to demonstrate the bottom line impact of TQM. Juran referred to the avoidable costs of quality as 'gold in the mine' (1951). The principle is simple: quality does not cost money, poor quality does, hence Crosby's notion of quality being free. Costs to be reduced are:

- prevention costs – checking and testing incoming components, auditing output, routine maintenance.
- failure costs – waste, scrap, rework, liability claims.
- appraisal costs – inspection, supplier surveillance, auditing activities.

However, there are costs, for example poor reputation and poor morale, which are more difficult to measure. A key point is that quality improvements need not necessarily lead to increased costs; rather, costs may actually fall because of a decline in failure rates, warranty costs, returned goods, and the costs of detection.

Organisational approaches. These include quality improvement or action teams, quality committees, cross-functional planning, self-inspection, exposure of employees to customers, more autonomous work units, and collaborative quality improvement with suppliers. At the apex of the organisation, quality planning is a component of strategic corporate management; while policy deployment ensures that quality policies at every level of the organisation, right down to the appraisal of individual members of staff, derive from and are congruent with the corporate plan. The new organisational infrastructure is seen as a necessary condition for TQM: it both enables the operation of total quality management and ensures its continued survival (Hill and Wilkinson 1995: 8–9).

'Hard' and 'Soft' aspects of TQM

Having discussed what is meant by TQM, in this section we look in more detail at two aspects of TQM, the so-called 'hard' and 'soft' aspects. The former, reflecting the production orientation of the quality 'gurus', emphasises systems, data collection and measurement. It involves a range of production techniques, including statistical process control, changes in the layout, design processes and procedures of the organisation, and use of the seven basic TQM tools used to interpret data (process flow charting, tally charts, pareto analysis, scatter diagrams, histograms, control charts and cause and effect analysis). The design process can also be improved by the seven new tools: the affinity diagram, relationship diagram, tree diagram, matrix chart, matrix data analysis, process decision program chart and arrow diagram. These new tools are often collectively referred to as quality function deployment (QFD). Other techniques include failure mode, effect and criticality analysis (FMECA), which studies potential failures to determine their effects and is often used at the design stage. TQM is based on the premise that all activities in a firm contribute to quality. Oakland (1989) emphasises the central importance of documented systems. Thus, it is important that a firm's activities and procedures are documented so that their effects on quality are understood by everybody. 1S09000 series establishes the methods by which a management system can be drawn up.

The soft side of TQM gets a good deal less attention. Thus:

> While solutions to the technical issues of designing appropriate systems and procedures are fully specified, there are lacunae in the treatment of the social factors. (Hill, 1991a: 556)

Clearly, such factors are likely to be critical, given the assertion that 'quality is everyone's business' and as firms are urged to move away from supervisory approaches to quality control towards a situation where employees themselves take responsibility. Associated with this is the notion that prevention rather than detection is the key (Juran, 1989). The soft side focuses on the management of human resources in the organisation and lays particular emphasis on the need to change culture. TQM thus comprises both production orientated and employee relations orientated elements; this highlights the tensions between, on the one hand, following clearly laid-down instructions whilst, on the other, encouraging employee influence over the management process.

TQM has implications for employee involvement, whether this be in terms of employees taking greater responsibility for quality and having accountability for its achievement, or in terms of the introduction of teamworking principles into organisations. TQM is rather different from quality circles, which also drew a link between employee involvement and quality. Unlike quality circles, TQM is compulsory and represents an integral part of the job rather than being a supplement to existing activity.

Conclusions

The language and assumptions of TQM strike a resonant note with those who see the world as having moved away from mass production to one of segmented markets, where quality acts as a euphemism for closeness to the customer. This view sees the trading environment in flux, full of uncertainty and calling for new and less formal organisational structures (Peters, 1989). The TQM concept of the internal customer is significant here. By introducing the 'market' into the organisation, TQM promises to break down the 'bureaucratic phenomenon' of latent conflicts within organisations, based on occupational and functional differences (Crozier, 1964). Arguably, such functional differences reflect barriers between departments, such as the separation of R & D from marketing and production, which isolated managers from customer needs (Burns and Stalker, 1961). TQM fits with Levitt's (1960) notion that a business must be a customer-satisfying process rather than a goods-producing process.

Within the context, TQM is seen as a way of overcoming organisational inertia. At Ford, working across horizontal boundaries was termed chimney bricking and was facilitated by TQM (Pascale, 1992: 135). Hill (1991a) has observed that TQM brings together the senior management concerns of innovation and strategy with those of finding more efficient methods of doing existing things, an important improvement activity which usually takes place at the operational level. Thus, TQM unites routine management and managing for innovation in one set of organisational practices and arrangements. However, TQM comes up against its most difficult implementation problems when it addresses inter-unit, departmental and plant issues. As TQM 'gives priority to different aspects of the business, compared to organisations that have not embarked on quality management, a likely consequence of quality management is the redistribution of power and influence' (Hill and Wilkinson, 1995: 17). Pascale (1991: 248) shows how quality management modified the previous balance of power among managers at Ford by providing engineering and manufacturing with a new countervailing influence *vis-à-vis* finance. Hill (1991a) notes that TQM – at least in theory – is also about the substitution of task-orientated ideals for traditional authoritarian top-down decision-making, and to bring this about in the UK would require a major shift in the corporate culture and style of managing for most firms. The extent to which this is achieved in reality is addressed on a number of occasions throughout the rest of the book.

CHAPTER 3

The Origins and Development of TQM

Introduction

The aim of this chapter is to trace the origins and development of the quality movement. We begin by discussing the origins of TQM in the writings of the US quality experts such as Shewart, Deming and Juran, and its adoption and development by Japanese manufacturing industry. We then review the development of quality management in the West, where interest arose in response to Japanese competition. The chapter thus puts TQM into its historical context and in so doing identifies the rationale and difficulties involved in its implementation, issues which are developed in more detail in subsequent chapters.

The origins of TQM

Given the current enthusiasm for the 'quality movement', there is a danger of assuming that the concern for quality is of recent origin. In fact, it is an age-old concern; for the craft guilds of the Middle Ages, for example, the maintenance of quality was one of their key functions, with only those workers who could achieve acceptable quality standards being admitted to membership. Until the advent of mass production, building quality into a product was the job of a craftsman, what Feigenbaum referred to as 'operator quality control' (1983). Skilled craftsmen produced high quality products and had pride in their work, and the association between craft/hand produced goods and high quality is still strong today in many industries.

Things changed considerably, however, with the advent of standardised mass production. According to Garvin (1988), the adoption of jigs and gauges, due to pressure from the defence establishment to mass produce reliable weapons with interchangeable parts, was the major breakthrough which enabled US manufacturing to benefit from economies of scale and still retain the ability to produce a reliable product. Scientific management emphasised the divorce of conception from execution and the substitutability of labour. With the division of labour, responsibility for maintaining quality was now separate from workers and eventually became a new 'quality control' function. Such a department had two main roles: responsibility for attempting to prevent defective parts arriving on the assembly lines and inspecting the final product. The role of the operator was simply to ensure that products were made to the set specification.

Thus, modern quality control has its origins in the mass production of components and in the need to ensure the interchangeability of products made in batches. The techniques and philosophy of modern quality control are usually seen as deriving from the work of W.A. Shewart, and his colleagues W. Edwards Deming and Joseph Juran. Shewart's text *Economic Control of Quality of Manufactured Products* (1931) is viewed as a landmark in the development of quality management.

Shewart argued that each process has variability built into it and that this variability is not within the power of the individual operator to control. All processes are inherently variable and this process variability is random. As long as the variation stays within the limits which can be calculated as random, due to so-called 'common' causes, the process is in as much control as the operator can expect, and little can be gained by the individual worker trying to trace the source of this natural variation, which is due to shortcomings in the work system itself. Common causes include such things as product design and poor lighting, and can be reduced only by systematic improvement of the production process. In contrast, variations which are outside these limits have specific 'special' causes, which should be investigated. Special causes arise because of special circumstances; they are not in the process all the time and do not affect everyone. They might include failure to clean equipment, poor raw materials, or errors attributable to the poor performance of a particular operator. They can be eliminated through quality controls by operational personnel.

For Shewart, the development of statistical techniques would enable management to determine whether the variation in the process was under control, in the sense of having dealt with the special causes. His application of the control chart to quality management, drawing on his experience at Bell Laboratories in the 1930s is seen as being especially influential. These ideas form the basis for the process control charts used to monitor industrial processes today.

Various statistical techniques were developed and applied to the mass production of US wartime goods by the Statistical Research Group. Deming, however, argued that whilst the application of statistical methods was necessary, it was not sufficient in itself. Indeed, the risk of such approaches was that quality management thereby came to be seen as a specialism, the remit of a dedicated quality department. This he referred to as the 'fire-fighting' approach, with quality specialists solving particular quality problems as they were diagnosed, but with no recognition of the fact that quality should be the responsibility of everyone in the organisation.

Whilst Shewart's ideas were influential during the war, the post-war boom brought end-of-line inspection back to prominence, as the onus was on quantity. By 1949, Deming believed that because there was no pressure from management for quality there was nothing left of the philosophy that had been developed. Quality control in Western business relied on statistical process control and end-of-line inspection. Inspection and testing facilities became an integral part of production plants, together with an acceptance of associated scrap and re-work levels. Reflecting this philosophy, the American Society for Quality Control focused engineers' attentions on ways of advancing statistical theory upon which most inspection systems were based.

The next quality era was that of quality assurance and included the concepts of costs of quality, total quality control (TQC), reliability, engineering and zero defects (Garvin, 1988: 12–14). Reliability engineering was developed to help minimise variability but tended to be an inspection-driven approach where responsibility for quality clearly lay in the hands of the process design engineers and the quality inspectors. It arose largely out of concern with the reliability of military components and systems.

In 1951, Feigenbaum argued that quality was not achieved merely through inspection, nor was it the responsibility of the quality control department alone. His theory of TQC viewed cross-functional working as critical and he claimed that until such a structure was developed, little progress could be made:

> The underlying principle of this total quality now is... that, to provide genuine effectiveness, control must start with the design of the product and end only when the product has been placed in the hands of a customer who remains satisfied... the first principle is to recognise that quality is everyone... . (quoted by Garvin, 1988: 13)

The concept of Zero Defects also developed in this period. The Martin Company, which was involved in the construction of the Pershing missiles for the American Government, had a very tight schedule, such that the normal inspection and correction programme could not be carried out. Martin urged employees to build it right first time with no defects. The programme was deemed a success and the company believed it was low expectations that had created an environment of defects in the past. Philip Crosby, who worked at Martins in the 1960s, adopted many of these ideas in his work.

Thus, the new TQC approach to the costs of quality overturned the unstated assumption that quality was costly. Juran (1951) discussed the economics of quality and divided costs of achieving quality into unavoidable costs (that is, prevention – inspection, sampling) and avoidable costs – defects, scrap and so on. He referred to the latter as the 'gold in the mine' because quality improvement would reduce these. Despite these changes in thinking, however, it was not the West but the Japanese who put the ideas into practice.

TQM and Japan

Indeed, the origins of TQM are usually ascribed to Japan's search for improvements. Ironically, in the 1950s, 'made in Japan' was regarded in the West as being synonymous with cheap and shoddy consumer goods. This reputation, in hindsight, was deceptive because it gave little indication of how Japanese industry was being reconstructed to compete on quality-for-price in emergent global markets in the automobiles and electronics sectors. Indeed, there is a double irony in that the recent Western quest to improve quality was to a large extent a response to the Japanese challenge, for many of the basic techniques of quality management were brought to Japan by Western academics and consultants who found that their ideas had a more sympathetic audience there than in the West (Wilkinson and Willmott, 1995a: 4–5).

Japanese industry was particular receptive to the quality message for a number of reasons. First, Juran (1993) has suggested that the long-established Japanese tradition of fine craftsmanship and attention to detail through miniaturisation, struck a chord with his ideas about how wastage rates could be substantially reduced and how the reliability of manufacturing process improved. Second, the strongly statistical flavour of the early work of Deming *et al.*, with its emphasis on quantifying variation in quality, fitted well with the Japanese penchant for numbers (Crump, 1992). Third, quality was seen as a national 'survival' strategy. It was felt that the only way Japan would be able to afford to import the food and materials that it needed, being poor in natural resources, was to export goods of high quality at low prices. Quality was thus the key to achieving this objective:

> Historically the modern Japanese concept of quality is closely connected to the post-war Japanese lifeline of exports. Quality was the condition for survival; without export earnings there would be no cash to buy food for a hungry nation. There was no time for elaborate speculation in the concept of quality. The single most important factor in promoting exports, besides a price advantage achieved through cheap labour, was seen to be quality. The first thing to consider was how to reduce the number of defectives; industry needed to rid itself of the evil of nonconformity to specifications. A production system that produced according to specifications was the first thing to achieve, and the first concept of quality was manufacturing-based.

Consequently the first methods of quality control were inspection and Statistical Quality Control (SQC). (Lillrank and Kano, 1989: 31)

After the end of the war statistical quality control was introduced into the telecommunications industry by the US occupying forces, and from here it spread to other industries. The American quality experts received a ready audience, with Deming giving seminars in the early 1950s on statistical quality control and problem-solving techniques.

In 1946, the Union of Japanese Scientists and Engineers (JUSE) was formed and in 1949 a Quality Control Research Group established. A committee comprising scholars, engineers, and government officials was set up and charged with improving Japanese productivity and enhancing the post-war quality of life. Both the research group and committee were highly influenced by the ideas of Deming and Juran. JUSE produced a journal, *Statistical Quality Control*, first published in 1950. The journal was designed as a vehicle for discussion in workshop quality control study groups led by foremen. In 1962 they published *Gemba-to QC* (Quality Control for the Foreman), as one of a series of three pamphlets on quality control, and the workshops for foremen were renamed 'QC circle activities' (Deming, 1982; Ishikawa, 1985; Tuckman, 1994). The aim of this was to ensure that ordinary workgroup members would read the journal rather than simply leaving it to foremen, so that the methods would be applied in the workplace.

Quality control education progressed during the 1950s, provided by such bodies as JUSE and the Japanese Management Association (JMA), and also through in-house training developed in the factory. Royalties from the publication of Deming's lectures, donated to JUSE, were also used to fund the Deming prizes for quality improvement. These prizes have been awarded each year from 1951 onwards to commemorate his contribution to TQM and spread the quality message. Winners include Hitachi, Komatsu, Toyota and, in 1987, the first non-Japanese winner, the Florida Light and Power Company. The mass media was utilised to reach foremen and group leaders. For example, radio broadcasts in 1956 introduced quality control to group leaders in the workplace and the period saw the publication of standard textbooks on quality aimed at foremen.

However, the initial years of quality initiatives, based mainly on the implementation of statistical process control (SPC) on the factory floor, were not an unmitigated success. Senior management were not closely involved and, according to Ishikawa (1985) the period saw an overemphasis on statistical quality control methods which many workers disliked because of their complexity. Many specifications and standards were created. Some, such as the Japanese Engineering Standards, were given legal status (Cole, 1979). These often had limited influence at the workplace, however, and top and middle managers showed little interest. Quality management in this period was thus limited in scope, rarely going beyond the shopfloor.

Juran visited Japan in 1954 on a lecture tour for senior managers and argued that quality was the concern of the whole management team. His 'quality spiral' suggested that every department was involved in producing a quality product, and that quality was too important to be left to a specialist quality control department. Both Deming and Juran were interested in the wider implications of quality and argued that quality control should be an integral part of the management control systems, in contrast to its traditional role as a policeman function. This developed into the notion that prevention rather than detection was the key, and the concept of 'managerial breakthrough', whereby 'continuous improvement', was held to be the ultimate goal (Juran, 1989).

The main Japanese innovations in quality control were facilitated by JUSE's role. These were quality control circles that were originally conceived as study groups for foremen but which evolved into quality circles involving company-wide control – sometimes called Total Quality Control or Total Quality Management. The elements developed by the Japanese are fundamental to modern definitions of TQM. As well as the introduction of quality circles this development of TQM in Japan is argued to have led to many other managerial innovations such as supplier partnerships, cellular manufacturing, just-in-time manufacture, and hoshin (policy deployment) planning (Ishikawa, 1985).

In sum, the road to TQM began with quality control and an emphasis on inspection. However, if defective products were produced at different stages of the manufacturing process, strict inspection would not necessarily eliminate the problem. This brought the emphasis in post-war years to quality assurance and the control of the manufacturing process as a whole, with the aim of building in quality rather than inspecting it. This ended the dilemma of appraisal versus failure costs. Even so, the emphasis on control of the manufacturing process was seen as too narrow. Manufacturing could not resolve issues of product reliability or economy if the design was wrong or the material poor. Hence all processes needed to be under a quality control programme (Ishikawa, 1985). Though these ideas were implanted by American production engineers, later development was facilitated by Japanese managers and by the Japanese Industrial Standards movement which consolidated the quality movement's efforts. By providing coordination and legitimacy, a similar role was played by JUSE which had close links with the business establishment and popularised the main concepts of quality control.

TQM goes West

Western firms have had something of a 'born again' experience with quality management, following the realisation by the 1970s that the Japanese economic miracle posed a competitive threat, not only in terms of price but more particularly in terms of quality. This sparked off a strong interest in Japanese management techniques, not least in quality management practices. Tuckman (1994,

1995) characterises the development of Western interest in quality management as follows:

> First phase: late 1970s to early 1980s some experimentation with quality circles. Mostly affects firms in direct competition with industrial sectors in which Japan had concentrated, for example, electronics and motor industries.
>
> Second phase: during the 1980s major companies, often affected by world recession concerned with control of suppliers and subcontractors.
>
> Third phase: from the mid 1980s a growing concern with customer service, particularly in the service sector.
>
> Fourth phase: from late 1980s penetration of concerns with 'customer service' into areas which previously had not recognised the existence of customers (for example, public services). (Tuckman, 1995: 67)

In this section, we develop this periodisation as a framework for our discussion of the development of quality management in the UK.

First phase: 'Japanisation' and quality circles

The late 1970s saw a series of visits to Japan by Western business people, for example the famous Pacific Basin Study mission organised by the Department of Trade and Industry in 1984. In the USA the 1980 NBC documentary 'If Japan Can – Why Can't We?', explained the influence of Deming in Japan in the 1950s. A large 'Japanisation' literature developed, both academic and popular (for example, Vogel, 1979; Ouchi, 1981; Pascale and Athos, 1982).

Quality circles (QCs) were identified as a critical tool, and were introduced in a number of major Western companies, as early as 1974 in Lockheed in the US. In the UK QCs first appeared on the scene in 1978, when Rolls Royce copied the practices of Lockheed. QCs took time to take root in the UK, with estimates of some 100 companies involved in 1980, increasing to 400 by 1985, largely in the manufacturing sector (Collard and Dale, 1989). The National Society of Quality Circles was set up in 1982 to encourage their development.

QCs were seen as a major innovation that would restore competitive advantage to ailing Western firms. Hill (1991a) identifies three reasons for such optimism. QCs were seen as possessing the potential to: increase employee involvement by means of direct participation, to provide a tool to change organisational culture, and to deliver enhanced business performance. Surveys found that it was the first of these hopes that most employers cited as the primary reason for introducing quality circles. Thus, studies by Dale (1984) found that the main motive behind QC introduction in the UK was improving employee job satisfaction.

However, QCs are now widely seen as being largely a failure, although many did deliver some improvements in business performance. As a tool to effect change in employee attitudes and organisational culture QCs were found wanting. At best it seems that they could produce a short-term improvement in attitudes and behaviours but this quickly waned after their novelty effect wore off (for example, Griffin, 1988). Few of the many research studies of QCs have been able to find much evidence of lasting improvements (for example, Hill, 1991a). Most evidence finds that QCs involved a very limited number of employees and had short life spans, often lasting less than a year.

The failure of quality circles has been attributed to many factors. Some of the most commonly reported are poor integration with existing structures, hostile middle managers, their voluntary nature and limited scope, and the problems of maintaining them in a period of organisational restructuring and associated redundancies. QCs were found to have many technical problems in their operation, including their restriction to a narrow range of issues, the separation of the identification of a solution from its implementation, their slowness in delivering results, their tendency to run out of things to do, poorly developed support structures and members' inadequate training and development to support the tasks required of them (Hill, 1991a). As well as these operational problems, it was often the case that circle members had to endure a less than supportive managerial environment. Middle managers and supervisors, who often felt threatened by successful circle activities, reacted at best with indifference and scepticism and at worst with outright hostility, sometimes denying circles the time and resources to carry out their activities. Similarly, the problems posed by quality circles being 'bolted-on to the main frameworks of organisational structures, the so called organisational dualism' (Goldstein, 1988) posed serious problem for circle survival. Not least there were the problems of complexity resulting in confused reporting structures and authority levels.

Second phase: company wide quality

By the mid-1980s, Tuckman argues, TQM's introduction in to the UK 'began in earnest' (1994: 740). As quality circles were fizzling out, TQM appeared to hold greater promise, not least because it offered the potential to address some of the problems identified by failure of quality circles in the UK (see Table 3.1). In essence the problem was that quality circles had been implemented in the UK in relative isolation from the *total* quality management system.

Increasingly, a wider commitment to quality improvement was sought from the workforce. Part of the failure of quality circles was the very limited participation of employees, often with less than 10 per cent of the workforce volunteering for membership. As competition increased, not least from Japanese companies, quality improvement could no longer be left to the minority of employees prepared to volunteer: quality was now everyone's responsibility. The voluntary nature of quality circles was perceived as having sent an inappropriate message about quality's importance: employees could opt out. In the new business environment this was no longer acceptable. If employees wanted job security and good conditions, then the price to be paid was the acceptance of responsibility for continuous improvement. Workers were not merely to be encouraged to make suggestions for improvement, they were now expected to become actively involved.

TABLE 3.1 Quality circles and TQM compared

	Quality Circles	*TQM*
Choice	Voluntary	Compulsory
Structure	Bolt-on	Integrated quality system
Direction	Bottom-up	Top-down
Scope	Within departments/units	Company-wide
Aims	Employee relations improvements	Quality improvements

Source: Wilkinson *et al.*, 1992

Whilst the organisational restructuring and associated redundancies of the 1980s can be seen as a major factor in the failure of quality circles (Dale, 1984), it also allowed TQM to be presented to the workforce in a very forceful manner. Adopting TQM promised nothing less than organisational survival.

The organisational restructuring of this period saw two other developments which fuelled the growth of TQM. First, the restructuring of manufacturing companies in the search for cost reduction and flexibility involved a considerable increase in subcontracting and outsourcing, giving rise to growing concerns with maintaining and improving the quality of suppliers' work. This led to a substantial increase in quality certification as large manufacturers demanded that suppliers be accredited to minimum standards. Thus, quality management practices were extended into the small- and medium-sized enterprise (SME) sector.

Second, the adoption of 'just-in-time' (JIT) inventory control by many manufacturers involved the reduction of stock to the bare minimum. Suppliers to a JIT firm are required to deliver components as and when the production process demands them, perhaps even every few hours. The problems caused by the delivery of sub-standard components are thus much great under JIT than under traditional manufacturing systems with built-in buffer stocks. The key requirement for successful introduction of JIT is a reliable supply of high quality components. Thus, the adoption of JIT led many firms to re-examine their quality management practices, not only on their own account but also to require similar commitment from suppliers who wished to remain on their approved lists.

This period, with the key concern for controlling the quality of suppliers, saw both government and multinational corporations keen to develop a TQM infrastructure. Thus, a group of 14 major companies set up the European Foundation for Quality Management in 1988, whilst the UK government provided considerable financial support to firms seeking to adopt quality accreditation standards.

Third phase: catering for the customer

Until the early 1980s it was the practices of the manufacturing sector which dominated much of the quality debate. The preoccupation of quality management writers with manufacturing can be seen in the development of concepts such as 'world class manufacturing' (Schonberger, 1986), and the first US Baldrige award in the service category was not made until 1990. Similarly, the main professional quality qualification – membership of the Institute of Quality Assurance – still has a very high engineering content, with such compulsory subjects as calibration systems, materials testing and metrology, reflecting quality management's engineering origins.

From the mid-1980s there was a growing concern with customer service in the services sector, including retailing, financial services and the hospitality industry, as competition intensified here also. The nature of service organisations means that the methodological and conceptual transfer of quality management practices developed in manufacturing was fraught with difficulty. However, some aspects of quality management are more easily transferred; the slogans of the quality gurus have been adapted to fit the service context. For example, while 'zero defects' is the goal of a manufacturing organization 'zero defection' of customers is seen as the sign of quality coming to services (Reichheld and Sasser, 1990). Before examining the development of quality management approaches in services, we briefly explore the key characteristics of services that necessitate a different approach.

Characteristics of services: challenges to quality

The features that characterise a service have been explored by a number of authors. Regan (1963) used a four category typology of: intangibility; inseparability; heterogeneity and perishability. Intangibility can be defined as the inability to see or touch the 'product' of a service. The simultaneous production and consumption of a service illustrates the feature of inseparability. Heterogeneity can be viewed as an implicit lack of consistency, whilst perishability gives rise to the problem of the immediacy of the service – a lost opportunity is a lost sale. Study of these aspects has been extended by a number of authors (see Edgett and Parkinson, 1993, for a summary and review of developments). We now examine these four issues with respect to the development of quality management in the service sector.

Intangibility. The most obvious thing about services it that they are intangible – they cannot be seen or touched. This poses great problems to the vendors in communicating to the buyer exactly what is on offer. In simple terms, a consumer cannot really evaluate a service until it has been consumed, although, of course, satisfaction with the service may influence repeat purchases or purchases by others where customers do have some degree of choice. As a result, Siehl and Bowen have commented that the 'service organization is in need of mechanisms by which it can reduce this input of uncertainty and acquire the information necessary for effective service production and delivery' (1991: 15).

Inseparability. Getting close to the customer is an unavoidable feature of service encounters. The encounter itself is the method *par excellence* for persuading, negotiating or damaging a customer relationship. Schneider and Bowen (1993), for example, describe the encounter as a relationship of 'physical and psychological closeness'. Customers have the opportunity to observe the detail of service provision, including significant interpersonal aspects such as non-verbal behaviour, linguistic competence and logical consistency between the development of ideas and definitions.

Thus, in services the organisational form can be seen as an inverted pyramid with a large number of individuals (the majority in most service organisations) coming into direct contact with the customer. In contrast, a goods producer typically has only a small handful of people – often only the sales force – who routinely engage in customer contact. Thus, for many organisations in the service sector there is no simple means by which the consumer can be separated from the person providing the service. The role of employees becomes much more critical, because to a very real extent the employees are the service, given the absence of any tangible artifact. They carry the responsibility of projecting the image of the organisation and it is in their hands that the ultimate satisfaction of the consumer rests.

Heterogeneity. One issue that complicates effective quality management in services, particularly at the level of the service encounter, is that services are different each time they are performed. This is mainly because each party to the service encounter – the service provider and the customer – is liable to introduce variation to the service, either by providing a service that deviates from the norm, or by failing to articulate needs. A service provider may not maintain absolute consistency throughout the day, even with well-defined service standards, nor is it always desirable to do so. Customer perceptions may also vary from one occasion to another. Some services may become dull or boring if there is no change in the offering; also, only rarely do we consume one service in isolation from another. Thus, many potential interactions are subject to variation leading to the possibility of 'service role ambiguity' (Berry *et al.*, 1989).

Perishability. If a service is not consumed it disappears. The airliner, having taken off, cannot fill further seats and the opportunity to maximise profit has gone forever. This is an economic cost to the organisation that cannot be recovered and which is critical to the very survival or the organisation. Consequently, the organisations often consider minimising costs or increasing flexibility. Perishability is a concern to all service providers but the method of managing this process will vary considerably, and sometimes to the detriment of quality or consistency.

Early work in service quality attempted to identify superior service providers. For example, Schneider (1980) differentiated between two types of management style, the service enthusiast and the service bureaucrat, whilst Peters and Waterman (1982) identified a number of 'excellent' service companies. The 1980s also saw some substantial theoretical developments, with the 'disconfirmation' paradigm of service quality. Here 'quality' is seen as being evaluated by consumers during and after the service encounter. They compare their (pre-service) expectations with the perceived (or actual) performance. Differences between expected and perceived performance give rise to disconfirmation – either positive (good) or negative (poor). This still appears to be the main theoretical underpinning of service quality models (for example, Gronroos, 1983; Berry *et al.*, 1985; Zeithaml *et al.*, 1990). Although the disconfirmation paradigm is now increasingly being questioned (Boulding *et al.*, 1993; Teas, 1993; Cronin and Taylor, 1994), nevertheless, no comprehensively superior model appears to have yet emerged.

A key concern was to develop ways to measure service quality in order to manage and improve it effectively. In 1985 Parasuraman *et al.* published their now classic article which led to a revolution in the way that service quality is dealt with. In that paper the results of their exploratory research were presented, including a statement of ten service quality determinants that appeared to be relatively important. Determinants represent the basic dimensions that a consumer uses to evaluate a service. In order to improve quality in a service organisation the first step is to identify the quality determinants most important or relevant to the company's target market (Berry *et al.* 1985) and then assess their own and their competitors' performance.

This early work formed the basis for the development of the service quality gap model and the resulting 'SERVQUAL' questionnaire (Zeithaml *et al.*, 1990). Service quality is defined as a function of the gap between customer expectations of a service and the perceptions of the actual service delivery. The SERVQUAL questionnaire has 22 pairs of Likert-type scales. The first 22 items are designed to measure customer expectations for a service and the following 22 to measure the perceived level of service provided by the firm. From this data, ten determinants are mapped on to five underlying factors. The factors were found to be:

Reliability: The ability to perform the promised service dependably and accurately.

Responsiveness: The willingness to help customers and provide service.

Assurance: The knowledge and courtesy of employees and their ability to convey trust and confidence.

Empathy: The caring, individualised attention provided to customers.

Tangibles: The appearance of physical facilities, equipment, personnel and communications material.

Of these, reliability was found to be the core issue in providing a quality service. Friendly caring staff in a pleasant environment do not compensate for an unreliable service. Although subject to increasing criticisms, for example problems of confusing negative statements and criticisms of the scales (Lewis, 1993), the SERVQUAL approach has been widely applied in private services and its use is increasingly being advocated for the public sector (Donnelly *et al.*, 1995).

Fourth phase: into the public sector

The late 1980s saw the adoption of quality management in the public sector services. Quality management appeared likely to be able to deal with a number of key concerns of public sector management. According to Clarke (1992), a common pattern was that of major upheaval and a striving to become more commercially aware, and TQM was seen as a vehicle to facilitate a move towards a more commercial culture. Other developments also fuelled its adoption, including legislation that gave more choice to consumers, competitive tendering, increasing pressures to contain costs and to deliver value for money, more demanding customer requirements, and not least the Citizen's Charter.

Quality management was seen as possessing the potential to facilitate a change programme that would start to answer the principal criticisms of public services: their alleged inefficiency, wastefulness and remoteness from those whom they are supposed to serve (Walsh, 1995). The capacity of quality management to reduce inefficiency derives from its claims to reduce the estimated one-third of an organisation's effort spent dealing with errors and check, and was thus particularly attractive. Quality management involves becoming 'customer-focused', 'client-driven' and 'market-orientated'. Some have even suggested that an emphasis on quality management complemented the transformation of public service from its 'Fordist' to 'post-Fordist' organisational form (Sanderson, 1992).

Pollitt (1993) saw the entry of 'quality' into the public sector from the late 1980s as involving three key elements. First, the introduction of 'quasi-markets' incorporating a much bolder use of market and quasi-market mechanisms for those parts of the public sector that could not be transferred directly into private ownership. Second, the decentralisation of the management and production of services; in this way the control through the hierarchical line of management is relinquished but control through contracts is substituted. Third, the use of the term 'quality' became 'positively promiscuous' with a constant rhetorical emphasis on the need to improve services.

A great deal was often claimed for the potential of quality management in the public sector. TQM has been proposed as the solution to all of the many, varied and complex problems of the public sector (Hammons and Maddux, 1990). The introduction of TQM has been proffered as the solution to making higher education more relevant to the needs of society (Bosner, 1992); as the key to improving productivity and cost effectiveness in the police (Butler, 1992; Flood, 1992); and as the route to efficiency and culture change in the civil service (Pickard, 1992). Sound quality management in the National Health Service is also seen as the vehicle to deliver efficiency, economy and effectiveness (Morgan and Everett, 1991). As public sector quality initiatives mature there are increasing numbers of case studies, often deriving from enthusiastic chief executives and consultants, reporting their success (for example, Industrial Relations Services, 1994). Many of these case studies claim wholesale organisational transformations as a result of introducing quality management. For example, Brent's conversion from being a fully paid-up member of the 'loony left', changing from 'Barmy Brent' to the 'Quality Council' with a mission statement to be 'simply the best local authority in the country' (Van de Vliet, 1994: 38) is a typical account. A sign of the growth of quality management in the public sector is that the British Quality Foundation's awards, originally restricted to 'for-profit' organisations was extended in 1995 to cover the public sector.

There are also many quality 'sceptics', however, who question whether quality management can be successfully introduced in the public sector. According to Gaster (1992: 55), it is all too often perceived as the latest political or senior officer fad, requiring lip-service to be paid in public but with little by way of serious implementation. Quality management in the public sector is thus often seen simply as a fashionable management practice (Davies and Hinton, 1993).

Increasingly, commentators are calling for distinctive systems of quality management for public services and warn of the problems to be encountered in the uncritical adoption of private sector practices (Walsh, 1990; Swiss, 1992; Dale, 1994b).The lack of a supportive infrastructure for the development of quality management in the public sector is seen by some as a key barrier to TQM's development. For example, Brockman's (1992) comparison of TQM in the US and UK public sectors laments the lack of a British equivalent to the Federal Quality Institute (FQI). The FQI was established in 1988 as a primary source of leadership, information and consultancy services on quality management for federal government.

Some authors have gone further, and have raised questions about whether it is possible to take a 'true quality approach' in the public sector because of 'red tape' and subservience to 'national dictat' (Pickard, 1992: 21). Others have suggested that quality management and the public sector are contradictions in terms:

> How in the world, I wondered, do we get bureaucrats to strive for 'continuous improvement'? They invented the status quo! (Sensenbrenner, 1991)

More critical accounts are also starting to emerge about the practice of quality management in the public sector (Walsh, 1995; Kirkpatrick and Martinez-Lucio, 1995). A number of concerns arise from these accounts. The 'success' of such initiatives is often seen as being at the expense of declining levels of service provision, job losses, the intensification of work for public sector staff, the undermining of trade union influence and employment conditions, and increases in the level of stress-related illness and ill-health retirements amongst public sector employees (see, for example, TUC, 1992; Industrial Relations Services, 1994). Competitive mechanisms ostensibly designed to improve quality seem to have as much to do with driving down costs as promoting enhanced quality (Pollitt, 1993).

It may be that quality 'talk' may be a substitute for actual quality improvement (Terry, 1994) and quality has been described as a 'distinctly murky concept' in the public sector (Gaster, 1992: 55). Pollitt also points out that:

> Quality is not some entirely new dimension of performance. On the contrary, it is likely extensively to overlap the more familiar performance criteria of economy, efficiency, effectiveness, equity etc. Service users, in other words, are likely to want fast, fair services which are effective but not wasteful. Second, most of the literature stresses that it is essential to respond to user (customer) requirements. Potentially, at least, this sets a sharp limit to the extent to which either public service professionals or managers or, indeed, ministers or councillors, can prescribe what the 'right' services ought to be. (1993: 153)

Thus quality provides an alternative ideology to that espoused by the 'professionals' such as doctors and nurses, and it is here that opposition to the new discourse has been most apparent. Pendleton (1995) sees the rhetoric of quality in British Rail as a response to past general failures to reform the organisation, and an overarching conceptualisation of all British Rail activities, both internal and external. He also notes its use as a legitimising force for a range of change initiatives.

The further element, which overlaps the quality approach, is the increased emphasis on 'user responsiveness' insofar as greater attention should be given to the wishes of the individual service consumer. But this may cause some problems in practice: do consumers understand what is on offer? Are they aware of resource constraints, or will they ask for the impossible? Finally, given the comparatively intangible nature of many public sector services, there is difficulty in reaching agreement over what is to count as 'conformance to specification' (Walsh, 1995). While customers may desire 'better quality services', it may not always be possible to specify what this means, or to develop an agreed method for measuring improvements. One attempt to solve this problem has been the centralised setting of precise standards and associated audits that are intended to guarantee levels of provision. Walsh notes how this move has, however, enabled politicians to distance themselves from responsibility for the management and delivery of public services. Equally, whereas the acid test of 'success' in the private sector is the continuing (profitable) sale of a company's goods and services, public provision is not directly governed by market forces. In this situation there is considerable pressure to demonstrate effectiveness in other ways – for example, through the adoption of other measures of performance, (seemingly regardless of cost), such as the accounting and information provision of systems that have found favour in the private sector.

Quality management: waxing or waning?

Having traced the origins and development of quality management it is useful at this stage to speculate on its future. It is evident from our analysis so far that there are a number of distinct possibilities. An optimistic view would suggest that although there have been setbacks for the 'onward march' of the quality movement, its principles and philosophy are generally sound, its practices are developing a coherent shape, and some of the early promise has been realised with considerable improvements in quality made as TQM programmes mature. Equally, despite academic scepticism about the intellectual credentials of TQM, there is an increasing body of knowledge and a number of promising theoretical developments. From this angle, TQM could be said to have established a secure hold on the agendas of both managers and academics. By continuing to apply its own principles of continuous improvement, the future for TQM would – on the face of it – seem to be full of promise.

The discussion so far, however, has also highlighted a number of significant problems with the development of TQM. Although it clearly has more potential than the quality circle phenomenon of the 1970s and early 80s, this may not be fulfilled. As we discuss above, its transfer from the manufacturing sector has been problematic and its uptake in the public sector has been controversial in many cases. Here, at least, it seems that rhetoric may be winning over the reality. Increasingly, doom and gloom prophesies have been made about TQM's decline in prominence and popularity. In short, sceptics see TQM as another, if slightly longer-lived, managerial fad that is already being replaced by the next generation of fashionable phrases and practices.

The aim of our empirical material, therefore, is critically to examine TQM's potential by posing questions such as: What has TQM achieved to date? What factors explain the successes and failures of TQM? Does TQM have universal application? What are the future prospects for TQM?

In Chapter 5 we examine the changing shape and character of TQM through a review of the survey-based research. In Chapters 6 to 10 we present a detailed picture of TQM in practice in several case study organisations. We have chosen cases in the various sectors of the economy in order to reflect each of Tuckman's four phases of quality management's development. Before we review the empirical material, however, we examine the 'soft' human resource management (HRM) and cultural aspects of quality management in more detail.

CHAPTER 4

TQM, Organisational Change and Human Resource Management

Introduction

As we have seen, the proponents of TQM define quality in terms of customer requirements, or 'fitness for use' (Juran, 1989). Those employees who do not have direct contact with external customers are encouraged to view their colleagues as customers, linked ultimately via a chain of internal customer relationships to the final (external) customer. In this way, employees in the organisation are exhorted to be customer-driven, with the aim of continuously improving customer satisfaction. There are implications for the workforce, as employers are urged to move away from supervisory approaches to quality control towards a situation where employees themselves take responsibility (Oakland, 1993: 31). Thus, the effective implementation of TQM requires that all employees, from top management to the shop or office floor, develop a commitment to continuous improvement as an integral part of their daily work. There is a need to develop a 'quality culture' (Hill, 1991b: 555; Dale and Cooper, 1992: 153; Glover, 1993; Wilkinson and Ackers, 1995).

The prescriptive literature on TQM, however, says more about what employers are *trying* to achieve in terms of employee commitment than about how this is to be achieved or the problems that may be faced in attempting to do this (Hill, 1991b; Wilkinson *et al.*, 1991; Snape *et al.*, 1995). The usual argument in the TQM literature is that employees, including supervisors and managers, are to be won over, not by compulsion but by leadership, training and by providing recognition (Oakland, 1993). The assumption is that employees in general will derive satisfaction from involvement in continuous improvement and from doing a job well. There is a notion of reciprocal commitment here, with the TQM organisation meeting the individual's needs for job satisfaction and self-actualisation, and receiving commitment to organisational goals in return.

However, Hill (1991a) claims that the proponents of TQM have understated the difficulties in getting staff at all levels in the organisation to 'buy in' to the ideals of TQM, and that they focus on too narrow a range of change levers. Traditional working practices and management styles may be inconsistent with TQM, and resistance to the ideals of TQM may be encountered not only at shop-floor level, where it may cut across traditional working and industrial relations practices, but also amongst professional, supervisory and managerial staff. Managers, for example, may feel that they have much to fear from TQM, given the emphasis on empowering their subordinates (Marchington *et al.*, 1992: 38), and the evidence suggests that TQM may make managers' jobs more demanding (Wilkinson *et al.*, 1993). Schuler and Harris (1992: 90–1) argue that TQM promises to empower front-line employees, giving them access to more information and greater responsibility, and in so doing undermines middle managers' traditional go-between role in implementing and monitoring the instructions of top management. Instead, middle managers are to perform the key function of providing leadership and support for front-line employees, which requires new skills and attitudes on their part. For employees, TQM means taking on greater responsibilities, often for the same pay, and there is a fear that TQM may involve job losses. Given all this, it is clear that we cannot take it for granted that managers and employees will necessarily respond with enthusiasm to TQM.

A practical key issue is how do top management attempt to build a quality culture? This chapter examines this question in detail. We begin with a discussion of organisational culture, which provides some insights into the implementation of TQM and highlights some of the potential difficulties faced in seeking to develop an organisation-wide commitment to continuous improvement. We then examine strategic human resource management (HRM), showing how HR policies and practices are expected to be in alignment with organisational strategies. The quality-enhancement strategy associated with TQM is likely to require a particular approach to HRM, involving an emphasis on winning employee commitment to organisational goals, rather than securing simple compliance through direct supervision and crude incentive schemes. This is followed by a discussion of HR policies and practices, the work context and job design, and employee involvement. A critical perspective is adopted, which allows us to examine the potential difficulties likely to be faced in the implementation of TQM.

TQM and organisational culture

TQM implies an open management style, with a devolution of responsibility. The aim is to develop a 'quality culture', whereby everyone in the organisation shares a commitment to continuous improvement aimed at customer satisfaction. However, according to an IPM-sponsored study:

> despite the growing awareness of cultural issues, comparatively little attention has been paid to the practical, day-to-day processes involved in creating, managing and changing organizational culture. (Williams *et al.*, 1991: 1)

Furthermore, much of the academic literature emphasises the difficulties in changing organisational culture, and recent years have seen a debate on the issue of 'can culture be managed?' (Williams *et al.*, 1991; Ogbonna, 1992/93). Edgar Schein (1985), for example, sees culture as very deep-seated, consisting of three levels. First, 'artifacts and creations' are the visible manifestation of an organisation's culture. This refers to the visible environment and behaviour of people in the organisation, including such things as the layout of offices (open plan or closed doors?), dress norms, and the way in which people in the organisation tend to express and deal with disagreements. On the second level, we can identify the 'values' of an organisation: views on what 'ought' to be, and how things 'should be done here'. Such values often emerge early in the life of an organisation, or when it faces a novel challenge, and will gain acceptance and be incorporated into the culture of the organisation to the extent that they provide workable solutions to the problems which the organisation faces. Gradually, certain core values come to be taken for granted by members of the organisation, and are transformed into 'basic underlying assumptions' – the third level of culture, which operates at the preconscious level. Schein's account thus underlines the complex nature of organisational culture, and counsels against the view that it is something which can be easily manipulated by management.

Others point to the existence of subcultures and competing occupational cultures, influenced by factors both internal and external to the organisation, questioning the notion of a single, shared culture which is easily manipulable by management (Meyerson and Martin, 1987). Even to the extent that it is useful to refer to a single 'organisational' culture, there may still be problems for the culture management view, in that the existing culture within an organisation may be resistant to change and thus act as a barrier to the successful implementation of TQM. At the very least, accounts of TQM implementation need to address the issue of resistance to change and avoid too simplistic a view of the possibility of managing culture.

What approaches have employers adopted in attempting to manage organisational culture? On the basis of a review of culture change programmes in 15 UK organisations, Williams *et al.* (1993) suggest that five main methods are commonly used by management:

1. Changing the people in the organisation, through selective recruitment and redundancy programmes, with a greater emphasis on selecting people with the desired attitudes, as well as technical skills and experience. This may involve the use of more sophisticated selection techniques, for example psychometric testing, assessment centres, and biodata.
2. Moving people into new jobs to break up old sub-cultures.
3. Providing employees with training and role models appropriate to the desired culture. This may involve getting supervisors and managers at all levels to act as role models and demonstrate personal commitment to new goals.
4. Training employees in new skills, and thus influencing their job attitudes. An example here is the training of operators in quality monitoring and improvement techniques, in a bid to win commitment to quality.
5. Changing the work environment, HR policies and management style generally.

They note that attempts to manage culture are likely to be more successful where change is preceded by some sort of 'precipitating crisis', such as a market slump, new competition, privatisation or financial problems. This helps to convince people of the need for change. Such developments are also often associated with a change in the leadership of the organisation, introducing fresh ideas and acting as the catalyst and champion of change. Schein (1985) appears to be in agreement with this, seeing structure, systems and procedures as significant but secondary mechanisms of change, with leadership and education, along with 'the deployment of organisational rewards and punishments' as the key levers of change.

The culture literature, then, suggests a complex and far-reaching change agenda for the implementation of TQM, encompassing management style, HR policies and the work environment generally. We begin to explore these issues in more detail in the next section, with a discussion of the strategic HRM implications of TQM.

Strategic human resource management

In recent years, there has been growing recognition of the contribution of HR strategies to organisational goals. In most accounts, this has involved a call for employers to adopt a strategic approach to managing their human resources. HRM is no longer to be seen simply as a staff specialism, concerned solely with people–management issues and separate from business management. As J. W. Walker puts it:

> The challenge of managing human resources is to ensure that all activities are focused on business needs. All human resource activities should fit together as a

system and be aligned with human resource strategies. These strategies, in turn, should be aligned with business strategies. (1992: 2)

According to this view, managing human resources is about achieving fit. There should be fit between the approach to managing people and the organisation's objectives, whilst the various HR practices themselves, for example on recruitment, development and remuneration, should also fit together as a coherent whole. Referred to as the 'matching model' of HR strategy (Boxall, 1992), this theme is now common in the literature. Schuler and Jackson (1987) explain how the three generic business strategies of innovation, quality enhancement and cost-reduction each require quite different employee 'role behaviours', which in turn require particular HRM policies. Similar typologies of business and HR strategy 'matches' have been produced by other authors, including Arthur (1992), again using Porter's generic strategies of differentiation and cost leadership; Purcell (1989), based on the Boston Consulting Group product portfolio matrix; and Sonnenfeld *et al.* (1992), drawing on the Miles and Snow categories of defender, prospector, analyser and reactor. This approach amounts to a contingency model of HRM, with the appropriate strategy depending on, *inter alia*, the nature of the product market, the nature of consumer demands, the stage of the product life cycle, the market share of the business unit, the structure of costs, and organisational structure (Storey and Sisson, 1993: 59–68).

Some writers have suggested that in many sectors the contingencies are shifting in favour of a high-commitment HR strategy (Walton, 1985). The usual argument is that markets are now becoming more competitive, due partly to the globalisation of competition and liberalisation by governments, whilst customers are becoming more demanding, not only on price but more particularly in terms of choice, quality, service and design. This means that more companies are now targeting their products at niche markets and attempting to respond quickly to ever-changing customer demands, rather than selling standard mass-produced goods (Piore and Sabel, 1984). In consequence, there is a greater emphasis on flexible, responsive organisations with multi-skilled workers and flexible technology, rather than on simply reaping economies of scale (McKinlay and Starkey, 1992; Cappelli and Rogovsky, 1994). There is in consequence a need to win employee commitment to the goals of quality and flexibility (Guest, 1987).

Such analyses suggest that we are seeing nothing less than the replacement of mass production with a new production paradigm, variously discussed as 'post-Fordism', 'flexible specialisation' (Piore and Sabel, 1984), or 'lean production' (Womack *et al.*, 1990). In the US (Beaumont, 1992), the UK (Guest 1987; Storey, 1989) and elsewhere, this has been associated with a debate about the development of a distinctive 'human resource management' (HRM) approach. A good example of this argument is Walton (1985), who argues that organisations are moving away from an HR strategy based on compliance, involving narrowly defined jobs, limited employee discretion and involvement, individual incentives and a hierarchical organisation, to one based on commitment, with broader, more flexible jobs, more teamwork, higher levels of involvement, a move towards group-based incentives, and a flatter organisation structure, with less emphasis on hierarchical, positional authority (see Table 4.1).

TABLE 4.1   From control to commitment: workforce strategies

	Control	*Transitional*	*Commitment*
Job design principles	Individual attention limited to performing individual job.	Scope of individual responsibility extended to upgrading system performance, via participative problem-solving groups in QWL EI, and quality circle programs.	Individual responsibility extended to upgrading system performance.
	Job design de-skills and fragments work and separates doing and thinking.	No change in traditional job design or accountability.	Job design enhances content of work, emphasises whole task, and combines doing and thinking.
	Accountability focused on individual.		Frequent use of teams as basic accountable unit.
	Fixed job definition.		Flexible definition of duties, contingent on changing conditions.
Performance expectations	Measured standards define minimum performance. Stability seen as desirable.		Emphasis placed on higher, 'stretch objectives', which tend to be dynamic and oriented to the marketplace.
Management organisation: structure, systems, and style	Structure tends to be layered, with top-down controls.	No basic changes in approaches to structure, control, or authority.	Flat organisation structure with mutual influence systems.
	Coordination and control rely on rules and procedures.		Coordination and control based more on shared goals, values, and traditions.
	More emphasis on prerogatives and positional authority.		Management emphasis on problem solving and relevant information and expertise.

	Control	*Transitional*	*Commitment*
	Status symbols distributed to reinforce hierarchy.	A few visible symbols change.	Minimum status differentials to de-emphasise inherent hierarchy.
Compensation policies	Variable pay where feasible to provide individual incentive.	Typically no basic changes in compensation concepts.	Variable rewards to create equity and reinforce groups achievements: gain sharing, profit sharing.
	Individual pay geared to job evaluation.		Individual pay linked to skills and mastery.
	In downturn, cuts concentrated on hourly payroll.	Equity of sacrifice among employee groups.	Equality of sacrifice.
Employment assurances	Employees regarded as variable costs.	Assurances that participation will not result in loss of job.	Assurances that participation will not result in loss of job.
		Extra effort to avoid layoff.	High commitment to avoid or assist in re-employment.
			Priority for training and retaining existing workforce.
Employee voice policies	Employee input allowed on relatively narrow agenda. Attendant risks emphasized. Methods include open-door policy, attitude surveys, grievance procedures, and collective bargaining in some organizations.	Addition of limited, *ad hoc* consultation mechanisms. No change in corporate governance.	Employee participation encouraged on wide range of issues. Attendant benefits emphasized. New concepts of corporate governance.
	Business information distributed on strictly defined 'need to know' basis.	Additional sharing of information.	Business data shared widely.
Labour-management relations	Adversarial labour relations; emphasis on interest conflict.	Thawing of adversarial attitudes; joint sponsorshipof QWL or EI; emphasis on common fate.	Mutuality in labour relations; joint planning and problem solving on expanded agenda.
			Unions, management, and workers redefine their respective roles.

Source: Walton (1985: 81).

The changing competitive environment, the need to come to terms with more demanding customers, the quest for flexibility and for employee commitment; all this echoes the earlier discussion of TQM. It appears that debates on strategic HRM and TQM have much in common. TQM implies the adoption of flexible organisation structures, with an open management style, a strong emphasis on two-way communications, the devolution of responsibility, and the establishment of problem-solving teams, possibly of a cross-departmental nature.

In fact, the above discussion of strategic HRM suggests that there are two views on the future of HR strategy. First, according to the contingency or 'matching' model of HRM, organisations might choose to implement TQM as part of a quality enhancement strategy, along with the appropriate high-commitment HR strategy. According to the contingency view, however, not all organisations will necessarily adopt this approach, with some choosing instead to emphasise cost reduction and the matching HR strategy. A second view sees the cost-reduction strategy as of decreasing significance, at least in the developed economies, with an attendant shift towards the high-commitment strategy. The suggestion here is that the adoption of a high-quality strategy is no longer a matter of choice. This goes back to our earlier discussion on whether TQM is seen as an option or an imperative. As we have seen, the TQM literature is unanimous in suggesting the latter.

TQM and human resource management

Regardless of whether the high-quality strategy is a matter of choice or of necessity, the above discussion suggests that TQM requires a particular approach to HR strategy if it is to be implemented successfully. In this section, we provide a detailed discussion of such a proposition at the level of HR policies and practices.

Devanna *et al.* (1984) argue that the various elements of human resource management should fit together as a coherent whole, as reflected in their 'HRM cycle' (Figure 4.1). This suggests that the bid to develop a quality culture begins with staff selection and induction, where the aim is to select employees with the required attitudinal and behavioural characteristics and to then induct them into the quality culture. Effective recruitment advertising is critical, including the careful choice of advertising media and the formulation of appropriate advertising messages. Job advertisements based on life-themes may be useful in attracting applicants with the appropriate attitudes (Snape *et al.*, 1994: 25), realistic job previews may be helpful in encouraging applicants to self-screen, whilst selection methods may be designed to test for aptitude in problem-solving and teamworking (Bowen and Lawler, 1992: 35). There may also be merit in involving members of the work team in the selection process. There is some evidence that organisations are identifying selection as playing a key role in TQM (Industrial Relations Review and Report, 1991), with more widespread use of psychometric testing and assessment centres. Storey (1992: 99), for example, describes Jaguar's use of tests in the selection of foremen and hourly-paid workers, to measure such dimensions as 'independence of thought', 'teamworking' and 'cooperativeness'.

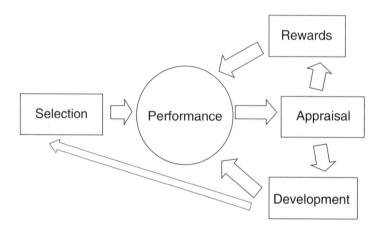

FIGURE 4.1   The human resource management cycle

Source: Mary Anne Devanna, Charles J. Fombrun and Noel M. Tichy – A framework for strategic human resource management. In Charles J. Fombrun, Noel M. Tichy and Mary Anne Devanna (eds) *Strategic Human Resource Management* (New York: John Wiley and Sons, 1984), figure 3.2, p. 41. Copyright © 1984 by John Wiley and Sons. Reprinted with permission.

Once employees are brought into the organisation, the HRM cycle focuses our attention on the management of individual and organisational performance through appraisal, rewards and development. Some have suggested that appraisal may play a key role in developing, communicating and monitoring the achievement of quality standards (Deblieux, 1991). Unfortunately, however, performance appraisal has often failed to live up its promise, and may degenerate into little more than an empty ritual (Snape *et al.*, 1994: 43). Furthermore, some of the quality gurus, most notably Deming (1986), have argued that performance appraisal is inconsistent with TQM. He argues that variation in performance is attributable mainly to work systems rather than to variations in the performance of individual workers; that quality improvements are thus found mainly by changing processes rather than people, and that the key is to develop cooperative teamwork. This, he claims, is difficult to do where the focus is on 'blaming' the individual, as in traditional appraisal, and where as a result there is a climate of fear and risk avoidance, and a concern for short-term, individual targets, all of which undermine the cooperative, creative, and committed behaviour necessary for continuous improvement. Some have argued that what is needed for TQM is a shift away from the traditional focus on results and individual recognition, towards processes and group recognition (Glover, 1993).

Western management, however, has been reluctant to dispense with appraisal. Even where organisations implement TQM, they have often done so alongside existing appraisal systems, in some cases even incorporating quality indicators into the appraisal (Bowen and Lawler, 1992: 37; Wilkinson *et al.*, 1993). Some commentators have argued that much can be done to make appraisal schemes more effective, one particular suggestion being to look beyond the traditional top-down approach by including people other than the manager in an individual's appraisal. Under TQM, the customer, whether internal or external to the organisation, is seen as supreme, so that it seems logical to include an element of customer evaluation in the performance appraisal. Similarly, peer review may help underpin cooperation and team-based performance, whilst appraisal of managers and supervisors by their subordinates may help develop a more open, positive management style (Redman and Snape, 1992).

Among the more sophisticated defences of appraisal is that of Fletcher (1993), who concedes much to Deming's (1986) view of assessment-based appraisal as a 'deadly disease' of Western management, especially given that external factors other than individual performance are a major influence on outcomes and that appraisers face difficulties in evaluating performance differentials and attributing their causes. Fletcher thus rejects the traditional assessment-based approach, especially where it includes merit pay, and argues instead for an approach based on the setting and reviewing of personal objectives, linked to a review of the training and development needs of the individual. This emphasises the developmental rather than the judgmental aspects of appraisal and moves away from the allocation of 'blame' towards the development of the individual.

Training and development has been regarded by most commentators as essential to the implementation of TQM. The proponents of TQM have tended to concentrate on training in the quality management tools and techniques. Employees are likely to need training in the principles of continuous improvement, problem-solving techniques and statistical process control. However, it is important to recognise that TQM also has implications for management development, particularly given the likely impact on management style, with an emphasis on interpersonal skills and leadership. In the longer term there may also be implications for career development paths, because the delayered, flexible organisation implied by many of the TQM gurus reduces the scope for hierarchical career progression, but at the same time places cross-functional experience at a premium (Bowen and Lawler, 1992: 36). 'Horizontal' career development is thus likely to become more significant, and career paths may become more complex and diverse. This suggests that there will be a need for individual career counselling.

A key element in the HRM cycle is to retain and motivate employees through the rewards system. The retention of high quality employees will require an innovative approach to rewards, particularly in competitive labour markets. Single-status terms and conditions can help to break down 'us and them' attitudes and promote a sense of shared responsibility for continuous improvement, whilst incentives may also have a role to play. However, incentive pay has been a controversial issue in the quality management literature. There is general agreement that output-related payment-by-results systems can undermine employee commitment to quality, but some of the quality gurus have gone even further. Deming (1986) is strongly opposed to attempts to underpin quality improvement with pay incentives and, as we have seen, he argues that performance appraisal and management-by-objectives (MBO) are inconsistent with the kinds of behaviours necessary for continuous improvement. Some of the TQM gurus have argued that the key to the development of the quality culture is the provision of recognition rather than reward, and have suggested the use of award schemes as a way of recognising outstanding performance or achievements. Such schemes may involve either tokens or prizes of significant financial value, but in either case the aim is to provide public recognition.

Others have questioned this view, suggesting that pay and appraisal may be used as part of the implementation of TQM, provided that management realise that incentives alone are unlikely to be sufficient to build the quality culture. Furthermore, employers could be well advised to link pay and quality. There may be an expectation amongst employees that they should receive increased pay in return for taking on greater responsibility for quality, and that they should share directly in the financial benefits of quality improvement (Drummond and Chell, 1992). Where this is not forthcoming there may be a risk of employees becoming disillusioned with TQM. One US commentator has suggested that quality management programmes often 'run out of steam' three to five years on, as employees begin to lose interest in token rewards and praise amid a growing expectation that they are due a share of the financial benefits of their quality improvement efforts (T. Walker, 1992). It seems that praise and a pat on the back may go only so far in a society where cash has traditionally been regarded as the true measure of value.

Clearly, this is a controversial area, and the implementation of TQM is likely to involve a search for new forms of reward. Developments such as group-based incentives, aimed at encouraging teamwork, and skills-based pay, aimed at encouraging individuals to broaden their skills, are likely to be consistent with TQM and may provide a complement or even a substitute for more traditional types of incentives (Bowen and Lawler, 1992: 37–8). Financial incentives may be directly linked with quality enhancement, for example by linking pay to customer feedback on service quality (Schuler and Harris, 1992). Kessler (1995) suggests that only a minority of organisations attempt to use financial incentives to underpin quality improvement. Among those who are attempting to do this, he identifies three approaches: setting individual quality improvement targets, linking pay to behaviours felt to contribute to quality and customer requirements, and linking collective bonuses to organisation-level quality targets.

As well as the above changes in HR policies and practices, it has been suggested that TQM may require a move away from detailed, fixed job descriptions (Bowen and Lawler, 1992: 37–8). This reflects the need to encourage flexibility, teamwork and a broadening of skills amongst the workforce, all of which might be undermined by an adherence to tightly defined jobs. The suggestion is not to reject job analysis altogether but rather to identify broader, more flexible roles, with an avoidance of too restrictive a delineation of jobs.

Much of the above discussion is predicated on the assumption that HRM can be utilised in the implementation of TQM through the management of individual performance. This might be termed the '*performance management*' view, with HRM focusing on the management of performance through the HR cycle, with appraisal, rewards, and development efforts all underpinning a commitment to continuous improvement (Table 4.2). From this perspective HRM thus provides key 'levers' of change in the creation of the quality culture.

TABLE 4.2 **TQM and the management of performance: two competing views**

	Performance management	*Deming TQM*
Focus for performance improvement	Individual performance	System performance
HRM implications	Individual appraisal	Avoid blaming the individual – 'drive out fear'
	Rewards	
	Development	Provide recognition, education and leadership

However, we have also encountered an alternative version of the relationship between TQM and HRM – what we might call the '*Deming TQM*' view. The key issue here is whether the main source of variation in organisational performance is the system or individual performance. The view implicit in the performance management approach is that organisational performance can be effectively managed by focusing on the performance of individual workers. In contrast, Deming (1986) argues that differences in the performance of individuals belong to the category of 'special causes' of variation in work performance, and as such are minor relative to the 'common causes' of performance variation. He argues that the latter are endemic to the system of work and are primarily attributable to system design rather than to the day-to-day work effort of particular individuals. The implication is that attempts to manage organisational performance through the performance of individual workers are mistaken.

Thus we have two contrasting hypotheses: one focusing on the management of individual performance, the other on improving the system. In fact, as we have seen, Deming goes further and argues that individual appraisal and incentives divert attention from the true causes of performance variation and actually undermine those employee behaviours which contribute towards continuous improvement. In making this additional step, he appears to argue that the two approaches are mutually exclusive.

Deming is surely correct to counsel against blaming individual workers for deficiencies in the work system, and it is widely recognised that evaluating workers against targets which are beyond their control is likely to demotivate. We have already seen, however, that the proponents of TQM have given too little serious attention to the question of individual motivation and commitment, and that there is a need to examine more clearly how HRM affects the implementation of TQM. Our view is that we need a synthesis of the two views outlined in Table 4.2. Thus, whilst HRM researchers and practitioners have tended to concentrate on the individual rather than on systemic determinants of performance, recent theoretical work has attempted to synthesise these. Waldman (1994), for example, proposes a theory of work performance in terms of both 'person factors' (knowledge, skills and attitudes, and individual motivation) and 'system factors' (including the work system constraints and demands). Aside from determining work performance, these two sets of factors are said to interact, for example with the work system impacting on skills development and motivation and with people also influencing the design of the system. This is in line with the suggestion that HR policies can be adapted to underpin the development of the necessary motivation, attitudes and competencies required for TQM. It also suggests that the work context and job design influence individual commitment to continuous improvement. It is to this that we now turn.

Commitment, the work context and job design

Oliver (1990) characterises TQM as involving a shift from a management strategy of 'direct control' to a 'responsible autonomy' approach, based on self-control and high levels of commitment. He suggests that attempts to develop employee commitment to TQM need to go beyond the exhortation approach of many programmes by changing the context within which work is carried out. He suggests how this might be done, building on the work of Keisler and Salancik on the psychology of commitment. The argument is that it is the *context* within which work is carried out that is the key determinant of behaviour. Thus:

> Unlike the approach which typically assumes that a change in attitude must precede a change in behaviour, this view regards behaviour as governed largely by the social context within which people are operating. Changes in behaviour, under this model, stem from adjustments to the context rather than from adjustments to attitudes. The model in fact goes further and considers attitude change as a consequence of changes in behaviour, rather than vice versa. (Oliver, 1990: 24)

The model is outlined in Figure 4.2. The context within which work is performed is seen as being made up of four elements. *'Explicitness'* refers to the need to make responsibilities clear, on the basis that individuals are more likely to avoid feeling responsible where goals are ambiguous. *'Revocability'* refers to the extent to which the individual worker's actions are irreversible. Thus, if we know that the work which we do is subject to little or no checking by others, then we are likely to exercise a higher degree of responsibility. *'Publicity'* reflects the view that where our actions and their consequences are visible to others, we are more likely to develop a sense of responsibility. The notion here is one of social pressure and the individual's need for approval. Finally, *'Volition'* refers to the extent to which individuals feel that they are in control of their own actions, in the sense of having a degree of real choice. The argument is that each of these contextual factors is positively related to the individual's sense of 'felt responsibility' or 'commitment', which then creates in the individual a pressure to act in a prescribed manner.

Oliver discusses how the work environment in organisations might be restructured in ways which underpin the development of a commitment to continuous improvement. His detailed suggestions include: the introduction of explicit performance indicators in order to develop explicitness and publicity; the removal of quality control inspection to increase revocability; and involving and empowering employees to increase volition.

Others have emphasised the importance of job design in winning employee commitment. James (1991), for example, argues that employees are only likely to show commitment when jobs are meaningful, involve significant responsibility and where the employee is able to get direct feedback on performance from the job itself. This requires jobs which utilise a variety of skills, result in an identifiable and significant outcome, and involve a significant degree of autonomy and discretion. As we have seen, such job design principles are also found in Walton's (1985) vision of the high-commitment HR strategy.

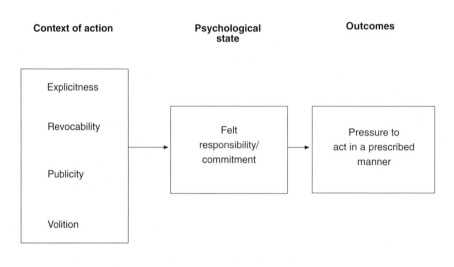

FIGURE 4.2   A model of commitment

Source: Oliver (1990: 24).

The interesting point for our purposes is that such contributions highlight the importance of the work environment itself in producing behavioural changes, and shift the emphasis away from attempting to change attitudes through exhortation. This contrasts with much of the TQM literature, which tends to emphasise the creation of attitudinal change through leadership and education, and extends the earlier discussion of HR strategy to encompass the impact of the work system on individual and organisational performance.

Employee relations and involvement

Much of the modern literature on quality management suggests that employees need to understand the process of continuous improvement and must be actively involved (Crosby, 1979; Deming, 1986). As Ishikawa puts it:

Top managers and middle managers must be bold enough to delegate as much authority as possible. That is the way to establish respect for humanity as your management philosophy. It is a management system in which all employees participate from the top down and from the bottom up, and humanity is fully respected. (1985: 112)

The emphasis is on autonomy, creativity, active cooperation and self-control from employees, with employee involvement a key theme.

TQM has been seen as including three elements of employee involvement (Wilkinson, 1994: 279–280). First, there is the educative process at company level, with briefings, videos, posters and newsletters being used to launch and sustain the TQM message. Second, participative structures such as quality circles, improvement and action teams may be established on an *ad hoc* or more permanent basis. These provide an institutional focus for problem-solving activity amongst the workforce. Third, as we have seen, TQM may be associated with changes in the organisation of work, including the elimination of inspectors, or at least a reduction in their number, more teamwork, a shift towards cell organisation and the establishment of semi-autonomous work groups. Again, the emphasis is on greater autonomy and self-control, with management delegating responsibility for quality and improvement, rather than seeking simply to blame employees for mistakes (Deming, 1986).

There are two key underlying assumptions in all this. First, the emphasis on commitment, self-control and trust implies a 'Theory Y' view of individuals: that if given autonomy and responsibility, workers will respond in a highly committed and motivated way. This contrasts with the traditional 'Theory X' view of workers as essentially lazy and in need of close monitoring and control. Thus, according to this assumption, TQM holds a positive, hopeful message to workers as well as to consumers, in that it offers opportunities for self-actualisation in a challenging but satisfying work environment.

The second assumption may lead us to a less optimistic conclusion. TQM contains an implicit unitarism, assuming that everyone in the organisation shares a set of common interests and values, with management's right to manage being automatically accepted as legitimate. The customer-defined goals of TQM are never really questioned, and management reduces to a technical matter of transforming inputs into outputs so as to maximise customer satisfaction. The overriding aim on the part of management is to enlist employees' commitment to meeting customer needs. Thus:

> employees are immersed in the logic of the market and are likely to be convinced of the legitimacy of company decisions. (Wilkinson *et al.*, 1991: 30)

Employee involvement, whilst a major element in TQM, is nevertheless focused on the task, rather than on broader issues of business strategy, investment or staffing. Indeed, TQM may reduce employee autonomy to the extent that participation in TQM is seen as compulsory (Geary, 1993), and the top-down approach advocated in the TQM literature may similarly limit real employee involvement in key decisions (Lawler *et al.*, 1992: 103). Continuous improvement requires the performance of individual tasks to be tightly defined and routinised, with improvements coming in the form of incremental changes to this specification (Oakland, 1993). The fact that employees are asked to participate in the design of tasks and that the individual's routine may now encompass a wider range of tasks may make TQM palatable to employees (Cappelli and Rogovsky, 1994: 207–8), but the fact remains that participation is restricted in scope. Critical evaluations have seen TQM and JIT manufacturing systems as part of an attempt to intensify work by eliminating non-productive time and increasing self-surveillance by the work group (Dawson and Webb, 1989; Delbridge *et al.*, 1992; Sewell and Wilkinson, 1992a, b). On this interpretation, TQM is simply another episode in the long struggle over the 'frontier of control' in the workplace, and one which sees management enlisting peer pressure and the legitimating device of customer awareness in the bid to extend management control. Thus there is a clear division of opinion between those who see TQM as leading to empowerment and those who argue that it involves intensification (see Table 4.3).

TABLE 4.3   Employee involvement and
TQM: contrasting perspectives

Bouquets	*Brickbats*
Education	Indoctrination
Empowerment	Emasculation
Liberating	Controlling
Delayering	Intensification
Teamwork	Peer group pressure
Responsibility	Surveillance
Post-Fordism	Neo-Fordism
Blame free culture	Identification of errors
Commitment	Compliance

Source: Wilkinson *et al.*, 1997b.

The issue of conflict is not addressed in most of the TQM literature, thus reflecting its unitarist and managerialist undertones. There is no consideration of the interests of workers themselves, aside from the assumption that TQM will offer scope for involvement and enhance job security for the majority. Not surprisingly, trade unions and collective bargaining are hardly mentioned. However, such omissions may be critical, given traditional patterns of pluralist industrial relations, which have accepted trade unions as the legitimate representative of employee interests, and recognised that such interests may on occasion conflict with those of management, on issues of pay, benefits and the organisation of work. Furthermore, the adversarial, low-trust pattern of industrial relations found in parts of UK manufacturing and elsewhere is in clear contrast to the commitment vision of both TQM and HRM (Guest, 1987; Wilkinson *et al.*, 1991).

To what extent have trade unions resisted the implementation of TQM? In some cases, union representatives have taken the view that the introduction of TQM is a management issue which does not directly concern the unions (Wilkinson *et al.*, 1992; Dawson, 1994: 84). But as TQM is implemented and the organisational and industrial relations implications become clearer, union representatives can be expected to become increasingly concerned. This was certainly so in a case study of a machine tool company completed by two of the authors (Wilkinson *et al.*, 1992), and Ferner and Colling (1991) show that unions at British Telecom eventually turned the quality theme around by calling for sufficient resources to enable their members to deliver on quality. Unions nationally have expressed concern about the impact of initiatives such as TQM, employee involvement, HRM and customer service programmes (Heery, 1993). Unions may fear that such developments threaten to marginalise their role in the workplace, by establishing rival channels of communication, and emphasising individual and small group over collective issues. They have also been concerned about the detailed impact on their members, for example about the risks associated with the wearing of name badges and dispensing with security screens in service organisations, about the possible use of customer feedback information to discipline employees, and about the implications of more flexible working hours and patterns (Heery, 1993: 288). Employees and their unions may also fear the possible impact of TQM on the intensity of work, and may see it as involving increased responsibility and pressure with little or no additional reward. This brings us back to our earlier discussion of TQM and pay; where there is an expectation that rewards follow additional effort, it may be difficult for management to resist this without the risk of resentment and demotivation (Drummond and Chell, 1992).

However, unions are not necessarily opposed to TQM. In 1994 the TUC published a report on HRM in which it suggests that management and unions can engage in a cooperative partnership in designing and implementing organisational change. A report from the Involvement and Participation Association, endorsed by senior managers and union leaders, also urges a partnership at workplace level (Marchington, 1995). Such views presumably envisage a form of enterprise unionism committed to the enhancement of productivity and quality, based on a firm acceptance of the common interests of management and employees. How widespread such a model can become depends as much on the precise nature of organisational changes and their handling by management, as on national union policy.

Thus, employee involvement techniques have been seen as an important lever of change in the implementation of TQM; indeed, involvement is at the very heart of TQM principles. However, TQM raises important industrial relations issues which are neglected in the TQM literature and which render the achievement of managerial objectives problematic.

Role of the Personnel function in TQM

Given the importance of HR issues in the successful implementation of TQM, what is the role of personnel specialists in all this? Clearly, they may be expected to be involved in the design and implementation of the new HR policies which are needed to underpin change. Such policies can act as critical symbols of the changes taking place, so that the contribution of the personnel specialist could in principle be moved to centre stage by TQM.

Personnel, however, has long been recognised as an ambiguous specialism, whose distinctive contribution may be difficult to assess. Personnel specialists have difficulty in claiming a well-defined and distinctive area of expertise; all managers are, after all, concerned with the management of people. What is so special about Personnel? Indeed, it has been argued that whilst recent years have seen a higher profile for HR issues in organisations, this does not necessarily translate into a higher profile for the personnel specialism, because line and top management are expected to show a greater awareness and assume more responsibility for HR issues (Storey, 1992). It may simply be the case that HR is too important to be left to Personnel, which as a specialism has for so long suffered from a lack status in the organisation, due to personnel specialists' limited awareness of the real issues facing the organisation, a lack of confidence in the department from top management, and Personnel's own lack of skills and/or self-confidence (Bowen and Lawler, 1992: 31–2).

In this section, we consider these issues from two perspectives. First, we examine the possible roles which Personnel may play in the implementation of TQM, in terms of the strategic nature of that role and the profile of the function. Second, we look more broadly at the implications of TQM for the future of the Personnel function.

A study involving two of the present authors helps us to understand the role of Personnel in the design and implementation of TQM programmes (Institute of Personnel Management, 1993; Wilkinson and Marchington, 1994). Drawing on in-depth case studies of 15 organisations, they describe four basic roles which personnel specialists were playing in the design and implementation of TQM. They distinguish between these roles along two dimensions: First, according to whether Personnel had played a strategic or an operational role *vis-à-vis* TQM. In extreme, the distinction is between an essentially routine administrative role, or alternatively being heavily involved in the design, implementation and evaluation of the programme. Second, they distinguish between high and low profile personnel departments, the former being highly visible to other managers and employees, and the latter being restricted to a behind-the-scenes role. The distinction between these two dimensions will become clearer as we examine each role in turn (see Figure 4.3).

FIGURE 4.3   The role of Personnel in total quality management

Source: Wilkinson and Marchington (1994: 14).

The first is the *'facilitator'* role. This was found in all the case studies, and involves the personnel department providing hands-on support for line managers in relation to the implementation of TQM, essentially at the operational level. This may involve responding to requests from line managers for assistance with training, or the organisation of newsletters and other communications media. For example, at Bedfordshire County Council, the personnel department had prepared the introductory leaflets on the Council's 'new management style', and had ensured that a statement of these new values was disseminated to employees. Although essential to the implementation of TQM, the facilitator role amounts to little more than the routine practice of personnel management.

The second role is the *'internal contractor'*. This involves the personnel department agreeing targets and standards for the delivery and administration of HR services to internal customers. Amongst their case studies, the clearest example of this was a computer software company which had achieved ISO 9000 series registration in 1987. Here, the personnel function had produced 'simple quality targets of Personnel products and services' following discussions with users. Ten areas were identified, ranging from recruitment to pay and performance review. In each case, the customers were clearly identified, and service standards set out. For example, offers and contracts were to be provided to managers within 24 hours of request.

Bowen and Lawler (1992) outline their vision of what such a TQM-based, internal contractor personnel department would look like. The aim would be, of course, to do things right first time, for example by avoiding the need to redesign failed training programmes or bonus schemes. There would be a clear focus on customer needs, providing services that may be customised, rather than providing standardised programmes to all. This would entail involving customers, for example line managers or employees, in specifying the design of services. The implementation of TQM in the personnel department would also involve the empowerment of those working in the department, and a concentration on continuous improvement.

Whilst the internal contractor, like the facilitator, works at the operational rather than the strategic level, nevertheless it is a higher profile role, given the attempt to highlight and publicise service standards. Such an approach treats Personnel as being responsible to its internal customers for quality standards, a key principle of TQM, of course. There may be an element of Personnel attempting to lead the TQM programme by example, and the application of TQM principles within the department may be seen as the first step in helping to implement them in the wider organisation (Clinton *et al.*, 1994: 11), but the internal contractor role still lacks a strategic input into the design of the TQM programme.

The third role is that of the *'change agent'*, which is both high profile and strategic. At the extreme, this involves the personnel department playing a major role in designing the TQM programme, preparing the ground for the development of the 'quality culture', and helping to drive the programme. TQM is thus seen as synonymous with organisational change, and Personnel presents itself as the function best able to define and lead this process. This role was seen in several of the case studies, most clearly at Ilford Ltd and Peterborough Priority Services. At Ilford, it was widely recognised within the company that the human resources function had played a major role in the development of TQM; 'creating the structure and culture within which TQM is possible', and acting as 'an engine of change', according to managers interviewed in the company. At Peterborough, the quality coordinator reported to the director of human resources and quality, who chaired the quality forum and played a leading role in other TQM structures. The personnel function had long taken the lead in developing quality initiatives; for example, the personnel director of the old District Health Authority introduced an employee charter and a positive action programme prior to the organisation implementing a patient's charter (in advance of Government initiatives in this area).

Finally, we have the *'hidden persuader'*. Here, the personnel department plays a key strategic role in TQM initiatives, for example by making a critical contribution to top management discussions. Unlike the change agent, however, the hidden persuader is not highly visible to other managers and employees, acting rather as a sounding board or mentor for senior management. Thus, at Racal Data Networks the managing director had chosen the human resources function to assist the quality manager in the development of the TQM programme because human resources was seen as neutral and able to take an overview of the change process, without pursuing potentially divisive departmental goals.

Perhaps not surprisingly, there are a number of pitfalls with these various roles. The change agent, whilst offering a visible and important role for Personnel, also carries the risk of alienating other departments if the TQM programme is resented or seen as a failure. In contrast, the hidden persuader faces the reverse risk of gaining little credit for success, a risk also faced by the backroom approach of the facilitator. The internal contractor carries the obvious danger of laying the performance and credibility of the personnel function open to public scrutiny, although it is fair to say that this is precisely what TQM is seeking to achieve for all activities in the organisation. A particular threat for Personnel is that as a staff function, the internal contractor approach increases the likelihood that managers will wish to contract for such services outside the organisation. Again, to the extent that such pressures lead to improved quality and effectiveness, TQM will be achieving its objectives.

A particular personnel department is not, of course, restricted to one of these four roles. Most will act as facilitators, as this is simply part of the normal role of a personnel department, but may take on one or more of the others. Thus it is perfectly feasible to act as a facilitator in the provision of support for training and communications initiatives, yet at the same time to make a strategic contribution to the design of the TQM programme and associated HR strategies, and also to implement TQM principles within the personnel department itself in the form of the internal contractor role.

The extent to which Personnel takes on one or more roles is not simply a matter of personal choice on the part of personnel managers. Much depends on three critical factors. First, the existing status and style of the function – a department which has hitherto performed little more than basic administrative work is less likely to have the expertise and credibility suddenly to take on a strategic role with respect to TQM. Second, the origin of the TQM initiative – schemes initiated by a marketing director are likely to have a different emphasis from those initiated by operations managers, and the content and concerns may affect the perceived relevance of the HR dimension. Third, the history of quality management within the organisation may also be important. Where earlier systems-based approaches to quality management are perceived to have failed, this may provide an opportunity for Personnel to claim a more strategic role by offering a new emphasis.

The role adopted by Personnel will not necessarily be constant. As a continuous process, rather than a fixed-term programme, TQM offers the opportunity for Personnel to be involved to a greater or lesser extent over time. There may be a heavy involvement in the initial design and implementation stages, only for Personnel to then slip into the background, encouraging line managers to take on greater responsibility for HR and quality-related issues. Personnel may be heavily involved in periodic evaluations and reviews of progress, for example through employee attitude surveys or comparisons with competitors.

TQM and the future of Personnel

What are the implications of TQM for the future of the personnel function? The response of the personnel function can be seen in the context of Personnel's long-term search for legitimacy in the eyes of managerial colleagues, According to Storey:

> personnel management has long been dogged by problems of credibility, marginality, ambiguity, and a trash-can labelling which has relegated it to a relatively disconnected set of activities – many of them tainted with a low status and welfare connotation. (1989: 5)

TQM provides a customer focus for the activities of Personnel, and thus promises to remove the structural and ideological ambiguities of the function. However, whilst most would agree that TQM can remind personnel departments 'to accept that their role is to serve their customers and not their egos' (Giles and Williams, 1991: 29), this begs the question of how customer needs are to be defined. To the extent that Personnel moves into a narrowly conformist internal contractor relationship, where line managers define their needs and are able to reject the services and advice of the personnel specialist, Personnel can do little more than reflect the competencies and values of such managers. However, as Fowler points out:

> The role of the personnel function is not solely to satisfy the heads of various line units. It is also to contribute to the achievement of corporate goals – a role which may sometimes require the stance taken by individual managers to be challenged. (1993: 29)

If Personnel is to maintain its professional integrity, it needs to transcend the narrow facilitator and internal contractor roles, and make a more strategic contribution. Fowler (1993) sees an effective personnel department as having the three key qualities of professional knowledge and expertise; relevance to the needs of corporate and line management in the achievement of the organisation's objectives in the short and long term; and a proactive approach, initiating proposals for action rather then simply responding to others. Given the crucial role of HR factors in the successful implementation of TQM, we suggest that TQM represents an opportunity for the personnel function to develop and demonstrate its effectiveness, but the question remains as to whether Personnel is able to display these three qualities.

We can provide an initial assessment of this question by reviewing some of the evidence on such qualities. On the first, the possession of professional knowledge and expertise, the Workplace Industrial Relations Surveys (WIRS) suggest that the proportion of personnel managers in British workplaces with formal professional or educational qualifications directly relating to their work stood at just over 54 per cent by 1990, having increased during the early 1980s and then fallen slightly in the later part of the decade (Millward *et al.*, 1992: 35).

The Institute of Personnel and Development (IPD), formed as a result of a merger of the Institute of Personnel Management (IPM) and Institute of Training and Development (ITD) in 1994, looks set to play an important role in developing professional standards in Personnel, developing codes of professional practice, training and educational services, consultancy, a locum service and a growing emphasis on continuous professional development. It must be recognised, however, that with only a proportion of personnel managers in membership, the influence of the IPD in practice is likely to be uneven, and whilst a growing number of Personnel job advertisements specify IPD qualifications, the Institute is far from being a monopolistic qualifying association.

All this suggests that we cannot take for granted that personnel 'professionals' necessarily have access to a recognised body of professional knowledge. Furthermore, it is to some degree unclear as to what exactly such a body of knowledge would be in the case of Personnel. The initial IPM training courses emphasised the behavioural sciences as a distinctive knowledge base for personnel practice, but recent developments in IPD syllabuses have placed more emphasis on 'professional skills'. It is by no means clear that possession of these is the distinctive feature of personnel professionals.

The extent to which the personnel specialist has so far been able to demonstrate relevance to the achievement of the organisation's objectives in the short and long term and adopt a proactive approach may also be questioned. Purcell and Ahlstrand's (1994: 55–61) review of the evidence on the influence of human resource issues in the formulation of corporate strategy is not encouraging. They suggest that personnel issues are usually considered in the implementation stage of strategic decisions on such matters as restructuring, redundancies and plant closure, but that such issues are rarely significant at the formulation stage, where financial and technical factors are of prime importance. The personnel function itself is revealed as having limited influence at the strategic level in most organisations, relative to other business functions.

However, Storey's (1992) study of human resource management in large British organisations suggests that whilst the personnel function may be marginalised when it comes to the major organisational change issues of the day, there is evidence that senior and line management themselves are recognising the importance of people–management issues and are increasingly taking on key responsibilities in this area. Thus, the majority of the organisational change initiatives in his 15 case-study organisations came from such managers, rather than from the personnel function itself. The implication is that initiatives such as TQM may proceed with or without the active involvement of Personnel. Our view is that, given the centrality of HR policies and practices to such initiatives, Personnel has something to contribute and that the probability of successful implementation can be increased through an actively involved personnel function. On the basis of our brief review of Personnel's past record, however, it seems that the function has much to do to achieve its full potential.

Conclusions

In this chapter, we have reviewed the human resource implications of TQM. We have shown that HR issues are central to its implementation, with the underlying assumption that employees and managers need to adopt the practice of continuous improvement. Whilst the TQM literature recognises the importance of HR issues, however, we find that the discussion is often superficial, with little on how exactly the quality culture is to be created, beyond relatively vague managerialist statements about the need for leadership, education and recognition.

The literature on organisational culture provides some guidance on the implementation of TQM, emphasising not only exhortation, education and leadership, but also HR policies and the broader work context. One hypothesis is that TQM requires the implementation of a high-commitment HR strategy, emphasising quality, flexibility and trust. Such a strategy has implications for management style and the organisation of work, as well as for HR policies and practices. In exploring these issues in detail we encountered two contrasting views of organisational performance, one emphasising the management of individual performance, the other focusing on the work system. We rejected the suggestion that these are mutually exclusive perspectives and suggested that a balanced approach would focus on the performance of individuals and on improvements in the work system, recognising the interdependencies between these two aspects of performance. Thus, we have argued that the contribution of HRM amounts to more than simply avoiding 'blaming the individual', and that changes in HR policies and practices, increased employee involvement and changes in the organisation of work may all have an important role in the implementation of TQM.

We have also noted, however, that the development of the quality culture is likely to be a difficult and lengthy process. Organisational cultures may be resistant to change, with some commentators questioning whether it is meaningful to talk about the 'management' of culture at all. We have argued that the TQM literature often masks an implicit unitarism, emphasising a top-down approach to implementation, and underestimates the difficulties in winning commitment to TQM in the presence of a pluralist industrial relations culture.

The perspective of employees and their trade unions may be difficult to ignore when it comes to the practicalities of implementation.

We have also examined the role of the personnel department in the implementation of TQM. We argued that this varies from a purely administrative support, low profile role in some organisations, to a more strategic and highly visible role in others. A range of factors was identified as influencing this role. We suggested that there is the potential for Personnel to make a major input into the implementation of TQM, but that this very much depends on the ability of personnel specialists to respond to the challenge. Admittedly, our review of Personnel's record as a contributor to strategic decision-making is hardly encouraging. It seems that the function has much to do if it is to maximise its contribution.

CHAPTER 5

TQM in Practice

Introduction

This chapter seeks to evaluate the significance and achievements of TQM. We seek to move beyond the euphoria of earlier accounts and to evaluate the emerging UK and US evidence. The chapter proceeds as follows: first, we review some evidence on the importance of quality in business strategies. What emerges from this is that quality seems to have a key role in competitive success. Second, we review the literature on the evaluation of TQM itself. Here the evidence is that TQM is difficult to implement, with many attempts failing in the early stages, although there is some evidence to suggest that it can contribute to organisational success. Finally, we try to account for this uneven performance by reporting on the difficulties in implementing quality management, drawing on our own UK study.

Quality and competitive advantage: the evidence

In the trading sector at least, especially in recent years, the pressure of competitive forces has been felt increasingly by employers – and then passed on to employees. The language of competitive advantage has become much more widespread, and employers have been urged to view competitors as opponents to be 'beaten' in the market place. If TQM is to represent a justifiable expenditure of effort, then it surely must be capable of delivering competitive advantage. In this section, we review the evidence on the contribution of product and service quality to competitive advantage and performance, and in the following section we present an evaluation of TQM itself.

Quality and competitive success

As part of the 1990 Workplace Industrial Relations Survey (WIRS), 'financial managers' in almost 500 establishments were asked which features of their product or service were most crucial for competitive success. The results appear in Table 5.1. 'Quality' comes out top, with 'price' in second place. Other aspects of quality, such as 'responsiveness to customer requirements', and 'delivery time/availability' also figure prominently. It appears from these results that quality, broadly defined, is the key factor underpinning competitive success.

TABLE 5.1   **What two features of your product or service are most crucial for competitive success? Evidence from the 1990 Workplace Industrial Relations Survey**

	Number of times mentioned	*% of organisations*
Quality	285	58
Price	235	48
Responsiveness to customer requirements	157	32
Delivery time/availabilty	79	16
Providing a distinctive product or service	54	11
Marketing/advertising	8	2
Others	6	1

Table shows number of responses (n = 489). Financial managers' questionnaire.

Source: Stevens (1992).

The profit impact of market strategy

A major study of the link between quality and business results was carried out by Profit Impact Market Strategy Associates (PIMS) using its database on over 3,000 businesses in North America and Europe. This contains price, quality, financial and market information, supplied by firms on a confidential basis. The quality measure used is a carefully constructed index of 'relative perceived quality', which takes a customer-centred view of quality, consistent with TQM (see Box 5.1). The data refers to business units rather than legal entities, covers at least five years for each business, and includes most types of business.

The PIMS data reveals a positive correlation between quality and profit, for both European and North American business. The higher the 'relative perceived quality', the higher both the average return on investment (RoI) and on sales

(RoS). Thus in the long run it seems that the most important factor affecting a business unit's performance is the quality of its products and services, relative to those of competitors (Buzzell and Gale, 1987).

BOX 5.1

The PIMS research: relative perceived quality

The PIMS work looks at 'relative perceived quality'; the perception of quality by customers, relative to the offerings of competitors. This goes beyond the 'conforming to requirements' definition used in quality assurance, and has more in common with TQM definitions. The measure is dynamic; as the company and its competitors improve their offerings, the customer's assessment will change. It takes account of all the issues which are important to customers; image and service, for example, as well as conformance quality.

PIMS's assessment process is as follows:

- A multi-function team of managers and staff specialists is asked to identify the key non-price criteria on which customers base their purchase decisions; these will include both product and service attributes.
- The team weights these criteria according to their perceived importance to customers.
- The team rates the performance of the company in question and of its competitors in meeting the criteria.
- From this information, an index of the relative quality of each company in a given market segment is calculated.

PIMS says that in 90 per cent of cases the assessments by managers are tested against customer surveys and where necessary the assessment is changed to reflect these views.

Source:　Binney (1992).

The studies suggest that profitability, both RoI and RoS, increase with relative perceived quality and with market share. Whilst market share increases profit mainly through lower costs, however, the impact of quality comes mainly through the ability to charge premium prices (Buzzell and Gale, 1987: 108). The finding is that relative perceived quality has little overall impact on relative direct costs. The explanation for this is that costs can be reduced through improved conformance to specification, as re-work and scrap are reduced, but that in many instances higher quality involves enhanced product/service attributes, which may involve additional cost. According to the PIMS research, the net effects on costs of improved quality thus tend to cancel out.

Having said all this, PIMS research rejects the traditional notion that attaining high levels of quality significantly *increases* direct costs (Phillips *et al.*, 1983). A recent study finds that the strategic positions most associated with successful firms (that is, those whose profitability is in the top third of the PIMS sample) are high quality/low cost, high quality/medium cost and medium quality/ medium cost, with the best position (in terms of RoI) being high quality/low cost, which many firms succeed in achieving (Cronshaw *et al.*, 1994). The bid to improve quality has a coercive aspect to it, to the extent that competitors which lag behind in terms of quality must either offer lower prices, thus reducing profitability, or lose market share and profitability in the longer term.

Studies using the PIMS database also suggest that improvements in perceived relative quality lead to improved market share, higher capacity utilisation, higher employee productivity and reduced unit marketing expenses (Buzzell and Gale, 1987: 114). Relative perceived quality emerges as the single most important factor affecting a business unit's long-term performance.

The conclusions of the PIMS research seems to provide support for the view that quality, defined in terms of customer requirements, is important for competitive advantage.

Evidence on the cost–quality relationship

A problem with relying solely on PIMS studies is that we may be understating the cost-reducing effects of enhanced quality and thus underestimating the potential impact of TQM. The concern is that as PIMS is based on data from US/European companies, often going back some years, this will tend to understate the true cost-reducing potential of TQM, because few if any, will have fully exploited this potential as yet. Arguably, more informative comparisons, when assessing the *potential* cost–quality relationship, are those between US/European and Japanese firms. This section examines some of the key studies that have attempted this, in particular the 'lean enterprise' research.

Lean production has emerged has a popular label to describe a group of manufacturing practices that are found in their purest form at the Toyota Motor Company. Car manufacture has formed the basis for much of the lean manufacturing debate, partly because of its origins in this industry but also because of the particular strategic nature of the motor industry and the fact that this industry, more than any other, evokes feelings of national pride and identity. Lean production is made up of a number of inter-related elements many of which are staple components of a TQM approach. The essence of lean production is, according to Womack *et al.* (1990):

- integrated, single-piece production flow, with low inventories and small batches made just-in-time
- defect prevention rather than rectification

- production pulled through the plant by customer demand rather than pushed through to fit machine loading
- flexible, multi-skilled and team-based work organisation with few indirect staff
- active involvement in problem-solving
- an emphasis on partnerships with suppliers and dealers

Following the considerable influence of the Womack *et al.* study, Andersen Consulting conducted the *Lean Enterprise Benchmarking Project* in 1992. This involved a study of manufacturing performance in Japanese and UK automotive components industries. The study's main finding was that Japan was outperforming the UK by 2:1 in productivity and an even greater margin in quality (Andersen Consulting, 1993; Oliver *et al.*, 1994). The second of the Andersen studies was reported in 1994 (Andersen Consulting, 1994). The remit of this study was broader, drawing on a worldwide study of manufacturing performance and management practices in some 71 plants across 8 countries. Of these some 13 plants were identified as 'world class', that is achieving both high productivity and high quality. A consistent finding was that there was a 2:1 difference in overall performance between world class and the other plants with the performance gap in quality the widest of all. Here world class plants outperformed others by 9:1 in seats; 16:1 in brakes and 170:1 in exhausts. The distinguishing features between the world class and other plants were disciplined process control and close management of the supply chain.

Not surprisingly, Japan had the majority of world-class plants (five) followed by US (three), France (three) and Spain (two). A regional analysis of all the plants in the study also showed that Japan outperformed other countries by considerable margins. In terms of quality US plants were the closest to the Japanese, who held an overall 30 per cent advantage. Japan held a considerably greater advantage over European countries in terms of quality, for example 4:1 over France and Germany and 8:1 over the UK and Italy. The performance of Japanese plants was also improving rapidly, increasing overall by over 38 per cent between the two studies. The conclusion of the study for the successful adoption of lean production in the UK is generally pessimistic, with the prime concern being that it is very difficult to build a world-class manufacturing base in a non-world-class economy (Oliver *et al.*, 1996). An IBM-London Business School study confirms the relatively poor performance of European plants, finding only one in 50 manufacturing plants in four European countries could be classified as 'world-class' (IBM, 1995).

The implications of these studies are clear. Lean production (with many characteristics of TQM) does reduce costs considerably; indeed, non-world-class plants pay a considerable penalty in terms of higher costs, particularly in higher direct labour costs and higher material costs that do world-class plants.

Evaluating TQM

The previous sections have established the potential contribution of enhanced product and service quality to competitive advantage and financial performance, notably through the impact on costs and the ability to charge premium prices. In this section, we turn to TQM itself. We review the studies of the implementation and impact of TQM, drawing in particular on studies conducted in the UK and the USA. Much of the preoccupation here is with the implementation of TQM and the processes involved, rather than its impact on firm performance and contribution to competitive advantage. Thus the danger here is that the point of TQM activity, business improvement, is often overlooked.

UK studies

In this section, we review the findings of six European studies on the effectiveness of TQM (Table 5.2).

TABLE 5.2   UK studies: summary

Studies	*Approach*	*Sample*	*Findings*
A.T. Kearney (1992)	Survey	Not specified	80% failed. Either had no information on performance or did not report improvement
London Business School (1992)	Self-assessment against the Baldrige Criteria Survey	42	Most firms in the UK sample would rate poorly against the Baldrige Criteria. This is not sufficient to apply for, let alone win the award
Durham University Business School (1992)	Survey	235	TQM is still an innovation and there are many uncertainties
Economist Intelligence Unit (1992)	Case studies	50 organisations (European, not just UK)	Report massive cynicism. TQ initiatives invested with TQ principles
Bradford	Externally reported information	29	A high proportion exhibit above average industry performance
Institute of Management	Survey and interviews	880	Only 8% claim QM was very successful

a) A.T. Kearney

This survey, conducted by consultants A.T. Kearney in conjunction with the TQM Magazine, reported that 80 per cent of total quality programmes had not yet demonstrated success. Of these companies 30 per cent reported no improvement and 50 per cent had no information on performance (although half of the latter claimed to be successful practitioners of TQ). Kearney characterised this approach as rose-tinted and argued that success should be demonstrated within 6 months and that companies are emphasising the quality at the expense of 'total', that is, largely examining process rather than results.

b) London Business School: in search of quality

This study by Cruise O'Brien and Voss of London Business School took a rather different approach. They asked managers to evaluate their organisations against the Baldrige criteria and concluded that 'the over-riding picture is that most UK firms are a long way from TQM and finding it difficult to get there'. They reported finding little sustained effort among managers although an optimistic view is adopted that this will emerge over time. They reported that whilst there was widespread use of quality systems (especially BS5750), most organisations were in the early stages of TQM and having problems developing it.

TABLE 5.3   London Business School findings

Category	Conclusion
1. Leadership	Many companies committed Difficulty in communicating Leadership often missing
2. Information and Analysis	More companies collecting data Little benchmarking Quality data often secondary
3. Strategic Quality Planning	Quality strategy in more companies Actions lag commitment
4. Human Resource Utilisation	New Programmes spreading Employee ownership of quality
5. Quality Assurance of Products and Services	Use of BS5750, ISO9000 Good process control, design Further room for improvement
6. Quality Results	Internal measures of quality Limited customer measures Feedback loops often poor
7. Customer Satisfaction	Few with customer standards

They suggest that TQM may suffer from 'too high' a profile and runs the risk of being 'flavour of the month'. Though many organisations have started to move down the quality route, and have achieved some of the technical aspects of quality standards, they were 'a considerable distance from achieveing total quality' (1992: 17). They express most concern about leadership. 'Too few organisations have adequate quality leadership at the top and of those that do have good quality leadership, some have problems translating that into quality commitment in senior and middle management' (*ibid*).

(c) Durham University Business School: the adoption of total quality management in northern England

This study involved a survey by Witcher and Whyte of 235 companies. They found little evidence that TQM had failed. According to their survey, two-thirds of companies have adopted TQM; most companies are still new to TQM; half of the expected benefits are being delivered with performance and involvement benefits high.

TQM appeared to be moving away from its narrow quality management origins to a fuller version of TQM. Thus there is now more company-wide development of TQM, more vision and mission statements, universal involvement of senior management, company coordinating mechanisms, surveys of external and internal customers and more use made of consultants.

They found that TQM experience is associated with greater long-term planning, a cooperative interpersonal climate, joint problem-solving, enabling management style, dynamic attitude to change and market focus.

They noted, however, that the evidence suggested that there was an internal bias in TQM – surveys are less frequent for external than internal customers and there was little use of marketing expertise in TQM initiatives. Hence TQM appeared to be rather more about addressing internal organisational issues rather than improving customer satisfaction.

According to Witcher and Whyte, 'the results indicate that pessimism about whether TQM is delivering has been overdone and that 'quick fix' expectations are misplaced. TQM is, after all, a radical new approach to business management. The true benefits will be longer term'. Some companies reported that they were using TQM to put their own houses in order before risking it on their customers. Ominously, however, Witcher and Whyte warn that TQM has to keep delivering to survive. If it produces diminishing returns, senior managers might weaken their commitment and look for 'another management fashion' to make an impact.

d) Making quality work: Economist Intelligence Unit

This study examined six 'star' companies in Europe who were renowned for quality. However, they point out that three of these, Nissan Motors UK, Club Med and Grundfos, have never had a TQ programme but have had success in applying TQ principles. The other three, Ciba-Geigy, Federal Express and ICL Product Distribution, have had programmes which produced only superficial change but made real impact when the quality programme was 'over-laid with other initiatives'. In 50 other companies examined, they reported 'massive cynicism' with TQ.

> In many companies a wide gap has opened up between the quality specialists who are convinced advocates of TQ, and both senior managers and ordinary staff who are deeply sceptical. As one manager said: 'We got the religion and then we lost it'.

They found that managers tend to go for the 'Big Bang', 'throwing people, structures and systems up in the air and hoping that when they land, things will be better. Usually they are not. Employees' sense of insecurity is increased and their willingness and ability to contribute to an improvement process is reduced'. They also pointed out that many of the processes adopted to implement TQ were themselves inconsistent with the TQ principles: they did not involve people but were imposed from the top; they did not foster learning but encouraged people to go through the motions; they did not foster co-operation between departments but encouraged competition; they did not push people to tackle root causes but allowed only addressed symptoms and they did not look outwards towards customers but were preoccupied with internal issues.

According to Binney:

> The most common barrier to effective implementation is failure to take the subject seriously. There are management teams which have TQ initiative because they believe they are required by head office to have one. They feel they have to show they are doing something; but they see TQ as yet another management fad. They acquire a simple first level understanding of TQ but they see no reason to invest time and effort in going any further. The realities of business have not changed. It is merely necessary to humour the bosses until they grow tired of TQ and go on to the next thing. (1992: 50)

e) Bradford study

A study by Zairi *et al.* (1994) at Bradford had positive findings. They relied on externally reported information and thereby hoped to avoid the problems of confidentiality and the difficulty of comparing performance based on a variety of internal measurements used by companies. The sample of companies was carefully selected for the study, based on direct knowledge and understanding of specific TQM approaches adopted by each individual company. Thus the 29 sampled did not represent any specific industry sector nor were the companies chosen on the basis of different resource availability or position in the market. The ability to generalise from the study is therefore necessarily rather limited.

TQM was defined as:

A positive attempt by the organisations concerned to improve structural, infrastructural, attitudinal, behavioural and methodological ways of delivering to the end customer, with emphasis on: consistency, improvements in quality, competitive enhancements all with the aim of satisfying or delighting the end customer. (Zairi *et al.*, 1994: 42)

Critical factors identified in these companies were leadership elements such as quality policy, strategic planning and mission, hard elements such as tools and systems, and soft elements such as teamwork, empowerment and innovation. The analysis focused on their performance over a five-year span (identified as a reasonable long-term indicator). The mean for each company was calculated over the five years for each performance indicator. The performance under each indicator for each company was compared to the appropriate industry median. The study reported that the companies exhibited above-average industry performance. For profit per employee 79 per cent of the companies showed positive quanta in comparison with the industry median. Average remuneration in 93 per cent of the companies studied is higher than their industry median. Total assets per employee is positively exhibited in 79 per cent of the companies. A total of 76 per cent of the companies showed positive returns on total assets. Turnover per employee in 79 per cent of the companies was higher than the corresponding industry median. A total of 76 per cent of the companies studied showed healthier profit margins than the industry median. A total of 72 per cent of the companies examined showed an above industry median fixed asset trend.

The number of employees employed trend is not conclusive but 17 of the 29 companies studied have, over the five years studied, increased rather than shed employees, and Zairi *et al.* concluded that there is a positive association between the TQM and tangible benefits. The overall conclusion of the study, however, was that TQM was simply a 'license to practice' rather than a source of competitive advantage in itself:

The results of this study by no means suggest that TQM leads directly to improvements in bottom-line results. TQM merely offers companies the opportunity to carry out improvements and focuses on getting closer to customers. It is only a license to practice. Companies must still have the right strategies in place, the right products and services, the right commitment, and the right investment strategies in order to be successful.

f) The Institute of Management study

In 1992/3 three of the authors carried out a survey of British managers for the Institute of Management, the aim of which was to answer the following questions:

1. How widespread is the quality management 'movement', and what approaches are being adopted by organisations?
2. Why are organisations showing such interest in quality management?
3. Who is responsible for quality, and how is it measured?
4. What has quality management achieved so far?
5. What are the main difficulties faced in the management of quality?

In this section, we focus on the first four of these, returning to question 5 in the final section of the chapter. As well as asking a set of structured questions on the above issues, the questionnaire also invited open-ended comments and was supplemented by a number of interviews carried out by the researchers in the second half of 1992 (Wilkinson *et al.*, 1993, 1994b, 1995).

The survey sample

A postal, self-completion questionnaire was sent to 4,000 managers who were members of the then British Institute of Management. Usable questionnaires were received from 880, a response rate of 22 per cent.

A majority of the sample described themselves as either 'board' or 'senior management', with less than 6 per cent placing themselves in the 'junior management' category. In terms of function, over 30 per cent worked in 'general management' jobs. Otherwise, the sample was fairly evenly spread across the various management functions, with 'production/manufacturing/ maintenance' and 'marketing/sales' being the next most common. Under 5 per cent were 'quality assurance/control' specialists. This spread of respondents in terms of job status and function is a strength of the present survey. Many earlier studies have concentrated on top-level managers, whereas we were interested in the views of managers at all levels. There was a reasonable spread of respondents by industry, with around a quarter from the public sector, and 15 per cent working for foreign-owned companies. Forty-three per cent of the sample worked for organisations with over a thousand employees in the UK, and almost a half worked for organisations with a turnover in excess of £50 million.

The extent of quality management

The survey suggests that quality management was becoming more widespread in the UK in the early 1990s, with 71 per cent of respondents claiming to have a formal quality management campaign, the great majority of them introduced within the last five years, and a further 11 per cent planning to introduce one. Forty-two per cent claimed to have implemented TQM in particular, with a further 7 per cent planning to do so. Fewer then 50 per cent said that their organisation had achieved a recognised quality standard, such as BS5750, although 25 per cent were currently aiming for one. Quality management seemed to be more well developed in manufacturing and in production industries such as gas, water and electricity than in services, but there was some evidence of 'catching up', in that those sectors where quality management had been less widespread had a higher proportion of organisations planning to introduce campaigns.

Almost two-thirds of managers said that 'customer demand for quality' had led to recent innovations in their approach to quality management, whilst over half said that there had been innovations due to competitive pressures to reduce costs and to improve service quality. Quality management appeared to be essentially market-driven, and only 9 per cent attributed developments in quality management to employee relations issues. Table 5.4 shows a high degree of consistency in the factors influencing quality management across different industries and sectors. Manufacturing industry seems to be particularly aware of market pressures to improve quality. Perhaps not surprisingly, foreign-owned companies were more likely to cite 'pressure from parent company' as a reason for quality management initiatives.

Implementing quality management

Two key issues in the implementation of quality management are, first, the allocation of responsibility for quality within the organisation and, second, the way in which quality is measured. On the first issue, quality was identified as a responsibility of all employees by 44 per cent of respondents and of senior management by 34 per cent. Only 9 per cent said that primary responsibility for quality lay with quality control specialists. This is consistent with the literature, which emphasises that quality management should not be left to a specialist department, but should be the responsibility of all employees, with senior management having particular responsibility for establishing a commitment to quality throughout the organisation.

TABLE 5.4   What factors have led to recent changes in quality management in your organisation?

(% of respondents selecting each item as a significant factor)

	All	Primary	Manufacturing	Construction	Services	Public sector	Private sector		
							All	UK-owned	Foreign-owned
Customer demand for quality	63	60	77	64	56	56	67	65	73
Competitive pressures to reduce cost	54	58	63	50	51	52	56	55	61
Competitive pressure to improve product design	21	2	40	20	13	11	24	20	37
Competitive pressure to improve service quality	57	58	55	54	58	52	59	58	65
New senior management	31	24	31	16	33	35	29	29	30
Pressure from parent company	14	5	22	11	12	14	14	6	42
Enthusiasm of senior managers	41	40	44	36	41	42	41	40	46
Employee relations issues	9	5	8	9	11	15	7	7	6
Department of Trade and Industry promotion.	5	3	6	9	4	5	5	6	5
Other	8	13	5	5	9	15	5	5	5

On the second issue, the main quality indicators used are customer feedback, complaints, delivery performance and reject rates. Thus, quality seems to be seen very much in customer-driven terms. Only 4 per cent said that they could not measure quality (Table 5.5). The pattern of quality measurement by industry and sector is broadly as one would expect. Manufacturing companies seem to use a broader range of quality indicators than do organisations in other sectors. Similarly, foreign-owned companies use a broader range of measures than do UK-owned companies.

Only 8 per cent rated their quality management programmes as 'very successful', with just over 2 per cent seeing them as 'unsuccessful'. (The results are shown in Table 5.6.)

There was no significant relationship between industrial sector and the extent to which managers rated their organisations' quality management programmes as being successful. However, private sector managers rated their organisations' quality management programmes as more successful than did their public sector counterparts. There was no statistically significant difference between the overall success ratings given by managers in UK- and foreign-owned private sector companies. This latter finding is perhaps surprising, given all that has been said about the allegedly greater managerial sophistication of foreign-owned companies in the UK.

Table 5.7 outlines the actual achievements of quality management in more detail. The most marked impact was in raising the level of quality awareness within the organisation, with over half our respondents seeing a 'major improvement' in this area. Most also claimed an improvement in customer satisfaction and in the level of customer complaints.

Although only a minority noted an improvement in returns, this reflects the fact that over half of our sample worked in services, where the notion of 'return' takes a less tangible form and is difficult to measure. Similarly, 38 per cent reported no effect on levels of scrap or defects, but again this reflects the presence of service organisations in the sample. When we look at manufacturing establishments alone, 69 per cent reported an improvement in returns and 83 per cent noted improved scrap/defect levels.

In the sample as a whole, fewer than half claimed that their quality management programme had led to any improvement in sales or profitability. Even among private sector organisations alone, only 8 per cent reported a major improvement and 42 per cent a minor improvement in sales as a result of the quality management programme, with corresponding figures of 11 per cent and 41 per cent for profitability. Some managers said that the lack of a clear impact on bottom-line performance made it difficult to maintain the momentum of quality initiatives:

> The worst problem for those of us who believe in quality excellence is the tenuous link between our success in the commercial environment and the quality of our service. Most of our customers buy on price, as long as there is an acceptable level of quality.

TABLE 5.5 How is quality improvement measured in the organisation?

(% of respondents)

	All	Primary	Manufacturing	Construction	Services	Public sector	Private sector		
							All	UK-owned	Foreign-owned
Failure/reject rate	38	25	72	27	23	21	45	43	52
Customer feedback	70	64	69	59	71	65	71	70	75
Number of complaints	50	57	56	34	49	51	51	50	52
Warranty claims	13	16	28	9	3	2	17	15	27
Delivery performance	39	25	50	27	36	35	41	39	49
Cost of quality	24	18	45	11	15	13	28	25	41
Do not measure	9	12	4	14	10	14	7	7	5
Cannot measure	4	5	2	5	6	6	3	4	3
Other	7	12	4	7	7	10	5	5	6

TABLE 5.6 **How would you rate the overall success of your quality management programme to date?**

(% of respondents, answering on a five-point scale)				
All respondents				
Very successful				Unsuccessful
8	39	37	14	2
Public sector:				
Very successful				Unsuccessful
5	31	47	14	3
Private sector				
Very successful				Unsuccessful
8	41	34	14	2

Base: Respondents reporting that they have or have had a formal quality management campaign.

A majority of our respondents reported an improvement in teamwork and in employee morale, although in most organisations this had not resulted in lower labour turnover or reduced absenteeism. Over 40 per cent did, however, note an improvement in safety as a result of the quality management initiative.

While the impact of quality management initiatives was generally seen to have been beneficial, a small but significant number reported some adverse effects. Almost 12 per cent of respondents claimed that there had been a deterioration in productivity as a result, whilst a similar number saw a negative impact on profitability. Nine per cent saw a deterioration in cost-efficiency and in employee morale. This suggests that whilst quality management techniques seem to offer benefits to organisations, introducing an initiative will not of itself guarantee benefits.

Summary

Most respondents were claiming a moderate degree of success for their quality management programmes, and private-sector managers were claiming a higher degree of success than were public-sector managers. Perhaps not surprisingly, the main impact of quality management is in raising staff awareness of quality issues, with most managers seeing a major improvement here. Improvements in customer satisfaction, complaints and in teamwork were amongst the other benefits reported by most of our respondents.

TABLE 5.7　What effect has quality management had on each of the following?

	Major improvement	Minor improvement	No effect	Minor deterioration	Major deterioration
(% of respondents)					
Quality awareness	60	35	6	0	0
Employee morale	14	47	31	7	2
Teamwork	22	53	23	3	0
Labour turnover	1	8	88	3	0
Absenteeism	1	10	88	1	0
Safety	9	39	52	0	0
Cost efficiency	18	51	22	8	2
Productivity	16	44	29	11	1
Scrap/defect levels	19	40	38	2	0
Customer complaints	23	48	26	4	0
Returns	14	31	52	2	0
Customer satisfaction	29	51	19	2	0
Sales	7	37	54	2	0
Profitability	10	37	42	10	1

Base: Respondents reporting that they have or have had a formal quality management campaign.

Managers were less likely to report an improvement in bottom-line performance, however, with fewer than half claiming even a minor improvement in sales or profitability. Some managers even remarked (either on their survey questionnaires or in interviews) that the lack of a demonstrable impact on financial performance could make it difficult to justify and maintain the momentum of quality management. It may well be that high expectations of quality management risk contributing towards a feeling of disappointment where the gains are not as significant as had been hoped.

While most of those surveyed felt that quality management programmes had achieved a reasonable degree of success, over 10 per cent of our respondents reported adverse effects, particularly on productivity, cost-efficiency, profitability and employee morale.

US-based studies

The overall view from the studies of TQM in the US provides a somewhat rosier assessment than that from those in the UK. Indeed, there is even now a mutual fund, the *General Securities Fund*, which trades purely in the stocks of TQM practising companies (Powell, 1995.) However, a recent analysis of the financial performance of the top 100 'quality leaders' in the US found somewhat more mixed fortunes (Schilit, 1994). The best performers had increased their stock value by six-fold over a five-year period, whilst the worst had suffered a 75 per cent reduction in value over the same period. Here we examine some of the major US-based TQM studies.

a) Conference Board studies

The Conference Board is a New York-based business research group whose first study on TQM in 1989 reported that some three-quarters of the large US companies it surveyed had quality initiatives in place. Over 30 per cent of these felt that TQM had improved business performance, with only one per cent believing performance to have declined as a result of TQM. Since this early survey the Conference Board has published more than 15 other studies examining particular aspects of TQM (for example, employee buy-in to TQM; practices in measuring quality; reward and recognition for quality improvement, and so on). These have ranged from broad-based postal surveys, in-depth analysis of large company quality programmes and meta-analyses of TQM studies (for example, Hiam, 1993). Overall, the studies can be summarised as endorsing TQM as a business strategy that works. Most of these studies, however, have used only management perceptions of TQM rather than harder data as the basis for reaching such a conclusion.

b) General Accounting Office study

A US study by the General Accounting Office (GAO) in 1990, in response to a request from the US Congress, attempted to link TQM and bottom-line results. The study entitled 'Management Practices – US Companies Improve Performance Through Quality Effects' focused on the top 20 scorers of the Baldrige Awards in the period 1988–89. Using both questionnaire and interview methods, the study asked the companies to provide information on a number of performance measures. The GAO reported that these firms had achieved better employee reaction, improved product quality, lower costs and improved customer satisfaction. They concluded that there was a cause and effect relationship, and TQM did improve corporate performance. However, questions can be raised over the sampling, the list of indicators and indeed the methodology. Detailed statistical methods were not used, the sample was only 20, not all companies answered all questions and the average response per question was only 9 per cent.

c) *Center for Effective Organization surveys*

This Center, based at the University of Southern California, has conducted a series of surveys of *Fortune 1000* companies, examining employee-involvement orientated organisational improvement initiatives. As TQM has grown in prominence the surveys have collected an increasing amount of data on TQM (Mohrman *et al.*, 1995). The 1993 survey asked about the use of TQM practices and their perceived effectiveness.

The latest survey found TQM still to be on an upward trajectory with around three-quarters of the sample having a TQM initiative, and with a quarter of these having embarked on TQM only after 1990. TQM was more prevalent in manufacturing (88 per cent) than services (61 per cent). The most used TQM techniques were customer satisfaction surveys and quality improvement teams, with other practices not finding widespread use. The evidence suggested that competitive pressures lead to the adoption of TQM. Companies which were experiencing more foreign competition and extreme performance pressures were more likely to use more TQM practices.

The study found a number of links between the adoption of TQM and organisational success. In terms of internal efficiency, the study found a positive relationship between TQM and employee productivity. There was also a relationship found between core TQM practices and market share for manufacturing companies, although, no significant relationship was found between TQM adoption and RoI, RoS or RoA.

d) *North-eastern US study*

This study, one of the more sophisticated methodologically and analytically, involved surveys of Chief Executive Officers (CEOs) and interviews with CEOs and quality executives in the north-eastern USA (Powell, 1995). A key finding of the study was that a resource-based theory of competitive advantage may explain why TQM adds value in some firms but not in others. Resource theory argues that success derives from economically valuable resources that other firms cannot easily imitate, and the question is thus raised of whether TQM creates such a resource.

At first sight it would appear not; all firms have equal access to management consultants, the books and videos by the quality gurus, TQM courses, business schools, and so on. Powell's study, however, in carefully disaggregating the different elements of TQM, found that success depended critically on executive commitment, an open organisation culture and employee empowerment, and less upon such 'staples' of TQM as benchmarking, training, process improvement and flexible manufacturing. The former elements provide the culture within which the TQM tools can work, but are less tangible and more difficult to imitate than the latter. They thus meet the criteria as resources capable of creating sustainable, competitive advantage, in that they have value, scarcity and imperfect imitability, the last presumably because of the social complexity of such factors as organisational culture and management style.

Significantly, Powell's research found these same factors were also associated with economic success in non-TQM companies. TQM firms without these attributes do not succeed and non-TQM firms with them do. Thus, for Powell, TQM's real contribution to business 'is in providing a framework that helps firms understand and acquire these resources as part of an integrated change programme' (1995: 31). This is a key finding from our point of view, because it underlines the critical importance of the 'soft' side of TQM, and indeed relegates the 'hard' tools and techniques aspects to a relatively minor role in organisational effectiveness.

e) *International Quality Study*

The 'International Quality Study', (IQS) a joint project of Ernst and Young and the American Quality Foundation involved examining selected quality practices used by over 500 automotive, computer, banking and healthcare organisations in Canada, Germany, Japan and the USA. It seems to be the most widely cited of all the TQM studies. Most organisations in the sample believed that quality was a critical factor in their strategic performance. However, quality was neither measured universally at the organisational level, nor was it linked to executive assessment and compensation. The study found that some TQM practices – particularly process improvement and supplier certification – universally improved performance, but that the effect of other TQM features varied considerably, depending on the firm's stage of development in TQM.

Thus the IQS findings challenged the assumption that any organisation, regardless of its current performance, can benefit from the widespread adoption of TQ practices. They argued that the hypothesis of universally beneficial practices was not supported by the evidence:

> Practices that are beneficial at one level of organizational performance show no association – or even a negative association – with performance at other levels. As a

result, a number of organisations are expending a tremendous amount of resources and energy on practices that have little or no impact for them. (1992: 7)

The report suggests that the lower performing organisations need to focus on a limited number of practices to achieve improvement, but as higher performance is realised they can add more sophisticated variants. For example, benchmarking is seen to deliver benefits to higher performing organisations but not to lower performers, partly because the latter have not sufficiently developed core quality infrastructures to gain advantage from the lessons learnt.

Evaluating TQM: a summary

As can be seen, there is a growing body of work on the extent of TQM and its impact on organisational effectiveness. A general finding is that TQM is increasingly being adopted both in the US and in Europe. According to many of the studies reviewed here there is a simple reason for this: most suggest that TQM can add value to an organisation's competitive strategy. The majority of the studies' respondents attribute a wide range of business performance improvements to the adoption of TQM.

Although firm conclusions are often reached, however, there are problems with many of the studies. First, many were carried out by consultants or quality associations and sponsored by bodies with a vested interest in positive findings on TQM. Second, there are methodological weaknesses in many of them, such as the use of very small samples, a concentration on large organisations, ignoring evidence on the performance of non-TQM companies, and not controlling for industry factors. Third, the evaluations of TQM's contribution to organisational success, although sometimes based on relatively sophisticated techniques of analysis, have generally neglected to establish the extent to which TQM was actually installed. Powell (1995) is among the exceptions here, with a careful attempt to measure the degree of implementation of 12 'TQM factors'. Thus a danger in many studies is that it is difficult to confirm that it is actually TQM that is being assessed, rather than some other managerial intervention. For example, Hackman and Wageman's (1995: 321) review of 99 papers on TQM found only four which assessed the degree to which TQM was actually implemented.

Such methodological problems aside, and they do not apply to all the studies, there is a growing body of evidence that TQM can result in significant improvements in organisational performance. The link between quality management and organisational performance, however, is not a simple one. There is considerable evidence that it is more successful in some organisations, fails in others, and results in worse performance in a small but important minority of organisations. We now attempt to shed some light on this uneven performance by examining in detail the difficulties faced in implementing quality management. We draw on our own IM study referred to earlier.

The difficulties with Quality Management

How can we account for the 'mixed' results so far achieved with quality management, and in particular for its failure in some organisations? Tables 5.8 and 5.9 summarise the main difficulties faced in implementing quality management, according to our IM study referred to earlier (Wilkinson *et al.*, 1993). It seems from Table 5.8 that lack of commitment from particular groups within the organisation can be a barrier in the management of quality, with 18 per cent seeing top management commitment as a 'major difficulty'.

TABLE 5.8   To what extent has lack of commitment from the following groups been a difficulty in the implementation of quality management?

	(% of respondents)	
	Major difficulty	*Minor difficulty*
Top management	18	19
Middle management	11	33
Supervisors	7	39
Employees	11	39
Trade Unions	4	16

Senior management came in for criticism from many of our respondents, particularly for failing to demonstrate their own personal commitment to the management of quality. They were variously accused of being sceptical, unenthusiastic, unwilling to commit resources, and of treating quality management with a 'short-termist' perspective:

I used to be Chief Quality Engineer here, I gave it up because of lack of commitment by top management.

Curiously the MD is not sufficiently enthusiastic.

I work for a Next Steps Agency into which the philosophy of TQM is just being introduced. Unfortunately it is being treated with scepticism and derision by senior managers immediately below Board Level. Until the culture is changed, it is unlikely to become an effective tool.

Some managers were concerned that quality management was given only 'lip service' in their organisation, rather than being embedded into the day-to-day life and fabric of the organisation. Some managers, particularly in the public sector, suggested that their own commitment to quality management was shared by few others in the organisation. One described it as 'a lonely crusade'. Others described their organisation's approach to quality management as essentially one of 'fit and forget'. For example:

> I honestly believe that quality (as a concept) is in danger of being widely abused. Organisations desperate to jump onto the quality bandwagon currently in vogue, are merely paying lip service to the quality ethos. They are eager to proclaim their quality status but on close inspection do not possess the necessary systems for quality to permeate their entire operations.

Lack of commitment from middle managers, supervisors and employees was seen as at least a 'minor difficulty' in the implementation of quality management by well over 40 per cent of our respondents in each case. Several suggested that quality management was being forced onto an unwilling and unreceptive staff. For example:

> Quality management appears to be seen as a necessary evil in my company, rather than as a positive benefit with potential advantages. This underlying factor, it seems to me, will inevitably ensure that its potential can only be minimally realised in the company. Companies whose attitudes are such as to favour intelligent management and the recruitment of bright people will, I believe, find QM easy to take on board, and to be advantageous. For those in an opposite condition, such as my company, it will be cosmetic in both adoption and effect. My experience is such, that sadly, most seem to fall into the latter category.

A few of our respondents even suggested that the way forward for introducing quality management lay in the removal of the 'quality sceptics'. According to one:

> The problem is a strong company culture which sees TQM as a threat to stability and established power bases. Improvements in TQ recognition in the last 18 months [have been] quite significant following a major early retirement programme associated with organisational re-structuring.

Interestingly, commitment from trade unions was seen as a 'major difficulty' by less than 4 per cent of our respondents, although this low figure may partly reflect the fact that not all organisations have a trade union presence.

Quality management seems to suffer from other limitations, with 'lack of resources' and 'cost constraints' emerging as two of the most important difficulties in implementation. As we have already noted, quality management may also be constrained by short-termist attitudes, with over 60 per cent of organisations seeing the 'emphasis on short-term goals' as a difficulty. As two managers put it:

The biggest difficulty in getting the quality message across are the banks and accountancy profession. Unless it can be shown to save overheads, they virtually don't give a
[xxxx] and can be hostile.

Our company is more interested in short-term goals such as surviving, invoicing,
shipping goods to try and not go past delivery deadlines. Quality is tolerated as a
sales tool to win contracts.

Problems in measuring quality, in communications and with a lack of
training also emerged as significant difficulties.

The quality of *employees* was seen as a 'major difficulty' by only 7 per cent of
our sample. Interestingly, this compares with 17 per cent who saw the quality of
management as a major difficulty. In total, over half of our respondents felt that
the quality of management presented at least minor difficulties.

**TABLE 5.9   Difficulties faced by organisations in the improvement
of quality**

	(% of respondents)	
	Major difficulty	*Minor difficulty*
Lack of resources	42	37
Cost constraints	38	36
Emphasis on short-term goals	34	29
Measuring quality	27	38
Communication	25	41
Lack of training	23	41
Clash with other initiatives	22	32
Recession	21	26
Quality of management	17	38
Lack of UK quality infrastructure	12	26
Seen as production/operations concern only	11	24
Quality of employees	7	40
Other	4	1

Forty-six per cent of our respondents saw the recession as presenting
difficulties for quality management. Recession increased the pressure on costs,

while redundancy and reorganisation undermined staff morale and commitment. Typical comments were:

> I also feel that training and general morale are low at this time due to concern over falling production schedules. To expect employees to aspire to the ideals of TQM whilst worry exists on jobs is perhaps wishful thinking.

> The recession has led to redundancies, slimming and abandoning of product lines and to re-organisation. This, coupled with instability, has inhibited progress on many of the quality initiatives over that past two years.

> In our engineering sections our unions are very sceptical of all management initiatives, including our recent TQM initiative. This is understandable because of the history of the last 8/10 years, where reductions in manning and increased capital investment has been our priority to remain competitive and survive.

One manager we interviewed described his frustration at his company introducing a TQM programme at the same time as it was planning a major rationalisation. This resulted in the introduction of TQM with very little training. With a planned reduction in the workforce from 3,000 to around 1,000, the company was reluctant to 'waste' training on those who would soon leave the company.

Specific sectors may face their own particular difficulties in implementing quality management, as the comments of a local authority manager illustrate:

> The need to improve quality of service provision is increasing, however in local authorities this is increasingly difficult with cash limited budgets, and the pace of change generated by legislative changes in recent years. This may appear odd, but consider the changes to taxation, compulsory competitive tendering, performance indicators, charge capping, etc. Quality initiatives may also be compromised by the political objectives of the elected members. Finally, a problem is also experienced with sceptical, old-style local government officers.

Some managers simply saw quality management as the latest in a long line of management fads. Thus:

> Quality has been perceived at my organisation as something that can be 'bolted-on' in the short term. It has been disastrous. Systemic quality management was built in to the business when it was founded, but subsequent senior managers have tried to make their mark by replacing systemic quality management by cosmetic 'fashionable' quality techniques.

Others were particularly critical of the increasing use of quality 'jargon'. According to one:

> I view the whole subject of quality management as a gimmick. Good leadership and effective professional management, produces good quality service delivery. 'Quality

management' is, to me, synonymous with 'effective management'. Jargonistic phrases such as TQM are superficial, theoretical rubbish. Effective leadership will produce high quality service, and I recommend people stop trying to make a new science out of simple truths and age-old principles.

Many managers suggested that quality management was developing into a mysterious and complex subject which could only really be understood by the initiated. This made it all the more difficult effectively to communicate the company 'vision' on quality to staff. Comments such as the following represent this view:

A great deal has been written and said about quality but the major barrier to achievement is the ability to translate the requirements into something sufficiently concrete and relevant to peoples' daily tasks.

TQM is being given a high priority from senior management and we have been talking about it for a year with little obvious progress, other than appointing TQM managers. Just what it is all about still remains a mystery to me.

The main problem facing us is that of communicating the corporate vision on quality in a way that allows us to get all 2,500 staff on board.

The introduction of quality certification, was sometimes described as being more a 'sales gimmick' than a major commitment to improve quality. This was succinctly put by one manager who suggested that 'BS5750 equals Kudos'. Another suggested that:

Companies emphasise the volume of output more than the quality of the product and obtain BS5750 to use as a selling tool more than a tool to increase quality. Companies expect to introduce a 5750 system but don't employ staff to make it work. A 5750 certificate does not ensure quality of product, but our sales boys sell 5750 as a quality product standard.

Associated with quality certification was the perception of a large and growing bureaucracy surrounding the notion of quality management. This was particularly the case in relation to quality certification, with BS5750 being singled out for particular criticism. Quality management was variously described as reducing to a 'mechanical approach', and as being 'paperwork driven' and 'bureaucratic', with the quality systems becoming an 'end in themselves'. All this meant extra work and was often perceived as adding little value. Typical comments were:

Acquisition of BS5750 Part 2 nearly six years ago has led to a near mechanistic approach to quality management, in which the system is merely maintained but seldom improved. New initiatives in our quality system are rare.

BS5750 gave rise to red tape being used for every event one performs.

I now believe BS5750 to be inefficient, cost consuming and time consuming. The documentation has become an end in its own right but has done little to change the quality of service which I receive.

Current emphasis on quality improvement strategy in the UK appear to be based upon getting the paperwork right rather than the product quality. BS5750 and all the hype and breast beating about it is typical of this emphasis on quality paperwork rather than quality products. If our products are to be sold competitively in the global market, paperwork exercises such as BS5750 become a nonsense. Japan doesn't give a damn about what our paperwork says, their main concern is that the product quality meets their requirements. No amount of paper is going to convince them that the product is of excellent quality if it isn't.

BS5750 was often criticised as being a costly process, and as giving little return to the organisation.

Eventually companies will realise that BS5750 is a very expensive club to join and remain as a member and will realise that the cost of membership far outweighs the benefits.

Criticisms were also levelled at total quality management:

There is a danger that TQM is yet another level of bureaucracy, which provides employment for those involved but which is a nuisance for those it is aimed at. The programme has to be accompanied by inspirational leadership – not forms.

TQM as a philosophy is an excellent concept but in my experience it has the danger of becoming an end in itself rather than a means to an end. Unless TQM is expertly controlled as a process, it runs the risk of supplanting the primary purpose of the company. Much time and effort is necessary to ensure that quality programmes actually have the desired effect.

Conclusions

The evidence suggests that quality management has become more widespread in the UK and in the USA. Furthermore, whilst there is evidence of successful implementation with a significant impact on organisational performance, the results are disappointing for the proponents of TQM in a large number of cases. In the previous section, we tried to account for this uneven pattern by examining some of the difficulties involved.

The most important difficulties to emerge from our survey were resource limitations, cost constraints and an emphasis on short-term goals. Recession was also seen as a problem, particularly by smaller organisations. The concern here is that recession intensifies resource limitations and the emphasis on cost-containment, whilst also possibly undermining staff morale and commitment to quality, especially where there are fears of restructuring or redundancies. Despite the array of quality indicators used, the measurement of quality is still seen as posing difficulties for a large number of organisations. Lack of commitment within the organisation was seen by many as a barrier to the implementation of quality management, with managers and staff at all levels receiving criticism in this respect.

A minority of respondents put forward a number of other important criticisms of approaches to quality management, seeing it as a management fad, as being dominated by increasingly obscure jargon, and as a sales gimmick. Quality management in general, and BS5750 in particular, was criticised by some managers for being too bureaucratic, and for placing an additional burden on organisations. The important point to bear in mind, though, is that managers tend to attribute any failings in TQM to *practical* issues, rather than having objections to or doubts about the *principles* behind TQM. To a large extent, managers appear to have bought the concept of TQM and the opportunities it offers to improve organisational performance through what they would see as more 'enlightened' and progressive management styles.

Where does this leave quality management? Quality management enthusiasts are inclined to attribute failings to implementation difficulties or to point to the need for evaluation over the longer term, whilst sceptics see more fundamental problems regarding TQM as yet another in a long line of management fads. It seems to us that much depends on the particular organisation, the approach that management adopts, and the commitment that is shown to its development. This is one of the key issues which we explore in the case studies that follow.

CHAPTER 6

Citizens as Customers: The Politics of Quality in Local Government

Introduction

Much that is written about quality and TQM relates, either implicitly or explicitly, to the private sector and in particular to manufacturing industry. To some extent this is understandable given that most models of TQM are drawn from manufacturing, and many of the tools and techniques have a specific resonance with the processes practised there. This is also reflected in the volume of articles and case studies which are written about TQM in manufacturing (for example, Dawson and Webb, 1989; Delbridge *et al.*, 1992; Wilkinson *et al.*, 1994a).

TQM proponents have argued that it has as much relevance to the public sector as to the private, and has a potential for use in local government – the subject of the case study analysed in this chapter. Several publications since the late 1980s have focused on the concept of quality (whether it be full-blown TQM, quality assurance or customer care) and the way in which it is being introduced into local government (see, for example, Stewart, 1988; Sanderson, 1992a, b; Pollitt, 1993; Morgan and Murgatroyd, 1994). Indeed, as Sanderson (1992b: 1) notes, 'it seems that nearly every initiative to improve public services is now launched under the banner of "quality" and the main political parties vie with each other to achieve the high ground in terms of policies to improve the quality of public services'.

While it may be true that political imperatives have stimulated greater efforts within local government to implement new quality programmes, it is not accurate to assume that quality was previously a neglected concept. Professional staff, of which there are many in local authorities, have long held that the quality of qualifications is a key element in the standards which are set and monitored for their occupations; librarians or architects are both cases in point. Quality of care is an issue which has been repeatedly at the forefront of discussions in areas covered by social workers or home-helps. Quality of representation, through democratically elected members, is an issue which never gets a mention in the private sector. A number of local authorities actively implemented quality programmes before the government initiatives of the late 1980s and early 90s. In short, discussions of quality, albeit often defined by the professions involved in providing the service, have always had a place in local government.

What is new for many organisations, however, is the more explicit focus on quality management, on the introduction of systems and processes designed to ensure that services are delivered with a greater conformity and standardisation than before, rather than through the sometimes haphazard efforts of different occupational groups. The perspective of the client or 'customer' has assumed greater prominence in recent approaches. It should be clear, therefore, that the implementation of new quality programmes in local authorities is likely to face resistance from (some) groups of staff who have quite different perceptions about how quality can be delivered, and who regard some of the recent initiatives as superficial attempts to measure performance which is difficult to quantify. Moreover, it is seen by many as a threat to their autonomy and jobs because it is being imposed by governments which wish to 'roll-back' the frontiers of the state and reduce public spending. As Sanderson (1992c: 37–8) notes, quality is not a neutral concept, despite its façade, but a political issue, which 'encapsulates a debate about the legitimate and desired purpose and role of local government... it is likely to be perennially controversial'.

This sets the scene for the remainder of this chapter, which aims to review the range and type of approaches to quality in local government within its political context. To understand the issues which inform the TQM agenda in local government, it is important to appreciate not only the ways in which local authorities have been subject to political interference over the last 20 years, but also the range of services which have been offered. The conflicts, complexities and ambiguities of TQM have a meaning which is more noticeable in the public sector, and which are often very different from those which confront large private sector organisations. Before moving on to analyse the case study of TQM in a metropolitan district (Marchington *et al.* 1993b) however, we need to examine the changing nature of local government and the models of quality which have been promulgated in recent years.

The changing nature of local government

British local government underwent a major reorganisation in 1974 which redrew the boundaries so as to create a series of larger authorities. The managerial implications of this political reconstruction were dealt with in the Bains report which popularised notions of managerialism, the establishment of a chief executive function and the importance of personnel management as a potentially influential occupation rather than a third tier administrative support function (Storey and Fenwick, 1990: 19). The development of corporate management during the 1970s was the result of two trends, according to Elcock (1993: 151–3): first, in order to achieve better coordinated and coherent central management within local authorities, there were moves to establish a central committee with responsibility for developing authority-wide policies and philosophies and a chief executive who led a management team comprising representatives from the range of council services. The second trend was the increasing acceptance of a 'governmental' role by local authorities which allowed them to take a relatively wide view of their responsibilities, including issues such as economic regeneration and links between public and private sector bodies.

The period from 1979 saw a major onslaught by the Conservative government on local authorities, putting them in a 'noose' (Bennington and Taylor, 1992: 165), in common with other parts of the public sector. At organisational level there were attempts to remove two-tier local authority structures. In the case of the metropolitan authorities (such as the Greater London and Greater Manchester Councils) this was achieved during the 1980s. The Government was less successful in the English shire counties, with the Local Government Commission recommending in 1995 that most should remain as two-tier authorities with county and district councils. About a dozen new unitary authorities were created, many of which were county towns such as Derby and Leicester, leaving the remainder of these counties as two-tier authorities. Rather than a radical reshaping of local government, the process can be characterised as a tidying-up. Over the whole period since 1979, local government has been forced to survive with lessening amounts of money from central government, even though in many cases demands for services have increased, for example in social services. The method of collecting taxes from local citizens has also undergone several changes (rates to poll tax to council tax), which has left senior managers and elected members unsure as to the source and amount of finance available. Finally, there has been a raft of legislation to enable the removal of services from local authority control via compulsory competitive tendering, first for manual operations in the mid-1980s and for white-collar jobs in the early 1990s. Tied in with this was the repeal of the Fair Wages Resolution in 1983 which made it possible for private sector contractors to submit cheaper tenders on the basis of paying lower wages to similar staff. The implications of all these changes for management in local government, and in particular quality, have been enormous.

Competing models of quality in local government

The twin notions of customers and quality have been used with increasing frequency in local government in recent years. Skelcher (1992: 463) suggests that the very use of the term 'customer' by local authority staff is a mark of the deep-seated changes which are now taking place, signifying a rejection of the view that model uniform services are delivered to passive recipients, who have little voice or influence over the process. Young (1993: 29) notes, on the basis of various surveys of Chief Officers, that 'quality' is the fastest changing area of management; by 1992, a third of all local government employers had an authority-wide policy on quality, whilst a further 40 per cent were preparing one. By the mid-1990s, there can be very few left without something in this area.

Bennington and Taylor (1992: 168–72) propose that there are three distinct approaches to quality management being practised, each of which is predicated upon different principles and ideologies. The first, termed **the New Right**, is based upon the assumption that 'private markets offer the best way of pursuing quality, through competition between producers and choice for customers' (Bennington and Taylor, 1992: 168). Economic positivism and philosophical individualism are its core values, finding expression in examples such as compulsory competitive tendering (CCT), the purchaser–provider split, and competition between schools, all of which are linked with notions of quality (Walsh, 1995: 87–94). In the 1992 Conservative Party manifesto, John Major (quoted in Tuckman, 1995: 77) wrote about the 'quality revolution' taking place in Britain, with government 'leading a drive for quality throughout our public services'.

CCT has been one of the principal mechanisms used by Government to restructure local government, and there is little doubting its impact. The proportion of contracts awarded to private sector employers has varied depending upon the service. For example, by the end of 1992, more than 40 per cent of cleaning contracts had gone outside local government, as had about a quarter of refuse collection and street cleaning, and about 20 per cent of vehicle maintenance and leisure management contracts. The vast majority of contracts had therefore been retained in-house, albeit with major changes to the ways in which the service was provided. Many local authorities had reorganised their direct works department into a direct labour organisation (DLO), reduced numbers employed and generally slimmed down all overheads to an absolute minimum. Service level agreements between the DLO and the internal customer had been drawn up, and quality systems such as ISO 9000 had been implemented (Paddon, 1992: 85–6). The Labour Deputy Leader of Bolton Council acknowledges (Harkin, 1994: 12–13) that CCT has encouraged local authorities to look more closely at management structures and systems, and caused them to refocus their attention on outputs and consumers. Some of the deals which have been struck in DLOs would have been unthinkable in the early 1980s.

There is less agreement about the effect of contracting-out on standards of quality and performance. Whilst government ministers and some local authority leaders point to major improvements in service to customers, as well as a lower cost base, the Public Services Privatisation Research Unit has maintained a database of scare stories following the contracting-out of services. This is referred to as 'quality destroyed' (Paddon, 1992: 73). It is clearly the case that some contracts were won by employers who lacked the resources or expertise to deliver services to agreed standards at the bid price (Paddon, 1992: 72–3; Elcock, 1993: 167). More detailed studies of contracting-out in particular services reveal significant changes in the delivery of the service, not always to the benefit of the customer and very often not to the benefit of employees (Kelliher and McKenna, 1988; Painter, 1991).

The Citizen's Charter represents a further example of the New Right's consumerist perspective on quality management. It has four main themes according to Sanderson (1992c: 20): improving the quality of public services; increasing choice for consumers; setting standards for services; ensuring value for money. The Conservative Government was adamant that it was not a short-term gimmick, but represents part of a clear strategy for reorientating our public services towards serving users rather than satisfying providers (Waldegrave, 1993: 11). The Citizen's Charter, as an element in the New Public Management, has similarities with the sort of TQM approaches that have been developed in the private sector, utilising the language of 'standards, quality, empowerment and customers, in contrast to the traditional language of professional bureaucracy that had developed in the post-war years' (Walsh, 1995: 82). Chartermarks were introduced in 1992 to recognise excellence in public service, and local government employers won almost half of those awarded in 1994. In total, there are nine Chartermark criteria, most of which relate to standards of quality and customer service. These are:

1. Setting challenging standards, monitoring performance against these, publishing results, and engaging in a cycle of continuous improvement.
2. Providing customers with full and accurate information in plain language about how services are run and how much they cost.
3. Regular and systematic consultation with users of the service and making use of these views in setting decisions about services and standards.
4. Courtesy and helpfulness, especially to people with special needs.
5. Putting things right swiftly and providing an effective complaints procedure with an independent review system.
6. Providing value for money, with efficient and economical service delivery.
7. Providing evidence of customer satisfaction.
8. Demonstrating measurable improvements in the quality of service over the last two or more years.
9. To have in hand, or plan to introduce, at least one innovative enhancement without any extra cost to the taxpayer or the consumer.

Despite the fact that the Conservative Government strongly promoted the quality message in local government, it would be wrong to place all the impetus at their door (Paddon, 1992: 67). Moreover, it needs to be recognised that the previous Government's quality message had a particular tone and emphasis which some found superficial and misdirected. This leads us on to the second broad approach, that of **the New Left** (Bennington and Taylor, 1992: 169). This is less easy to define as a single entity than the New Right approach, but it includes (1) an analysis of the failings of centralised statist approaches and an 'assertion of the need for more decentralised solutions to problems of social need and economic restructuring', (2) an acceptance of the legitimate and positive differences in people's needs and wants, and (3) a policy of empowering citizens rather than demeaning and disabling them. Examples of this approach would be the strengthening of public participation, rights for customers and citizens, worker involvement, and changing management and professional cultures.

The Labour view is that quality local government should provide 'value for people' as well as 'value for money' (Sanderson, 1992c: 21). This extends beyond the consumerist perspective to include the welcoming of participation by citizens as well as innovation in service delivery. It also acknowledges that notions of consumerism and empowerment are complex phenomena, not easily reducible to simple analysis and appealing phraseology. The pursuit of quality involves the redress of imbalances in power towards those who use and experience local government services. As Sanderson (1992c: 23) argues, 'it is important to recognise that the "empowerment" of some can imply the disempowerment of others'. Local government managers need to make sure that a consumerist strategy does not merely empower those most able to look after themselves, that is those who can articulate their requirements more effectively and vocally than disadvantaged groups.

An example of the New Left approach could be found in Islington (Thompson, 1992: 194–200), one of many Labour-controlled authorities quoted in the party document, *Quality Street*. The Council there has instigated the following techniques in order to develop a quality system: consumer research, through exit polls and neighbourhood forums; consumer care, through the avoidance of negative messages; consumer rights, through the use of plain language and a good complaints policy; consumer contracts for consulting with residents and employees. Also, 'quality audits' are used which comprise a range of different perspectives on issues, none of which are right or wrong but all are partial (Thompson, 1992: 209). It should also be noted that the word 'consumer' is used in Islington, rather than the terminology of the New Right – 'customer'.

The third approach is labelled **the New Managerialism**. This is the least explicit of the three, encompassing aspects of both the New Right and the New Left. Its principal emphasis is on the 'pursuit of quality through changes in the management of services, rather than through changes in market relationships, as promoted by the new right, or in political processes, as argued by the new left' (Bennington and Taylor, 1992: 170). Examples of this approach would be guarantees of standards of service (for example, minimum response times for letters), improvements in signposting, quality of waiting areas, courtesy of front-line staff, level of information about services, and the simplicity and clarity of forms.

Many chief executives have pioneered these developments, for example by having direct telephone lines for people to ring in with problems, by undertaking personally the work of front-line staff for a day or a week, or by establishing surveys of service users (Bennington and Taylor, 1992: 171). The underlying ethos behind this is that if senior management is fully committed to TQM, it will want to involve all parties (employees, managers, the general public, councillors). It is argued that quality should be measured in terms of 'strategic direction' to the community as a whole rather than in terms of service delivery alone, and there are clear similarities between TQM and a 'Public Service Orientation' (Stewart and Clarke, 1987), which refers to service for the public and places emphasis on the public for whom the service is provided, in contrast with service to the public which places emphasis on the service.

Having placed quality within the broader political framework of local government, we can now turn to the case which analyses the approaches taken by one authority in the mid-1990s. This draws principally from the perspectives of the New Right and the New Managerialism. Following the case, we re-evaluate the prospects for TQM in local government.

Modern Metro: quality for customers

Organisation structure and policies

Modern Metro is a Conservative-controlled metropolitan council which emerged in its current form following the local government reorganisation of 1974. At the time of writing, it employed approximately 8000 people across eight departments – Town Clerk's, Finance, Education, Social Services, Housing, Environmental Health and Trading Standards (EHTS), Libraries and Arts, and Technical Services – and so provided the full range of council services. Numbers employed are likely to fall during the latter part of the 1990s as Modern Metro moves further towards the position of an 'enabling' authority, contracting out more of its traditional core services to private sector companies. At the same time, the organisation has already made major changes to its human resource policies and systems, as departments have been obliged to reorganise their activities in an effort to continue delivering services which have been put out to tender.

Each of the eight departments is represented on the chief officer's group along with the deputy chief executive and the chief personnel officer. This is the group which is responsible for managing the authority in line with its policy plan and in conjunction with the elected members. Accountability is maintained through the Council's committee structure, which covers each area of organisation's interests, and through management boards for certain sports and leisure activities. Over the period, 1992–95, the Council's objectives included the following which are relevant to and set the context for quality issues:

1. To serve the Council's customers.
2. To improve the quality of service to customers within the resources available.
3. To introduce a style and structure of local government which ensures that Council services are provided in the most effective, efficient and equitable way.
4. To train, develop, inform and motivate staff to ensure quality and high performance throughout all Council services.
5. To ensure that services are provided in the most cost-effective way possible.
6. To promote the Council's services within the Borough and to communicate effectively with staff, residents and visitors.

In common with the rest of local government in the mid-1990s, the authority is facing major changes in the way it is run, the most important for the purposes of this chapter being the extension of compulsory competitive tendering (CCT) to white collar and professional staff, the implementation of internal trading units, and the impact of the Citizen's Charter. Numbers employed have fallen slightly over the last few years, primarily due to CCT for manual workers, although the majority of contracts have been won by in-house tenders. At the same time, the Council prides itself on being able to deliver a quality service to customers with one of the lowest ratios of staff:population living in the borough.

A number of trade unions are recognised by Modern Metro, the largest of which are UNISON and the GMB. Density of unionisation is a little under 40 per cent overall, although for the manual workers it is less than a third of all eligible employees. As with the rest of the public sector, there is a long tradition of trade unionism, especially amongst full-time and professional staff. The relationship between management and unions has been good, and there have been few industrial relations problems in recent years. Modern Metro claims it is committed to keeping all employees and trade union representatives informed of major policy changes, and seeking their views wherever appropriate.

The development of quality management

The current initiatives in quality management and customer care started in 1986 with the initiation of a Customer First Programme, well before any moves by central government in this area. The chief executive referred to this as 'a top priority' for Modern Metro, which 'recognises the role of every employee in delivering a high quality, responsive and courteous service while seeking to improve, and keep on improving, standards of service delivery'. The Customer First Programme initially incorporated training in the principles and practice of customer care for all front-line staff. This included sessions on how to address residents and visitors over the telephone and in face-to-face meetings, how to deal with complaints, and how to ensure that the Council is seen in a positive light by the general public.

Customer First has now been subsumed under a more wide-ranging and general programme entitled 'The Metro Style', which has been publicised to all residents and employees via a short booklet. This details the service that customers can expect to receive from Council employees. It stresses that quality management should not be seen as a revolution in standards but more as a 'continual refinement in service delivery, a passionate belief that excellent customer service is at the heart of local government services, which have set us on the path of **continuous improvement in standards, achievement and fresh approaches to customer care**'. Key elements both of customer care and TQM jargon are clearly evident in this commitment by Modern Metro: continuous improvement and refinement of services, delighting of customers, establishing and monitoring standards. Indeed, senior management received presentations from staff at British Airways prior to unveiling 'The Metro Style', perhaps explaining why this statement could just as easily apply to a private sector organisation. There is hardly any reference here or in the Council Objectives to the equally important public sector issues of representing residents, consulting with staff and unions, or of citizens other than as individuals who may require services which the authority has on offer. Modern Metro draws its ideas from the New Right and the New Managerialism, rather than the New Left, perhaps best exemplified in the language of 'customers' for Council services rather than citizens.

Customer care finds expression through a variety of routes. A regular hotline was introduced in 1986 for customers with concerns about Council services to speak directly with the chief executive between 9.00 and 10.00 am every weekday morning. The Council made a commitment to customers that telephone calls would be answered promptly and letters would be answered within five working days. These standards are monitored by management on a monthly basis for each department, and the results are fed back to the departments concerned; during the first full year of the programme, for example, it was estimated that over 7500 more callers have been able to get through to staff each month. Employees are now expected to answer telephone calls by providing their name, department and employer, and ensure that callers who have rung an inappropriate or incorrect number are given assistance. In this area, as in others, indications are that residents are very satisfied with the performance of the Council; a MORI poll ranked it third out of 22 local authorities that were assessed, and there were sizeable aggregate improvements since the previous poll in the late 1980s. Employees are not quite so happy with the customer care initiatives however. Interviews with some professional staff highlighted concerns that the 'charm' approach conflicted with other duties, as for example when an important and pressing task was constantly interrupted by a series of telephone queries. There is also a feeling that the customer care message betrays a superficiality in dealing with enquiries which is more appropriate for a fast-food chain than a professional office. Ansafones have become more common, as too have the 'soothing' tones of piped music as telephone callers wait to relay their message. On the other hand, there is little doubt that the customer care message has heightened awareness about the off-hand and off-putting approaches used by some staff which have alienated or frightened off enquirers in the past.

Access for, and information to, customers was also improved during the early 1990s. Reception areas have been refurbished to make them more welcoming, and signposting has been clarified to guide customers to their destinations. Newsletters to all residents are now part of the Council's communications strategy, as are exhortations to use plain language in all communications with customers and potential service users. Departmental customer surveys are a regular feature, especially for service users in areas such as sports, arts and libraries.

Customer First was followed by a quality management initiative in 1990, which comprised quality action plans and targets for all departments and an encouragement to establish quality service teams (QSTs) within sections and departments. A quality award scheme was introduced in 1991. In parallel with this, although to some extent separate, some departments have chosen to go for ISO 9000 series registration. This has already been achieved by two departments: Environmental Health and Trading Services, and Technical Services. Unlike some authorities, Modern Metro had decided not to go for organisation-wide registration for the simple reason that services varied so fundamentally across the whole Council. At the same time, each initiative has to be firmly located within 'The Metro Style' and the Council's primary objective of serving its customers via a strategy that is 'orientated towards the twin objectives of performance and quality management'.

The overall mission and style of Modern Metro is reinforced by departmental statements. For example, in Corporate Personnel these refer to 'developing people and shaping the future' and 'providing the best service to our customers'. The department also has a quality service team of its own, and has drawn up a 'quasi-service level agreement' with its customers. The Corporate Personnel department has made a major contribution to the quality initiative through management development activities programmes such as the senior management development programme (SMDP) and the life skills course (LSC). The SMDP was developed in collaboration with a local university in 1988, and it is designed such that participants are able to gain management qualifications for their work there. It was extended in 1992 to include about 250 first line managers with the Council; the senior officers are convinced that this programme is essential to underpin effective quality management. The life skills courses are run internally and operate in a cascade format, with responsibility for training passing down the management hierarchy within departments. This aims to encourage managers to explore ideas, work in teams, and generally adopt a more open and sharing approach to problem-solving. The managers who were interviewed about this programme differed considerably in their evaluations; some viewed the course as, at best, vague and nebulous, whereas others considered it essential if more open management styles were to be fostered.

Although initiated within the personnel function, these management development activities were developed with strong support from the chief officer's group, and it has led to the promotion of champions for quality within Modern Metro. Much of the work undertaken by Corporate Personnel has attempted to empower line managers to take responsibility for improving quality within their own departments. Accordingly, its role is to generate ideas, act as an internal consultant, and support and facilitate the process. Crucial though this is to making quality work, the contribution of Corporate Personnel is not particularly visible to departmental managers and staff, and this input therefore runs the risk of being forgotten. As we argued in Chapter 4, whilst the 'hidden persuader' role of Personnel may be effective in terms of getting things done, it is ultimately reliant upon continued senior line management patronage for its long-term viability.

Perhaps the most effective way of illustrating the range of quality initiatives within Modern Metro is to examine three separate departments which have followed different paths: the first, Environmental Health and Trading Standards, has gone for ISO 9000 registration; the second, Home Care Services (within the Social Services department), has opted for Quality Service Teams; and the third, Adult and Community Education (part of the Education department), has focused on improving access and student feedback. Each of these will be considered in turn.

Quality assurance in Environmental Health and Trading Standards

The Environmental Health and Trading Standards department (EHTS) comprises three sections: occupational health, pollution and administration – which covers issues such as air pollution, waste disposal, and health and safety at work, in shops, pubs and restaurants; food, housing and general – which deals with matters such as blocked drains, pest control, and a dog warden service; and trading standards – which oversees consumer protection items relating to the quantity, quality and price of goods. The whole department employs less than 100 people.

A series of pressures during the late 1980s and early 90s each combined to put quality assurance firmly on the agenda within EHTS. Certain parts of the authority's work – for example in catering and cleaning, and aspects of transport and highways – had already been required to be put out to tender, and it was anticipated that the contracting-out process would be extended to EHTS. The second stimulus was internal, due to developments within Modern Metro which required departments to draw up quality action plans. The catalyst that turned this into a quality assurance programme and the quest for ISO 9000 was the attendance of the head of the department at a PA Consulting Group presentation to trading standards officers. He came back convinced that this was route for EHTS.

This began in 1991 with a visit from consultants who had been hired to help EHTS achieve ISO 9000 within the year. There were presentations, reviews of current activity, and the attendance of all staff at a series of workshops which explained the meaning of quality assurance, followed by the establishment of a steering group. One manager was given responsibility for guiding the process through, in addition to his normal duties, and a considerable amount of time and effort was spent working with staff, helping them with paperwork and ensuring that they were committed to the project. Apparently the use of existing staff was crucial in gaining the acceptance and cooperation of the few staff who were dubious about the exercise. Notwithstanding this, the project lost momentum as it became apparent that much more work was required to establish systems which would be acceptable to the inspectors. It was agreed to second the coordinator to the project three days a week and employ an administrator on a temporary contract until accreditation was awarded. Well within the year, during 1992, EHTS was awarded ISO 9000.

The most obvious signs of quality management, apart from those which operate across the whole authority, are in the quality manual and the leaflets which now publicise the work of the department. The former contains the quality policy statement, which is derived from and complements the objectives of the Council. For example, phrases abound in the statement about 'the highest quality of service', 'meeting customer needs', 'high levels of quality awareness amongst staff', 'structured quality systems', 'continual quality improvement', and 'communication with, training of, and ownership by' staff of the quality policy and process. The leaflets explain in straightforward terms the range of services which are offered by EHTS, along with cartoons illustrating rat-infested kitchens, underweight packs of sausages and unlicensed taxis. The impact of gaining ISO 9000 on EHTS, its services and customers is harder to gauge, but there is little doubt that the process of seeking accreditation helped to increase feelings of common identity within the department. Modern Metro's senior management team were certainly pleased with progress in the department and keen to publicise its success.

Quality service teams in Social Services

Social Services is one of the larger departments within Modern Metro, and a number of support services, including human resources, are provided at departmental level. This provides an extra layer which dilutes the impact of initiatives stemming from Corporate Personnel. The Home Care Service, which employs a total of 360 home care assistants, is run by an assistant director, and assists nearly 3000 'customers' each year. A full range of help is available between 8.00 am and 6.00 pm seven days a week, and an evening care service operates through until 11.00 pm to assist people who need help with getting to bed or a late evening 'check'.

The Home Care Service altered its name from the Home Help Service in 1988 to portray a more customer-focused approach, following a visit from the Social Services Inspectorate which identified a number of areas for improvement. Other changes included the implementation of a work plan system, whereby customers are provided with a 'contract' drawn up in conjunction with the direct carer, his or her manager and the customer. A copy of the work plan is retained by the customer so that he or she can ensure that all tasks are completed to the required standard and over the correct time period. Further developments have taken place within the Home Care Service since the late 1980s to clarify the department's mission and vision, its core purpose and activity, and in the establishment of more extensive training programmes and quality service teams.

The core business of the Service is to provide 'personal and practical care of excellent quality to the Department's clients within the resources available... in order to enable them to remain in the community (if they so wish) with dignity, comfort and self-respect'. Its vision is 'to know that our customers feel they are being provided with a service of excellent quality and choice'. The Mission Statement is 'Home Care gives Quality to Life through Quality Service'. The Home Care Service draws much of its inspiration from private sector sources such as Marks and Spencer or Scandinavian Airline Services (SAS), and in their training manuals and programmes there is great emphasis on models of excellence (Peters, 1989) and moments of truth (Carlzon, 1987). In relation to the latter, team members are encouraged to identify examples of bad service, including when the provider appears off-hand, is discourteous, lacks expertise, jokes about something which is upsetting you, or makes promises that are not kept. By contrast, ten techniques are outlined which ensure good customer service:

1. smile
2. ask for name and use it
3. listen by giving full attention, don't do other things at same time
4. be punctual
5. be informed and give correct information

6. keep customer involved
7. don't smoke or eat while dealing with a client
8. don't patronise or judge people
9. be polite
10. be understanding

A major feature of the Home Care Service, within the framework of the Modern Metro Style, is the quality service team (QST). Twenty-eight teams have been established since 1990, built onto the existing communications systems and structures within the Service. The teams are each led by a senior home care assistant responsible for a particular area, and they comprise ten to fifteen assistants. Teams meet for approximately one hour every six weeks to examine ways of solving quality problems and improving levels of service to internal and external customers. The impetus for this came from a variety of sources: the Council's broad commitment to quality and senior management's decision to sponsor 'champions' within the organisation, the effect of the management development programmes initiated by Corporate Personnel (in particular the SMDP and the LSCs), and a Masters project completed by the department manager.

All the home care staff have been on training courses connected with Customer First and quality, supported by a grant from the Local Government Management Board. It is felt that QSTs have led to improvements in staff morale and communications, and labour turnover halved during the first year of the new developments. Home care assistants indicate that they are now more involved in the work of the Service, they feel closer to management, and reckon that problems are solved more rapidly as all parties are more open in dealing with complaints. New methods of working with customers have been implemented, and a new annual 'Home Care Standards of Service' audit has now been agreed after a pilot scheme and feedback to staff. The home care managers also won one of the first quality awards in the Authority. Much of the process has been driven by line managers within Home Care, with a substantial involvement from Personnel staff who played a key role in setting up the training system for all staff, and in helping to facilitate the sessions themselves. Corporate Personnel has provided the basic building blocks of the quality initiative, playing a major role in designing and delivering the first training programmes and in facilitating the work of the QSTs.

Access and student feedback in adult and community education

Like Social Services, Education is a major department within the Modern Metro organisation, although its role has changed markedly in recent years as more schools have chosen to opt out of local authority control. The focus in this case is on adult and community education (ACE), which is organised into three area offices across the Council, each of which acts as a centre for the provision and organisation of classes. The type of class that is offered depends to a large extent on local demand, but includes topics such as modern languages, word processing, first aid, yoga, and arts and crafts. There is also a strong tradition of courses for women returners, supported by money from the European Social Fund. Classes run only if a minimum number of students is enrolled, and an army of tutors is employed on part-time, temporary contracts. Apart from the courses for women returners, most of the classes are offered in the evenings and occasionally at weekends. A crèche is provided for women returners, again staffed by individuals who work on a part-time basis. Each area office is managed by a full-time member of staff, who also teaches on some courses, and by several administrative and secretarial staff (mostly part-time) depending on the size of the programme.

The question of how to introduce a quality initiative into ACE is thus rather more complicated than in the previous two departments given the very large proportion of part-timers employed by the Council. Another complication is that, unlike the situation in Home Care Services, many of these staff hold professional qualifications and have strong views about the assessment of teaching. Moreover, all are on temporary contracts and have no obvious commitment to the work of the authority; indeed, they may also be employed by other local authorities in the region, each of which has different policies on quality and customer care.

The introduction of a dedicated quality programme in ACE is a more recent innovation, stimulated partly by pressures to develop further the Metro Style but also by the actions of a new manager in the department who is committed to improving service to users and teaching standards. It takes two specific forms which are central to the work of ACE. First, in order to promote the activities of the department and improve access, there is a clear commitment from senior management to ensure the use of plain language in all communications with potential service users. Seven golden rules are highlighted to ensure that a good piece of written work will be:

1. clear and concise, so the reader can easily understand it
2. accurate and relevant
3. no longer than is necessary
4. well presented
5. personal rather than impersonal, according to the purpose and the audience
6. capable of only one interpretation
7. grammatically correct

This is especially important in publicising classes to potential service users, explaining the level of the course (beginner or intermediate, for example), its content, its length, timing and location, and fees (especially for unwaged individuals). Plain language is also important when customers visit the ACE centres to enrol on courses or speak to members of staff. In both cases, special consideration has to be provided for members of the community for whom English is not their first language. As with the rest of Modern Metro, plain language and courtesy are key aspects of customer service when dealing with telephone calls and other casual enquiries.

The second aspect of quality assurance in ACE is questionnaires for students and tutors, designed to 'help ensure a quality service through continuous improvement'. These have been introduced in order to gauge student feedback on particular classes as well as the standard of administrative support at the centres. Every student attending a class is asked to complete a questionnaire by the centre manager and return it to the tutor half-way through the course. Completion is optional, and students can choose to fill in the forms anonymously, or can give their names if they have a specific query on which they would value feedback. Students are asked questions about the organisation and level of the course, the value of learning materials provided, and the tutor's teaching style. Students are also asked for feedback on the adequacy of buildings and classrooms (including access for those with disabilities), crèche facilities and administrative support, as well as marketing for the course. They are also asked whether the course has met expectations, whether or not they would advise others to attend, and what ideas they have for courses which are not currently offered. Students who have left the course are also contacted and asked for comments.

The system has been running only for one academic year so it is too early to make any definitive judgements about its success. About half the students returned evaluation forms, some of which were quite critical of the teaching styles and approaches adopted by tutors. As this is a new initiative at Modern Metro, some tutors have been rather negative about the whole process, regarding it as an intrusion into their own professional world (in much the same way that some university lecturers sought to resist the monitoring of teaching standards by the Higher Education Funding Council for England). Students with previous experience of higher education and in managerial/ professional jobs have written extensive additional comments about classes. Other students with less confidence to make judgements about courses and teaching styles have been less prepared to complete the forms, other than in a fairly neutral manner. As mentioned above, this is a problem that is particularly pronounced in local government, not only in ACE but also in housing, because users often lack the confidence and resources to challenge the work of professional staff. If notions of customer responsiveness and quality are to be taken seriously, these rely heavily on professional staff being open to constructive criticism about their standards of performance even if they reject 'market' notions of the customer. Whilst surveys of customers are a necessary ingredient of attempts to provide better standards of service, they need to be located within a broader democratic framework of accessibility to services, representation by Council members, and notions of community and citizenship (rather than as *individual* customers).

Summary of TQM at Modern Metro

The quality initiatives at Modern Metro appear to operate at several layers within the organisation, which is hardly surprising given its size and complexity. At the corporate level there have been a number of initiatives under the broad umbrella of 'management style', in the areas of management development, customer care and quality management. At this level the Corporate Personnel department played a sizeable role, although this is not always easy to observe given that much of the effort has been to facilitate a change in culture and empower line managers to lead new developments. Its role at departmental level – in developing ISO 9000, quality service teams, or student questionnaires – has been restricted to the design and delivery of training sessions. Even here, however, some initiatives have proceeded without any explicit contribution from human resource practitioners. As we have seen in other cases, HR can play a number of roles in the development of TQM, depending upon both the issue at hand and the organisational level at which the contribution is made. In the case of Modern Metro, the HR function showed evidence of all four roles analysed in Chapter 4.

Whilst there are clearly pressures to develop TQM in local government, its philosophy can vary depending upon the political complexion at national and local level. Given such a diverse organisation – both in terms of the range of services offered and in the geographical location of establishments – much also depends upon the motivation and ability of line managers, many of whom are professionally qualified, to make quality work. These problems are further compounded because customers for many of the services offered by local government lack the confidence or the resources to fight for quality, or the opportunity to take their custom elsewhere.

Quality management in local government: an alternative model?

It should be apparent, both from the introduction to this chapter and from the case study of Modern Metro, that there are important differences in the philosophy and practice of quality management between local authorities and private sector firms. These are summarised below.

First, unlike the private sector, party-political pressures (both national and local) directly influence the practice of quality management at the workplace. At one level this is manifested in choices about the language that is employed to define service users, such as customer, citizen or consumer. At another level it can be observed in the priorities that are accorded to particular attempts to enhance quality, such as those to improve access and rights for residents, or the 'charm' techniques of customer care alone. Either way, it is clear that there are strong tensions in the patterns of quality management in local government. As Walsh (1995: 83) suggests, 'the contrasting approaches to the reform of public service management reflect different views about the nature of government. On the one hand there is the idea that public services are provided for citizens as *individuals* [emphasis added] who have rights as consumers... . On the other hand there is the concept of citizenship as the expression of community membership, involving duties as much as rights'. Therefore it is 'possible for the same service to be seen as being of high quality from one perspective, and low quality from another... . The debate over the nature of public service quality is a debate over the values of the public sector' (Walsh, 1995: 86). The dominance of the New Right perspective nationally throughout the 1980s and mid-90s sets a clear context for quality initiatives which Conservative-controlled authorities, such as Modern Metro, have been keen to develop. Even Labour-controlled councils, whilst attempting to create a different agenda locally, have not been immune to the language and practice of the New Right and have been obliged to acknowledge – grudgingly or not – the value of some aspects of the consumerist perspective.

A second difference relates to the complex meanings accorded to quality in local government which lead some observers to differentiate it from the private sector, and in particular from manufacturing. The provision of services is in many respects different from the supply of manufactured goods, and it can be difficult to specify standards of conformance for an intangible relationship. Where this is done in parts of the private service sector – as in some fast-food chains, airlines or supermarkets – employees sometimes complain about superficiality and a lack of discretion, whilst customers may ridicule the mechanistic and parrot-like delivery of learnt phrases. In many parts of local government, such as social services, housing or education, service users might be keener on attention to their own problems rather than having to listen to a standard response. In some situations, especially when dealing with complex emotional issues, establishing trust through the construction of close relationships is much more important than the perfect delivery of a meaningless one-liner which serves only to alienate clients.

The evaluation of services can also vary considerably between users. In ACE, for example, where it is common to have mixed-ability classes, it is difficult to satisfy all learners. In some cases, it is also problematic to evaluate the service during or immediately after its delivery, and it is only some time later that its impact is felt; again, teaching and management development are good cases in point. In yet other cases, for example in Planning and Highways, it may prove difficult to determine whether or not the service has been delivered at all, and users may be reliant upon the professional expertise of the council officer (Walsh, 1991: 513). Perhaps, as Morgan and Murgatroyd (1994: 43) note, quality in services is therefore about increasing 'the skill repertoires of staff so that they may more appropriately meet wide variations in demand'.

But not all aspects of local authority work are concerned with professional or personal services, and it is important to recognise that some departments do undertake activities that have much closer similarities with the private sector;

indeed, in some cases, following the introduction of CCT, local authority workers may be in direct competition with private sector contractors for the future provision of services. The principles of quality assurance may have a more obvious meaning in what Sanderson (1992c: 17–18) describes as 'technical services', as in the case of Environmental Health and Trading Standards at Modern Metro, than they would in Social Services or Education (the 'people-orientated' or 'social improvement' activities). Whilst elements of quality assurance may be relevant for these latter services, on their own they are likely to be insufficient.

A third potential source of difference between public and private sector initiatives in TQM relates to the nature of the customer in local government. In many cases, citizens who are the most frequent users of services (for example, in Housing and Social Services) lack the power to make their voice heard (Bank, 1992: 3). Reliance here solely on models of customer care borrowed from the private service sector may mean that the needs of disadvantaged individuals or groups are ignored as time and effort is concentrated on the most vociferous users of services. In other words, citizens to whom improvements in the service should be targeted are disenfranchised or have their legitimate needs unmet. In situations such as this, 'delighting customers' may deny other citizens sufficient access to a range of council services. Moreover, as Sanderson (1992c: 29) notes, we have to recognise that users of local government services may lack the information or financial/informational resources to make choices and judgements in their own best interests. Furthermore, the views of individuals must be balanced against those of a wider public interest; local authorities must therefore ration services to match constrained resources, with the result that people may well be dissatisfied that they are not getting all that they want. Unlike private sector companies, who have more freedom in this respect, it is often impossible for local authorities to increase the supply of a service to meet demand. This problem is further exacerbated if better publicity (of subsidised or free access to courses and crèches in ACE, for example) leads to increased demand without the provision of extra resources for its delivery. There are clearly limits to the applicability of free market principles in local government due to problems in defining the meaning and interests of customers.

Finally, the ethos of professionalism has much stronger roots in local government than in most parts of the private sector, with staff often more prepared to identify with their own specific occupational group than the council for which they work. Conflicts over the implementation of quality programmes have been most apparent here, albeit at the level of cynicism and negative reactions to customer care initiatives rather than outright struggle. Morgan and Murgatroyd (1994: 47) suggest that resistance to change is greater in the public sector than in manufacturing because of this professional orientation. Opposition may be articulated in a variety of ways: the methods proposed for evaluating quality are superficial and/or inadequate; professionals already have their own methods for assessing quality and do not need 'interference' from managers; quality can not be assessed by users because they are not always aware of what their needs are; quality is being implemented only as part of an economy drive to intensify work. Undoubtedly many of these arguments are valid, but there are also nagging suspicions that some professional workers are keen to maintain their current level of autonomy, seeking ways to minimise surveillance from managers and audit bodies. Pollitt (1990: 442) proposes that local authorities are left with two options in dealing with these groups of professional staff, either to encourage the professions to establish their own standards and systems, or for management to specify the design features of quality assurance systems and require comparisons with similar occupational groups working for other employers.

Morgan and Murgatroyd (1994: 98) see this as especially problematic in the education sector, where there is a strong anti-management tendency and a cynicism about ideas drawn from the private sector which are somehow seen as anti-caring. They offer (1994: 169–75) the concept of 'contrapreneurship' to characterise this behaviour; it is 'the effective and creative use of skills and competencies to prevent significant change from occurring...The kinds of resistance encountered are active rather than passive, creative rather than blunt rejection, and powerfully effective rather than being just a nuisance'. It takes three distinct forms: resistance, due to fears that the widespread adoption of TQM will lead to job loss and work intensification; resentment, due to feelings that quality management represents nothing more than the latest fad; and technical objections that these approaches are not relevant for professional workers in the classroom.

Conclusion

This chapter can be concluded by reiterating three major points. First, quality management in local government has been subject to a range of different pressures from that which is experienced throughout the private sector. The most noticeable of these are the party-political axis, the varied meanings of quality, problems in defining customers, and professional resistance to quality initiatives. Second, despite these broad differences between the sectors, some local government departments have adopted quality assurance techniques similar to those in the private sector, typically in response to or in preparation for CCT or other forms of market testing. Their take-up across whole authorities, however, has been somewhat less common. Third, different patterns of quality management are emerging *within* local government between different authorities, most obviously between those subscribing to the New Right and the New Left philosophies. The case of Modern Metro is an example which has greater resonance with the former than the latter, but techniques were implemented which aimed to increase the involvement of citizens as a whole. If a Labour-controlled authority had been analysed, the emphasis would have been somewhat different, and it is likely that there would have been even greater differences from the best-known private sector model. Whatever the political complexion of the local authority, however, Pollitt (1990: 436) summarises the issue well when he suggests that quality is a contested concept. It is likely to remain so given the conflicting and contradictory pressures on local government.

CHAPTER 7

Making TQM Work in a Tough Environment: British Steel Teesside Works

Introduction

British Steel is the world's fourth largest producer of steel, producing over 12 million tonnes of crude steel in 1994. The company's 'Cinderella' like transformation, from a record loss-making nationalised producer to the most profitable (in 1990) steel company in the world, has often been depicted as nothing short of an industrial miracle (for example, Heller, 1995). After years of ridicule the company has recently been described as one the UK's few truly 'world-class businesses' (Johnson and Scholes, 1993: 433). Surveys of corporate reputation amongst the UK's senior managers report British Steel as one of the most improved companies. British Steel increased its ranking from 189 in 1992 to 54 (out of 260) during 1994. This was achieved on the back of markedly higher scores for the quality of its management, products and service (Hasell, 1994). The effect of this transformation is keenly felt by the company's managers. According to one manager:

> If someone asked me in the pub 'Who do you work for?' I used to be embarrassed to say British Steel. I knew what was coming, the jokes and mickey-taking about losses, productivity, overmanning, quality. We used to be a laughing stock. It's not like that anymore. I'm proud to work for British Steel. We are now a respected company.

In 1993, British Steel restructured into a 'two-tier organisation'. The new structure comprises a headquarters with executive directors and functions in finance, legal, personnel, corporate communication and commercial services, and shared specialist support functions of research and development, information technology and supplies and transport. Headquarters is responsible for the overall strategic direction and for ensuring that the individual businesses achieve agreed performance targets. Below headquarters are four businesses grouped in 'portfolios' covering long products, flat products, distribution and associated companies and subsidiaries. Each group is led by a managing director with responsibility for the operational and strategic management of the business. Each manufacturing business also has full responsibility for marketing its products. The restructuring has many implications, not least the removal of a divisional layer of management along with the divisional titles of 'Strip Products' and 'General Steels'.

This case is based upon Teesside Works, located in the north-east of England. Teesside is one of British Steel's four major iron and steel-making sites in the UK and is an integrated works producing iron from raw materials, converting these to steel, which is then cast into semi-finished products before final conversion to finished products in the rolling mills. Teesside's products include heavy sections for the building industry, flat products and medium sections for a wide variety of applications. The majority of Teesside Works' 4900 employees (as at March 1993) are employed on the Redcar site. British Steel continues to invest substantial sums at Teesside Works with some £167 million already invested in the 1990s, including enhancement to the universal beam mill and replacement of the pipe mill. Teesside Works is a key employer in an economically depressed area. Its presence on Teesside has recently been estimated to support over 600 local suppliers employing a further 5882 employees on Teesside Works contracts. Such local support, however, is not always fully reciprocated. The company withdrew its long-standing sponsorship from Middlesbrough Football Club in 1995 when the construction of the new stadium mostly used German-produced steel.

Teesside Works sits within the Sections, Plates, and Commercial Steels (SPCS) business. The SPCS, itself part of the Long Products division, has been formed at a difficult time for the steel industry. Falling prices, product substitution, excess capacity in Europe, growing imports from eastern European countries keen on foreign currency earnings, market penetration by the more aggressive newly industrialised producers such as South Korea and Brazil, continuing fierce Japanese competition, restrictions in the US, all on top of weak domestic demand, have made life very difficult for the recently privatised British Steel (Butler, 1991). Competition is also increasing from the small, innovative, flexible and lean mini-mills, such as the US-based Nucor group (Birat, 1987; Dickson, 1991; Overman, 1994).

The steel industry is highly cyclical. The record profits of 1990 were followed by a profit collapse in which the company recorded losses in two of the following three years. However, results for the financial year ending in March 1995 again saw a return to strong profits. In such a challenging business environment, many steel producers are increasingly emphasising quality management as a key element of business strategy (Franz, 1991).

According to SPCS's Managing Director:

> High quality, cost competitive products delivered on time and with a sound technical and commercial backup service must be the ongoing objective if the new Business is to survive and prosper. (Ward, 1993: 1)

The competitive strategy of Teesside Works, with a strong emphasis on cost leadership and customer service, also echoes this emphasis on quality management. The mission statement of Teesside Works includes the following aim:

> Teeside Works will be a profitable, efficient, and environmentally aware innovative leader in the international volume steel market. Our aim is to provide all customers, internal and external, with quality products and services and to strive for continuous improvement. (Campbell, 1992)

Total quality management at Teesside Works

The introduction of total quality management in British Steel was originally agreed with the trade unions in 1987 in the joint council on pay and conditions (Industrial Relations Service, 1990). Due to concerns about the overtly managerialist overtones of TQM and the desire to gain the agreement of trade unions to its introduction, the British Steel quality management initiative was christened 'Total Quality Performance' (TQP). The decision to introduce TQP at Teesside was taken by the works management committee in 1988. Research into what quality management approach to adopt was conducted by a small, newly appointed team of two led by a TQP manager.

The team examined the literature on quality management, especially the writings of the American quality gurus, received many presentations from management consultants, and visited companies already started on the total quality management process, including a study tour of leading US 'quality' companies. However, because of concerns about the unique nature of a steel works, described by one manager as 'a big, dirty industry spread all over the place', and by another has having a 'grey, unexciting image and product' the eventual decision was to design a tailor-made programme for Teesside Works using the assistance of management consultants.

The introduction of the TQP initiative had a mix of hard and soft managerial objectives. In relation to the former there were some major quality-related issues to be tackled at Teesside as customers were becoming more demanding and costs were under intense pressure, not least because of governmental subsidies to some of British Steel's international competitors. Yields, product conformance, stock levels, delivery reliability and costs were all areas where improvements were sought (Williams, 1993; Zellweger, 1993). An example of changing customer demands for improved quality is that for 'blue' steel. Newly produced steel has a blue tint and if protected from the environment this colour remains. Although this characteristic is of only aesthetic value, customers were less willing to accept rusty sections. Such a requirement places more pressure on order scheduling and delivery performance to ensure finished products are not left open to the environment long enough to become oxidised.

There were also softer HR and 'cultural' objectives underpinning TQP's introduction. In the hostile marketplace for steel many firms are increasingly seeking to manage their workforces more strategically in the search for competitive advantage (Adams, 1988; Franz, 1991; Oswald *et al.*, 1991; Waters, 1993; Overman, 1994). British Steel's attempts to refashion its traditional industrial relations structures and HRM practices are well documented (Upham, 1980, 1990; Dobson, 1981; Hartley *et al.*, 1983; Kelly, 1983; Bamber, 1984; Avis, 1990; Blyton, 1992; Morris *et al.*, 1992). In support of such changes, managers at Teesside described a search for a new and more appropriate management style via TQP. The old autocratic and tenacious management style (typical of management/employee relations in steel making in 'adversarial' countries such as the UK, US and Canada [Docherty, 1983; Bain, 1992] and traditionally very characteristic of British Steel) was seen as having been an asset in securing survival in the earlier part of the decade. In the late 1980s, however, Teesside was profitable and an aggressive management style was now seen as a barrier to further progress on some of the goals outlined above.

The introduction of TQP was described thus:

> Suddenly we were making money. We were successful. We looked around and said we are not going to get any better than this if we carry on as we are. We have to start bringing people on board, involving them. The improvements we will make now and in the future will come from down below. We also recognized that we were not going to get improvements from the shop floor if all they are used to is being yelled at when it goes wrong. We needed to remove the whole culture of uncertainty and fear which we operated in. (Personnel manager)

> TQP was about managers changing their styles, from the old aggressive style that we had to have in this company in order to survive. What we said to them (middle managers) was 'We may have to kick that out of the window now. You cannot have that any more. We need a partnership to get the best out of people'. If you think about it, it's exactly what the unions have always wanted. (TQP manager)

One manager described how, after years of being told to 'kick arses', he was now expected to operate in a radically different fashion under TQP:

> I was told, 'This is how we want you to manage people now. We don't want you to shout at them when they get it wrong. We want you to sit down with them and tell them why they got it wrong so we can ensure it doesn't happen again'. But they don't see the raw material that I've got to work with. (Engineering manager)

The management of the TQP programme reflects this emphasis on HR and cultural change. First, the role of the TQP team was seen very much as a facilitative and catalytic one. The aim was for ownership to be firmly located with line management and employees. To this end the central team was kept deliberately small, a TQP manager and an assistant supported by others seconded to the initiative, to ensure early transfer of ownership. Second, both the TQP manager and his assistant manager had personnel and training backgrounds rather than technical or engineering ones that could perhaps be expected in a steel works. The role of the TQP team has changed as the initiative has matured and the TQP manager describes it as being now 'less and less about nagging and more and more about public relations and building confidence'. A good example of the public relations aspect is the recent celebratory 'World Quality Day' (based on the European Organization for Quality proposal for such events) held in November 1994, which involved presentations, exhibitions, and videos by teams from the Works as well as suppliers.

Given these broad demands upon the TQP programme, a major investment in training was required (Procter *et al.*, 1990; Procter, 1992). A training programme designed to introduce the principles, tools and techniques of total quality was introduced in April 1988. The main aim was to raise awareness and generate employees' commitment to the programme. Particular emphasis was placed on the concept of internal customers; all employees under TQP are considered as suppliers and/or customers. The importance of the internal customer concept was described by a manager thus:

> You could go to anybody in this plant and 95% of the people you would talk to could tell you what's happening in the plant in terms of yield. What's happening in term of performance like wastage, returns, yields, complaints. They all know because that information is always there. But one of the things we were very aware of is that everybody is focused on their own little area. It was something that came out of the quality programme. We started pushing internal customers. It's great if the blast furnace get their act together but they still need to be aware of what the steel makers want. It is a natural progression that you actually come to the end customer. (Production manager)

The target was to train the entire workforce in TQP within two years of launch. This was a major logistics challenge in itself, necessitating the training of over 150 senior managers, 1000 middle managers, 460 foremen and supervisors and around 5400 other employees. Consultants were brought in to train senior managers and then a cascade training process was developed, using internal trainers or 'facilitators'. These were 'suitable' managers, defined as 'proficient in their area of operation, respected by fellow managers and workforce, and who had already exhibited communication skills' (Procter, 1990: 270). Senior management wanted to use only highly committed and effective managers rather than those who were merely 'available'. In the words of the works director 'If you can spare them, I don't want them'. The initial training programme was completed by autumn 1990.

The programme for shop-floor employees involved training in brain-storming, cause and effect diagrams, measurement tools and an introduction to statistical methods. The training for managers gave considerable accentuation to cultural and HRM issues in contrast to the technical, that is, systems, audits, tools and techniques, and certification, emphasis of much TQ training (Dale *et al.*, 1993). For example, the training for middle managers comprised eight modules (Procter *et al.*, 1990):

1. What is TQP?
2. Customer first
3. Managing for TQP
4. Teamwork
5. Tools and techniques
6. People make quality
7. Barriers to TQP
8. Making TQP a permanent part of our culture

Training continues to be given a high priority at Teesside as a key lever for gaining employee commitment to, and capability for, continuous improvement. British Steel has won more national training awards than any other UK company (Donaldson, 1994). The Investors in People award was achieved in 1996. All employees will be provided with their own personal training plan linked to departmental and works quality objectives. The works has also embraced National Vocational Qualifications (NVQ), formally endorsing the Government's national target of achieving at least 50 per cent of employees qualified to NVQ Level 3 by the year 2000.

A decision not to use quality circles as part of the TQP initiative was taken at the outset. The main issue influencing this decision was that circles had been introduced in the mid-1970s and had failed. The re-introduction of a previously failed technique, with many employees still employed by the Works who had experienced the quality circles, was thought to be ill advised. Instead quality improvement teams (QIT) were developed as the main vehicle of employee involvement in TQP. Unlike the quality circles, QITs were disbanded once a problem was solved; when a new problem arose, volunteers were asked to form a new QIT. Part of the rationale here was to involve more of the workforce in problem-solving and also to put less pressure on individual team members who could move in and out of membership more fluidly. By mid-1993 more than 150 schemes had been successfully completed and a further 150 were under development.

To date, QIT projects and the TQP initiative have mainly concentrated on the production and distribution areas and have generally been much less active in the administrative and support functions. This was partly to start TQP with the 'success stories' that it was thought these areas could provide and the difficulty of measuring quality improvement in service areas such as the personnel and finance functions. Further, it was felt that the shop-floor employees would be more responsive and less cynical about TQP than the non-managerial administrative staff. However, some administrative QIT projects have been very successful. For example, a project to reduce the error rate in letters of credit (estimated by the clearing banks to be on average 60 per cent nationally) has achieved a result of 92 per cent correct first time and an annual saving of more than £250 000.

Evaluation: is TQP working?

Overall, management at Teesside Works consider the TQP programme to have been a major success. In 1991 the works director set up a progress review team to evaluate TQP's progress, determine performance measures and establish milestones for the future. Workshops for managers were also conducted to develop an evaluation strategy. The result of a vigorous debate was that it was decided that TQP would be evaluated against three key areas, process improvement, attitude and culture, and customer focus. In this section, because of the market-sensitive nature of much of the data collected on customer focus, we concentrate on the first two of these areas. Each area has a number of key sub-themes: process improvement is subdivided into health and safety, environment, efficiency and supplier strategy; attitude and culture is subdivided into management style, communications, employee involvement and values and behaviours.

Other areas against which TQP could be evaluated were considered but the above were identified as the most important to support the business strategy of the Works. For example, TQP could be evaluated against how it has helped maintain jobs. The Works management takes considerable pride in not compulsorily laying-off any workers in one of the deepest recessions it has ever had to face. The belief amongst senior managers is that in a large part this stems from the business being in a much better shape, because of the TQP programme, to be able to weather economic downturns. TQP has thus undoubtedly saved jobs at the Works but the programme was not formally evaluated against this area as it was a 'card the company did not wish to play'.

Health and safety

The link between improved health and safety and effective TQM is a strong one (Krause and Finley, 1993). The TQP programme has had a positive impact on Teesside Works' safety record. Given the nature of steel production the potential for serious accidents is a considerable one. The Works safety department developed, with academic help, the application of total quality principles to safety management. The resulting 'zero accident' principles mirror those of TQP: prevention not detection, management led, everyone responsible, cost of safety, right first time, company-wide and continuous improvement. This was a considerable change in the traditional accident prevention approach in the Works, characterised as a remote corporate management setting safety objectives with little local management or employee involvement in the process. This resulted in what was described as a 'combative' rather than a consultative approach to safety.

A feature of the TQP training programme is the linking of accident prevention to total quality. When quality improvement plans for a department or section are produced, elements of health and safety are automatically incorporated. Some 30 departmental safety improvement teams have been established, with members from all levels. A wide range of projects has been completed using TQP principles and tools. For example, a customised kinetic handling course designed for Redcar Coke Ovens; the design of a new glove to prevent burn injuries in the Continuous Casting Plant; and the development (to the point at which a patent application was processed) of a new load binder for securing structural sections to road trailers (Jamieson and Procter, 1990).

The zero accidents initiative has produced major improvements. For example, since its introduction there has been a 45 per cent reduction in lost-time injuries, and a 25 per cent reduction in all injuries (Ball and Procter, 1994). The Redcar Blast Furnace is a good exemplar of the impact of the new approach to safety. During 1990–91 the furnace witnessed its heaviest lost-time accident total in its history, some 15 occurrences. Following the introduction of the zero accidents programme it became the first major plant to record no lost-time accidents over a year for the second time in 1993–94, surpassing its previous record of 425 days, this time with a total of 594 days. The monthly all-injury accident rate has also fallen from an average of 8.1 accidents per month to 3.1 after the introduction of the programme. However, following such a breakthrough in accident prevention, early analysis of 1995 statistics suggests a slight rise. This rise seems to be mirrored both locally and nationally and managers believe that the high temperatures experienced in a long, hot summer in the warmest year on record may well explain this.

Environment

Public statements form British Steel place a high priority on improving environmental performance and the group committed some £150 million to introduce additional environmental controls over 1991–95 (Scholey, 1991). A number of improvements in environmental management have resulted from the total quality initiative. In a reaction to increasing public and corporate awareness about environmental issues, legislation and local concerns, an environmental commitment was added to the works mission statement in 1991. This was a direct result of a recommendation from the TQP progress review team (Zellweger, 1993).

An environment committee and an ecology group have been established. Environmental improvements in coke oven emissions, iron oxide fumes from the blast furnaces, and reductions in wind-blown dust from the raw material stockpiles have resulted from the TQP initiative. The environmental improvements at Teesside Works have achieved external recognition. The Works was awarded the Premier Award in the 1994/5 Business Commitment to the Environment Awards. This was gained for an 'outstanding environmental training programme for employees, suppliers and contractors' (*Green Bits*, 1995: 13).

Efficiency

Teesside's benchmarking suggests that it is now the world's second lowest cost producer. One internal estimate is that TQP contributed greatly to this, saving over £50 million in its first five years of operation and the use of SPC alone is estimated to save over £1 million per annum. For example, the reduction in time taken to unload ore trains from three hours to 20 minutes, reduction in firing costs of coke ovens saving £100 000 per annum, the reduction in coke moisture saving £84 000 per annum, improvements in roll wear in the Universal Beam Mill saving over £300 000 per year. Although it is very difficult to attribute directly to the programme, TQP is viewed as a major contributor to a number of dimensions of Teesside Works' improved performance. For example, between 1988 and 1992 the company stripped out over £30 million of operating costs; man hours per tonne of liquid steel have dropped from 3.4 to 2.7; and stocks held have been reduced by £20 million per annum. In terms of product quality, major improvements and investments have been made, particularly in conformance and aesthetics. Investment in on-line dynamic measuring systems have helped increase yields and reduce scrap by producing a higher quality product that does not require further re-work before dispatch. Since the introduction of TQP absenteeism has also reduced from more than 7 per cent in 1988 to 4.5 per cent for manual workers in 1995.

Lastly, on-time delivery performance has markedly improved, from 'under 80 per cent to over 90'. The company has set itself a target of 95 per cent on-time deliveries by 1996, which at current production levels would still mean some 175,000 tonnes not being delivered on time. Within the industry, however, this would still represent a strong performance and one which managers believe would provide the Works with a competitive advantage over rivals in a critical area.

Supplier management

Suppliers play a vital role in any organisation and Teesside Works, like many others, greatly increased its use of subcontractors in the 1980s (Malloch, 1991). Initially their use was a typical form of distancing strategy which makes labour management 'somebody else's problem' (Atkinson and Meager, 1986: 54) and was driven largely by manpower reduction and cost reduction goals. Company policy was to select many suppliers in order to encourage price competition, invariably selecting on a lowest cost basis. Thus by 1990 Teesside Works had over 3500 suppliers. Contractors were often harshly managed, with little loyalty extended from one contract to the next. One manager described the relationship with contractors as the 'bloodsport of contractor bashing'.

In the TQP workshops, however, it emerged that the use of subcontracting was posing an increasing number of problems for managing quality. High turnover and 'corner cutting' by the contractor working under very tight margins were both products of a hard use of subcontractors. The result was an increasing range of quality problems associated with contractor performance. Thus contractors, as other research has noted (Cole, 1993), were increasingly recognised by management as a weak link in the quality management chain. A QIT was set up, comprising members from engineering, production, services functions and supplies personnel, to examine this problem.

In 1991 the policy was changed. The number of suppliers was to be reduced and closer ties with the remaining ones developed. A Pareto analysis of suppliers found, in classic fashion, that some 87 per cent of spend was with 22 per cent of firms. During the early 1990s Teesside Works ran a series of 'Managing Contractors' seminars to put across the new purchasing strategy and the message of 'partnership' with subcontractors. Over 45 seminars were held for more than 1000 representatives of about 25 per cent of suppliers.

According to the TQP manager:

> We keep saying to them 'We don't want win–lose situations any more. It's not a case of screwing the contractor for everything you can get. We have got our rates down. We have got a situation where we have got very competitive rates coming into the company from contractors because we are big enough to demand that. We can't go soft and it's still a business relationship but if we are going to get quality out of them, there has got to be something in it for them. That is not always necessarily money. Nowadays we are looking for partnerships with our contractors.'

Teesside works termed the new approach one of 'strategic purchasing' and a newly formed site contracts team was formed to work with the purchasing department and operational personnel to manage the supplier improvement programme. Suppliers are now selected not on lowest cost but on 'total quality' cost and undergo more detailed appraisal before selection and ongoing monitoring by supplier and contractor 'owners'. Training for suppliers has also been introduced. Total quality workshops for contractors staff are run by line managers from Teesside Works. All suppliers were also told that by 1993 they should have achieved BS5750 if they wanted to continue to do business with Teesside Works; evidence from the interviews, however, suggests that this has not been fully implemented, especially with some of the smaller suppliers.

The new partnership approach has moved away from ultra-tight specifications for contractors, which were seen as stifling flair and improvement, to one where there is room for, and an expectation of, suppliers using their skills and experience to help solve joint problems. The ultimate aim is thus to support the continuous improvement of the Works by the suppliers' own continuous improvement, and the suppliers in turn will be able to pass on benefits to their customer, Teesside Works. The awarding of longer contracts was seen as part of the solution to achieving this partnership.

One manager described the newly sought-after relationship with subcontractors as follows:

> We shouldn't have to threaten them. That's not the way we want to do business any more. We shouldn't hold things over their heads and say do this or else. We should be able to co-operate with them, to talk to them. They should understand our needs and we should understand their problems. It sounds idealistic but that's what we now want.

Pressure on subcontractors from employees for high-quality performance is also in evidence. This is partly spurred by employee concerns about poor contractor performance affecting the local lump-sum bonus schemes (LLSBS) which include quality indicators in their computation (see Snape *et al.*, 1996). According to various managers interviewed, employees put 'tremendous pressure on contractors'; 'are quick to criticize'; and 'mercilessly hassle the under-performers'. The transport manager said:

> I know for a fact that if they [contractors] slip up, there will a be a knock on my door. The constant whinge I get nowadays is not that we are using contractors, that's now well established and accepted, but that the employees say 'They are not as good as we are. They are reducing our bonus'.

Suppliers have been considerably reduced and further reductions are planned. In 1993/94 a total of 2608 were used. These were made up of some 2036 companies who supplied products, and a further 572 subcontractors who serviced the Works by providing an average of 1000 personnel per day at a cost of over £60 million. A good example of the reduction is provided by the use of contracting companies supplying fitters, electricians, and boilermakers. Before rationalisation in 1991 some 19 firms were used but by 1993 this had been reduced to six.

Changing employee attitudes and building a quality culture

In line with the 'good practice' recommended by many TQM writers (for example, Collard, 1989; Oakland, 1989), management at Teesside Works decided to carry out a survey to assess employee attitudes towards the TQP programme. The survey was partly motivated by concerns that TQP was 'running out of steam' as it matured and that the easier, major breakthroughs in improvements had already been achieved. Further, the hard times of recession had returned; there was a concern that managers were 'reverting back to type' and the old aggressive, authoritarian managerial style was slowly returning.

According to one manager:

> Recession came along, pay was effected, we were still making redundancies. Managers were feeling the pressure and starting to revert back to type. I don't think we took our eye off the ball but we had so many other pressures coming on us it was unbelievable.

Such a development was keenly felt by those below top management. A production supervisor described the growing indifference of some managers to the TQP programme during this period thus:

> TQP is working back to front here. We are trying to keep it going but they [management] don't seem bothered. They should be encouraging us to keep the momentum going, not the other way round.

The survey was conducted in February 1992. It consisted of some 79 questions divided into seven main areas: TQP philosophy; leadership; management and teamwork; customer requirements and performance measures; communications; reward and recognition; and employee information. The anonymous survey was distributed at the workplace but returned via prepaid envelopes to an independent body for scoring and collation. It was also stated that the questionnaires would be destroyed once they had been analysed. Some 5068 questionnaires were issued and 1809 returned, representing a 35 per cent response rate. Using a weighted analysis an average 'footprint' of results was produced for the Works and separate ones for different categories of employee, for example, senior managers, middle managers, supervisors, production and craft employees, and so on.

A key finding to emerge out of the attitude survey was although there had been a considerable degree of success in terms of the 'hard' objectives of efficiency and customer service, the desired 'softer' attitude and cultural changes had not been fully achieved. This is consistent with the findings of other research (for example, Wilkinson, 1994). Unsurprisingly, senior managers were the most positive about TQP, with a steady decline down the hierarchy to craft workers, who were the most negative of all groups. The survey did highlight many strengths. Most of the workforce understood what TQP was about, recognised the importance of gearing all activities to customer satisfaction, were supportive of the internal customer concept, accepted that quality improvement was everyone's responsibility and a continuous activity, and that the attitude towards teamwork was improving.

A number of real concerns emerged, however, not least that the maturity of TQP had not achieved managerial expectations, total quality was still perceived as being apart from the normal way of doing business. The effect of the attitude survey shattered a number of managerial illusions about the TQP's progress and recriminations were the order of the day:

> People accused us of letting them down. They expected overnight change. They expected it to be wonderful. (TQP manager)

> The attitude survey said people didn't believe us any more. Didn't believe we meant it. Didn't believe TQP had worked. (Production manager)

Eighty-two per cent of all negative responses were related to four areas; low morale, management style, communications, and commitment to TQP. The most negative attitude was related to staff feeling they were not assessed and rewarded according to the quality of their work.

After analysis of the survey, and feedback to all employees of its results, a number of developments have occurred. First, TQP has been 're-launched', again using consultants but in a much lower-key way compared to the original high-profile introduction. Second, an 'attitude' task-force was set up. The task-force formed sub-groups to examine the key areas of concern. The task-force made many recommendations and so far a number of these have been implemented. The works director now devotes three days each month to managerial briefings, which are then cascaded down to all employees. The briefings give particular prominence to meeting customer requirements and improving operations, as well as to production and sales data. This initiative has involved the training of almost 600 team briefers and a survey in 1995 found that some 60 per cent of employees consider the briefing sessions to be their most important source of information. Team briefing sessions are also used to conduct more frequent employee attitude surveys. The Works has also introduced quality 'story boards' (in production areas some are as large as 60 feet long by 20 feet high) into all areas with 'owners' responsible for updating the display of a wide range of quality-related data.

A director's video is produced quarterly to supplement the briefings. Special editions of the internal newsletter, *Steel News*, are devoted to quality two or three times a year, and quality competitions, such as designing a poster for a safety campaign have been used. A director's annual award for the most successful quality improvement projects has been introduced. The aim here was to attempt to encourage more employee involvement and to publicise and acknowledge quality success stories. The 1993 winners of this award also had contractors as a part of the team. A separate 'supplier of the year' award for contractors was introduced in 1994; and in order to encourage more commitment to TQP philosophy and practice amongst the administrative functions a specific award for this group has also been introduced.

Management also examined and adopted some of the practices of particular plants within the Works, plants that had a strong reputation for employee involvement practices. Particularly influential was the so called 'Shelton Model'. This was a 'second stage' TQM programme based at the Shelton Works, Stoke-on-Trent, called 'Managing Change'. It comprises a wide range of employee involvement practices including: training and management development to support employee involvement; face-to-face interviews to find out the workforce's views; and multi-functional quality improvement teams. This initiative also brought with it the language of 'empowerment' to Teesside.

A range of other employee involvement (EI) support mechanisms have been introduced. The company now makes an increasing use of study tours to other 'quality companies', organised via its membership of the European Foundation for Quality Management (EFQM). Shop-floor employees are also included on every study tour undertaken by a manager. In the managerial appraisal process at least one objective for every manager will now result in a quality improvement project which involves a wide section of the workforce. A sharp criticism from the attitude survey was that employees needed time and facilities to get involved in continuous improvement, and in many departments this was difficult to obtain. The company has responded by introducing a 'create time/facilities' support initiative targeted at a local level. It has also dedicated and equipped work space throughout both production and administrative areas so that staff can meet together more easily to work on quality improvement. The number of employees purely dedicated to the TQP initiative has been increased by the appointment of full-time quality support coordinators to act as 'encouragers' for local initiatives and as 'bridges' for translating Works quality policy into a meaningful local action plan. A commitment to repeat the attitude survey regularly and achieve improvements has also been made.

Much of the literature on TQM emphasises the importance of active EI in order to achieve a quality culture (Blackburn and Rosen, 1993). For example, Hill (1991a: 400) suggests it is 'the central mechanism for improving business quality'. As Hill (1991b: 565) also notes, however, there is a danger of becoming 'starry-eyed' about the effectiveness of EI practices to support TQM. The results of the employee attitude survey brought the stark reality into clear view for managers at the Works when it showed that the heart of the TQM approach, employee participation, was ineffective. TQP was not yet embedded into the company culture nor had it captured the 'hearts and minds of staff'.

This is not an uncommon scenario in maturing TQM programmes. Wilkinson *et al.*(1992) describe TQM as going through a series of phases: an initial introductory phase with a high profile and much flag waving; a second phase of hope and enthusiasm; and a third phase often characterised by disappointment and disillusionment as the gains expected by managers or the influence employees hoped for fail to materialise. Such a framework aptly describes the Teesside Works experience. Unlike the cases described by Wilkinson *et al.* (1992), however, rather than TQP slipping in to obscurity and decay, management demonstrated their sustained commitment to it in a number of ways. These included redoubling efforts; more effectively integrating participative activities into daily work practices; and committing more resources to make involvement effective and bring about the attitude changes necessary to support TQ. Early evidence from more recent surveys would suggest that such efforts are paying off. For example, a survey of those attending briefing meetings in April 1995 found 70 per cent of employees reporting that they were actively involved in quality improvement.

Conclusions

The future expectations of TQP's progress at Teesside are high. The company has set itself some exacting targets for what it hopes to achieve. When TQP is next reviewed, some of the main benchmarks for success will be: two man hours per tonne of liquid steel produced (equivalent to a world-best performance of plants with similar configurations to Teesside); £40 million of further cost reduction; 95 per cent on-time delivery; 25 per cent improvement in customer service across a range of indicators; 10 per cent reduction in all injury and lost-time injury frequency rates (for BS employees and contractors); 80 per cent of employees involved in quality improvement activities; 30 per cent reduction in suppliers and contractors; and zero contraventions of the permitted release levels of pollutants and a 10 per cent reduction in waste. The company now uses the EFQM award as a self-assessment and an internal benchmark of TQP's progress, and has conducted site audits in 1996 with initial targets of a shadow application in 1997, UK entry in 1998 and European one in 1999. Targets have also been set on improving the levels of employee commitment to TQP, as assessed by attitude surveys, to make progress on process charting/mapping , and for all areas to have BS5750. Further aims are for TQP practices to be more widely adopted in the administrative areas and for supplier rationalisation. These are hard, measurable, demanding and important performance targets for the Works and provide a very real indicator of the success of a TQM initiative (Redman, Snape and Wilkinson, 1996).

The company's managers strongly believe that TQP has been central to its considerably improved business performance over the last decade. These gains have not been won easily, managers have had to take 'on the chin' some often difficult setbacks to TQP's progress, in particular the disappointing results of attitude surveys and lack of progress amongst white-collar groups. The development of a sustainable 'quality culture' has been much more difficult to achieve than managers anticipated at the start of the programme. Very real questions were asked of managerial commitment to the programme by the depth of the recession in the industry in the early 1990s. Economic downturns place great pressures on achieving short-run returns and thus many organisations neglect long-term, 'journeys without end' – TQM initiatives – often with fatal results. A particular casualty in such times is a reduction in a company's investment in training and the quality infrastructure. The scope of the initial training and its continuing development via the introduction of NVQs and Investors in People, as well as an expanded support system for TQP activities, are all indicators this did not occur at Teesside Works.

The continuing restructuring of the industry and associated redundancies in this period made winning and maintaining employee commitment to TQP all the more difficult to achieve. Where such difficulties have often proved fatal for other TQM initiatives, however, it was managers' strong belief in the value of TQP, fuelled by its early successes, that helped sustain the programme through a very difficult period. The Teesside Works case provides some support for the view that gaining competitive advantage from TQM depends critically on executive commitment, building a quality culture and employee involvement, rather than such 'technical' TQM staples as benchmarking, tools and techniques and so on (Powell, 1995). The essential role for the TQP programme at Teesside Works is thus one of providing an integrated vehicle for management to understand and acquire these key skills and resources. The Teesside Works case illustrates that such resources and organisational competencies, despite the claims of much popular TQM writing and many management consultants, are not easily gained but are painstakingly acquired. The aligning of managerial practices, in particular the use of subcontractors and HRM systems (especially employee involvement and remuneration), to the aims and philosophy of the TQP programme have also helped sustain it. As economic conditions improve for the steel industry the company expects to reap the benefits of this commitment; better than expected financial results in the mid-1990s and future forecasts indicate that this may well be occurring.

CHAPTER 8

Fads and Fixes – Waving Goodbye to Quality in Financial Services?

Introduction

Until the 1980s the building societies, which had their origins in the mutual self-help organisations of the eighteenth and nineteenth centuries, had the home loans market largely to themselves, and operated an interest rate cartel, with the Building Societies Association (BSA) publishing recommended rates of interest. Building societies did, however, face strong competition in the market for deposits, with the banks and National Savings all seeking to attract the savings of the personal sector. The building societies enjoyed fiscal privileges over other financial institutions, and their investors received favourable tax treatment, while the tax regime discriminated in favour of borrowing for house purchase, the building societies' primary function.

During this period there was little price competition in the home loans market and societies competed with one another, mainly through advertising and through the development of branch networks. The number of branches increased rapidly, with a growth of 12 per cent per annum in the 1970s and a corresponding increase in the number of staff employed (Rajan, 1987). The growth in the size of the movement was accompanied by a reduction in the number of individual societies, however, as mergers led to increasing concentration.

The 1980s saw the entry of the banks and other financial institutions into the home loans market, and the unique tax advantages of the building societies were eroded as the Government sought to promote competition in the financial services markets. The banks, spurred on by their worries over Third World debt and attracted by the high returns on mortgages, increased their share of the home loans market from 7 per cent of net advances in 1980 to 36 per cent in 1982. While market shares have since varied considerably from year to year, with building societies accounting for 50 per cent of net advances for house purchase in 1987 and 75 per cent by 1990, the days of the building society monopoly in home loans were over (McGoldrick and Greenland, 1992).

The building societies responded by abandoning their interest rate cartel in 1983. They adopted a tougher marketing stance, and began to use their extensive branch networks to offer a wider range of financial services. They introduced cheque accounts and moved into insurance products. Automatic teller machine networks were developed in collaboration with other institutions. The growth in the number of branches slowed to around 3 per cent per annum in the early 1980s as societies looked for cost reductions and more cost-effective forms of competition (Rajan, 1987).

Competition was also intense in the bid to attract deposits because of the introduction of interest-bearing cheque accounts by the banks and privatisation issues. Societies developed premium interest accounts for depositors, designed to protect their share of deposits; by 1987, 80 per cent of deposits were in higher interest accounts, compared with only 45 per cent in 1984 and 10 per cent in 1974.

By removing some of the restrictions on their activities, the 1986 Building Societies Act allowed them to develop their diversification strategies on a more equal footing. While their primary role was still to be the making of secured loans on residential property, societies could now become involved in unsecured lending, and in activities such as property investment, estate agency, insurance broking, and personal pensions. The period since 1986 has been one of further diversification as societies experiment with the new powers (Macey and Wells, 1987; Ennew and Wright, 1990).

In summary, there has been a trend towards the 'one-stop shopping' idea in financial services, with building societies and banks attempting to meet the whole range of financial services needs of their customers (McGoldrick and Greenland, 1992). The aim is to cross-sell a range of products to customers, rather than simply to provide them with a mortgage or savings account. From a staffing point of view this places much greater emphasis on selling and customer services skills than in the past. Add to this the need for a broader range of technical product knowledge and it is clear that there are likely to be significant implications for human resources.

Given these changes, building societies have sought to adapt their management styles and organisational cultures (Smith, 1986; Macey and Wells, 1987). What was appropriate in a predictable, stable environment was no longer suitable in the more competitive, dynamic environment of the 1980s and 90s (Wynne, 1990) (see Table 8.1). Given the limits to the ability of financial institutions to pursue differentiation in terms of the nature of their products, partly because of the ease with which competitors can match any innovation (Speed,

1990), individual building societies have attempted to differentiate themselves from their competitors by branding and advertising, and by improving the quality of customer service. Thus the quality and performance of staff has increasingly been seen as a key contributor to competitive advantage in the financial services sector (Snape *et al.*, 1993; Wilkinson 1995a).

TABLE 8.1   **The building society movement and the 'new' building societies**

	The building society movement	*The 'new' building societies*
Philosophy	Social good	Commercial
Structure	Centralised and bureaucratic	Decentralised and market-driven
Management style	Paternalistic	Performance oriented
Role of branch manager	Financial GP	Sales person
Role of staff	Compliant 'moneyboxes'	Pro-active
Key actors	Generalists	Specialists
Employment relationship	Secure and caring	In flux, move towards more market-oriented relationship
Career prospects	Good, internal labour market	Uncertain as specialists come in
Pay	Seniority	PRP, appraisal, profit share
Employee involvement	Collective joint consultation and downward communication	Increase in downward communication and upward problem solving

Sources: Macey and Wells (1987), Nellis and Litt (1990), Snape *et al.* (1993)

Smith's (1986) description of the desired change in management style suggests a greater emphasis on business development, on decentralisation, on the management of performance, and on the recruitment and training of specialists. The aim is to retain the loyalty of staff but at the same time to encourage them to go beyond mere compliance to administrative rules by showing greater personal initiative and flexibility. This implies that the centralised, bureaucratic approach of the past is to be replaced by a more market-driven approach, with human resources as a key element in the business strategy. Building society mission and policy statements increasingly reflect this approach (UBS Phillips and Drew, 1991). Emphasis was thus to be placed on the strategic fit between business and human resource strategies, with employee commitment, adaptability to change and improved service quality identified as the goals and HR strategies seen as central to the successful implementation of business strategy, on paper at least consistent with characterisations of HRM (Guest, 1987). Essential to this new direction is the encouragement of employee initiative and commitment. Management in building societies, as elsewhere, have often seen quality initiatives (such as TQM and customer care programmes) as offering a means to achieve such goals.

In this chapter, we examine the development of quality initiatives in a large building society. Our aim is to examine how the changing competitive pressures have affected the management of human resources, and in particular the growth of quality initiatives in the context of the existing employee involvement (EI) schemes.

We see three phases or waves of interest in management's attempts to promote greater involvement with their staff (see Table 8.2). First, the long-standing schemes of representative participation and downward communication dating from the 1970s. Second, a phase of commercialisation whereby management sought both to 'educate' staff about the market and the organisation and provide a performance-based pay system designed to align individual interests with corporate interests. A third phase saw the development of a quality initiative which sought to build on the previous waves by establishing a quality culture so that staff would not only understand the reality of the 'market' but would look to contribute to organisational success through a variety of vehicles under the Partnership programme. It is this third wave that we focus our attention on in this chapter. However, it is important to see this initiative in the context of earlier initiatives, given that the stagnation and perceived failure of the previous initiatives affected the perception of the new initiative. As Watson's use of a wave metaphor suggests we often find '[ideas from the past] existing alongside their would-be successor' and 'every wave both collides with its predecessor and combines with it… the pattern that is left is rarely a neat one and it is never predictable' (1986: 46–7).

BuSoc

In the 1980s, in common with other societies, BuSoc diversified into estate agency, housing trusts and fund management. It now has some 1500 sites, including 900 branch offices, and employs more than 10 000 staff. The mid-1980s had seen disappointing financial results attributed to post-merger rationalisation and re-organisation costs, losses suffered in the estate agency section and provision for bad debt against its residential mortgage book. While the ratio of costs to income soared during the merger, the society sought to reverse this through rationalisation (with 400 redundancies in the branch network during 1988/9), and by the early 1990s, senior management pronounced BuSoc as being 'leaner and fitter'.

As with most financial services organisations, staffing policy has been characterised by a high level of management prerogative and paternalism. A unitarist view has been promoted which encourages an ethos of teamwork, shared interest and a commitment beyond the cash nexus. The internal labour market also encourages loyalty. The small size of branches facilitates informal communication and reduced 'them' and 'us' attitudes. The nature of branch work encourages job rotation with a wide range of tasks and an uneven flow of work. Financial services remain highly centralised bureaucratic organisations, and several volumes of practice and procedure lay out in detail the work activity of the branch.

This period also witnessed changes in management style, due to greater competitive pressure and the fusion of the merged societies' cultures. This reflected a conscious attempt by senior management to become more commercially orientated with the appointment of a number of new executive directors and an infusion of senior management from outside the building society industry, described by one manager as 'real hard-headed business people' rather than the 'soppy paternalists' of the building society tradition.

The new emphasis on sales was expressed through changes in visual identity: a new logo, corporate colours and branch redesign. There was a move towards more sophisticated targeting of branches, previously only done on an *ad hoc* basis for particular products. Structural reorganisation involved greater management specialisation, modernisation and rationalisation. The new structure involved a smaller branch structure and a 'delayering' of the organisation, with the reduction of district managers from 400 to less than 100. Within branches, restructuring was designed to give greater emphasis to sales with the introduction of a new financial advisor position and a clearer division between sales and support roles. There was also a move towards a more open-plan branch design. Some work was also removed from branches, centralising in specialised administrative centres dealing with mortgages. This split what staff had regarded previously as a whole task and meant that they now had to liaise between customers (who were annoyed at their inability to deal directly with staff in the branches) and the centralised unit which experienced long teething problems in establishing systems.

The status of branch managers has probably increased as a result of the new structure (with district sales managers having a less hands-on role than the old district managers who often resided in the same branch). The surplus district managers were counselled into alternative employment or took voluntary redundancy. A newly created post was that of sales consultants who were effectively a direct sales force, working from home.

Given the restructuring of the branch network, fears of redundancy have affected branch managers more than other staff. Furthermore, the pressure was now on managers to deliver. They in turn were expecting more of their staff. Sales targeting was gradually being introduced, based on tills (rather than individuals), with weekly awards of wine and chocolate. In its early stages this was welcomed as bringing interest to the job. As one manager described it, 'It's a good thing, a game, the girls get a bit excited'.

According to one branch manager, it was 'survival of the fittest', staff must perform. 'It was a business, not a service, it was no longer acceptable to chat with an elderly customer for 15 minutes when depositing £25'. According to another, however:

> More and more is being expected of staff at all levels of the society. This is seen by staff as being introduced with very little consideration for the pressure they are already under and no end to these pressures seems to be in sight.

The HR function has traditionally been highly centralised and managed using standard procedures. Thus the Personnel manual has over 200 pages, covering working hours, health and safety, data protection, personnel administration, pay and allowances and training. Industrial relations disputes tend to be immediately referred to the staff association and the personnel department. However, in a move to introduce more HR responsibility into the line, area HR managers have been introduced who in turn, report to the area general managers.

Personnel managers claimed that the function's importance had increased in the late 1980s, although they admitted it was long way from a full strategic role. There appeared to be some frustration that while the personnel people were trying to introduce a strategic perspective this had not yet penetrated the highest levels. Thus, while Personnel was a good professional HR department with all the tools, it tended not to have the influence it sought. Line managers tended to take decisions and sort out problems later. According to the chief executive 'tough times need tough management' and the right to manage had been exerted more frequently of late. According to the union, past experience had led to Personnel recognising the futility of attempting to point out the error of their ways and embarking on a policy of not upsetting top management. This meant that in practice the department adopted very much a 'facilitator' role, (Wilkinson and Marchington, 1994), not questioning the aims of management, nor the means designed to achieve them, but merely responded to top management needs as perceived by top management, and implemented the top management line.

There were significant IR and HR issues arising from the merger, consequent on a belief that the new organisation was 'over managed'. As part of the merger agreement, however, a 'no redundancy' promise had been made and this was invoked by the union, although rejected by the management, on the grounds that the redundancy of a district manager related not to the merger but to changing competitive conditions. Branch rationalisation (around 100 branches closing) also resulted in a protracted process of managerial exit (early retirement, voluntary redundancy, counselling into alternative jobs, redeployment and so on). While few non-managerial staff departed, this was a severe cultural shock for the organisation and caused particular problems, given that it was managers who were responsible for facilitating change that were most affected.

Commercialising staff: employee involvement (EI) and quality initiatives

The first phase: information and consultation

Over the years BuSoc have introduced a number of initiatives designed to educate staff and gain their commitment. These include a joint consultation and negotiating council (JCNC) and a number of downward communication schemes, including a staff newspaper. The paper appears monthly and is a combination of news, features and competitions. It is seen as having an 'important role in linking everyone together'. It was particularly important during the process merger with 'special editions' every few months providing details of progress, and containing a question and answer section. Most issues present a mix of features on departments/regions/branches, news section on births, marriages and retirements, a variety of events, quizzes, competitions sports and special events. There are different versions of the paper for different sections/divisions to make them more localised and relevant. Their main function is to 'educate' staff and increase commercial awareness.

TABLE 8.2   Involving employees: the three phases of initiatives

	Form	Objective
Phase I 1970s	JCNC Newspaper	Information, education and consultation
Phase II mid-1980s	Briefing Employee report Financial EI	Commercialisation
Phase III late 1980s	Quality initiatives	Staff input, creation of a quality culture

Collective representation developed in the 1970s in the form of an internal staff association, reflecting the fact that building societies lack the strongly pluralist tradition (which has been seen as a barrier to HRM in other sectors) (Guest, 1989). The JCNC is the main formal, collective participation structure and operates on a centralised basis, although there were plans to introduce local

consultative procedures with one per 200 branches and at each of the administrative centres. The JCNC consists of five members nominated by the chief
executive, one of whom acts as chairman to the committee together with five
members nominated by the staff association elected from within the membership. BuSoc provides a permanent secretary to the committee meetings, which
are quarterly, and joint statements are issued after each. In recent years,
managers have taken a harder line – 'Yes, a bit of negotiation, a bit of consultation, but then the game's over – That's it!'. From our questionnaire analysis it
appeared staff had very little knowledge of the body, although they rejected the
notion that it dealt with items of a trivial nature, and asserted that it was vital
that their representative was involved.

The second phase: commercialisation

The merger process had placed a great deal of emphasis on communication, but
uncertainty was the central message. For example, while staff reductions had
been mooted, precise details were unavailable for several months as discussions
continued with the staff associations. The result was, in the words of the head of
Personnel, 'staff were all screwed up'.

Team briefing

Briefing was introduced in the mid-1980s and carried out in weekly sessions,
following Industrial Society principles. The aim was simply to inform and
educate staff concerning developments in the market and within the organisation. After the initial high-profile launch, however, briefing stagnated as it
became a lower priority for branch managers in the context of increasing
branch pressure; nor was it ever monitored by head office. It operated in full for
about 18 months, and although it has not officially been abandoned it has
simply stopped happening on a regular basis. Training sessions do, however,
contain elements of the briefing process but this varies in each branch. At one
branch it was described as a 'blast from the past' and few remembered much
about it. At another, elements seemed to have been incorporated into training
sessions, although briefing as an entity had simply been forgotten.

Annual employee report

Part of the process of educating staff included a new four-page report with an
address by the chief executive and financial results presented in various forms.
While generally welcomed, a report at the time of the research caused some
controversy, pointing out the good performance of the building society with
improved profits. Staff failed to see how their profit share fell in this period. The
fact is that the profit share is a group scheme and outside the retail area the

society fared poorly. Clearly, there was a lack of integration concerning the contents of employee communications.

Paying for performance

A new remuneration package, 'Profit through Performance', was introduced as part of the commercialisation process. The aim was 'to help staff realise the importance of their performance to the success of the Society and become fully committed to their role within their team and within the Society as a whole'. There were to be four elements in this package: *profit share*, linking payments to the achievement of profit targets; *individual merit pay*, which replaced the existing system of general awards and merit increments; and *team* and *individual bonuses*, one-off payments drawn from a bonus pool funded from profits.

Management say they are disappointed with the impact of the package. They are considering giving notice to end the profit share scheme, which is too expensive and which they admit to rushing into following publication of the 1988 Finance Act. The connection between performance and pay is also undermined by the absence of a bar to profit sharing by those who receive poor appraisals. Team bonuses were never implemented, not least because the design was never resolved. Individual bonuses were to be paid where either an individual had received the top of the pay scale, and thus would not receive merit pay, or for exceptional work above and beyond the call of duty. The process was quite tightly controlled; nominations came from the area manager, and were vetted by the personnel department. At the time of our research only 50 staff (out of 11 000) have received rewards, ranging from £250 to £1000. While merit pay initially appeared to be welcomed by staff, in practice resources were lacking to provide real incentives.

The third phase – creating a quality culture

Quality initiatives and organisation change

The QM initiative was concerned essentially with customer care by creating a quality culture. The programme seemed impressive on paper, especially in its espoused connection with corporate strategy and other EI initiatives. According to the official view:

> Communication is vital and we use team briefing for a constant dialogue with staff throughout the Society. In addition, I and other senior managers spend a great deal of time on branch and departmental visits and training courses to ensure that we communicate as directly as possible with staff, and indeed hear back from them. Secondly, we encourage staff to participate in the process of improving service we

give through our Partnership Programme. This operates in all branches and departments. It is designed to encourage staff to think hard about our relationship with our customers and with each other. The result is a constant process of improvement in the way we operate emerging from our staff as a whole.

Hence this official view envisaged an integrated EI policy with quality as the latest manifestation to be incorporated under the broad EI umbrella. In practice, however, it was less impressive and its achievements superficial (Wilkinson *et al.*, 1992).

It was designed to be 'a long-term, sustained campaign to secure more customers by instituting measurable standards of improved service'. The programme had two phases. The first was described as a 'religious phase', the communication of the company's values through mission statements cascaded through the organisation. The second phase was concerned more with practical implementation – the design and application of principles and practice. The central component of the programme was the establishment of a service culture and standards in the areas of environment (that is, the branch setting), 'the area we serve our customers in', hospitality – 'the way we serve our customers', product knowledge – 'the information we give our customers', and telephone service – 'being courteous to callers'. The programme sought to encourage staff to think about quality issues relating to their day-to-day work and be 'empowered' rather than to train them in a standardised approach to service. Staff were invited to attend, after hours, travelling roadshows that explained the concepts behind the programme. If earlier initiatives had been designed to educate and commercialise staff, this programme was designed to tap into that awareness and get employees to change the way they did their work and focus on continuous improvement, not just 'doing the job'.

The programme was set up and run by the customer service group, part of the business development unit, and a facilitator was appointed in each branch. It is important to note that this was not controlled by the branch managers, nor was it monitored by them – a very different approach from that taken by many other organisations which have stressed the importance of the line manager. Three main mechanisms were set up to pursue TQM goals: first, setting standards (see Table 8.3) via action plans for both departments and individuals; second, external customer evaluation via a series of customer questionnaires and the establishment of customer service groups (customer circles); and third, internal customer evaluation, again by questionnaires and quality circles. Unlike the earlier EI initiatives this demanded the active involvement of staff and seemed to be the most serious of all the initiatives.

In the early days staff were strongly supportive of the programme, although branch managers were suspicious, inasmuch as it undermined control. There was an elected staff member in each branch who met regularly with representatives from other branches; comments from the meetings were conveyed to the area general manager. Staff enthusiasm, however, seemed to decline after a

TABLE 8.3   **National minimum service standards – branch achievements**

Key Service Area	Standard
Personal service	Greeting/offer of help/assistance Polite and helpful service Conclusion/closing remarks Professional appearance/dress Apology for delay when queue forms Mention BuSoc Answer within 5 rings
Window display	Neat and tidy Absence of rubbish
Inside branch appearance	Clear floors and tables (Absence of waste paper) Neat and tidy counter area Name at counter position or on person
Partnership board	In good order Photographs Signed certificate 'We Value Your Opinion' leaflets displayed
Point of sale material	Poster frame complete with interest rates Leaflets displayed in dispensers and available Handbooks displayed in dispensers and available

few months as staff were unable to meet specified targets (which were self-monitored) and the awards were perceived as going to small branches which did not suffer from the pressures of large city-based ones. In fact, the award scheme created considerable antagonism between competing branches such that, on one occasion, a winning branch asked to be withdrawn from the award because of this ill feeling. The perceived arbitrary nature of awards also extended to individual awards and created irritation within branches. Staff were also upset at organisational changes which removed certain back office functions concerned with mortgage administration; they saw these as contradicting the notion of a quality service because their relationship with the customer for the provision of mortgages was lost. Many staff felt it was more of a public relations exercise, with little in the way of benefits to staff (or indeed customers), rather than anything to do with extending employee involvement, or increasing customer satisfaction.

This staff assessment was shared to a large extent by the managers, who at best regarded the initiative as an irritant and little more than a 'smile campaign'.

Moreover, they pointed to current surveys showing 90 per cent acceptability ratings of staff by customers. Customer circles had brought to light only a handful of issues, for example product knowledge, which could be tackled at the local level. The overwhelming majority of issues related to head office administrative departments, which the programme never really addressed. Internal customer surveys never got off the ground and, even if they had done, it seemed unlikely that there were the resources or managerial will to solve these problems. The scheme had not been designed to tackle serious political issues which such an objective would necessitate. To a large extent it became seen as a 'fad', led and championed by head office careerists who wanted to make their mark and then move on, and who were perceived as less interested in improving customer satisfaction than making a high profile 'splash'. This feeling could be seen as part of a broader disillusionment with head office who were regarded by both branch managers and staff as out of touch with the 'real world' of branch life. The high-profile launch and subsequent demise of earlier initiatives, such as briefing and paying for performance schemes, produced an air of tired cynicism; staff felt that once again they were going to have to jump through the hoops for the latest corporate game.

Branch managers tended to go through the motions, doing enough to satisfy the reviews undertaken by the customer service group, (see Table 8.4). Furthermore, it is significant that the regular audits of branch operations did not include explicit reference to quality issues or to the TQM programme itself. In other words, the control mechanisms did not afford a high priority to quality issues. The tone of the programme also conveyed superficiality – the staff magazine which gave a high profile to Partnership included poems such as 'Ode to Securities' and award winning ideas such as winning branches displaying letters of thanks to customers. The gimmicky nature of the awards did not help either. Branch awards were badges and a plaque for the branch, with vouchers for meals out and so on. Individual service awards were T-shirts, desk-sets, mugs and so on. The pinnacle was the Platinum Award, a hotel weekend event involving 150 staff from the top 12 branches at which each branch presented a four-minute video on a day in the life of the branch that was judged, in Eurovision style, by the contestants. A rather more useful idea to come out of the programme was to hold weekly planning meetings in branches to report on the workload and to allocate resources. This was to give staff an insight into branch operations and a greater say in the running of operations.

At the time of our research the programme had effectively died away, although there was speculation that it would be 'reheated' as a new dish. Certainly, within the branches the view was that TQM had finished and there was little evidence of enduring effects although the customer service group claimed it had successfully raised commercial awareness.

TABLE 8.4   Quality of service research – individual branch report

ADDRESS

OVERALL POSITION IN REGION:

AWARD RECEIVED:

OVERALL PERFORMANCE	SCORE	NATIONAL STANDARD ACHIEVEMENT
BEST IN REGION AVERAGE IN REGION AVERAGE IN AREA		STANDARDS ACHIEVED PERSONAL SERVICE WINDOW DISPLAY BRANCH APPEARANCE PARTNERSHIP BOARD POS MATERIAL
(MAXIMUM POSSIBLE	2500)	
		% ACHIEVING STANDARD IN REGION
		% ACHIEVING STANDARD IN AREA
		% OF MAXIMUM ACHIEVABLE

	Branch	Best in Region	Region Average	Area Average	National Average
Customer Satisfaction Customer feedback					
Branch Appearance Customer feedback Personal visitor					
Service performance Customer feedback Car loan Travel services					
Product knowledge Car loan Travel services					
Business performance Travel services					

Quality management – fad or fixture?

Since the mid-1980s there has been more experimentation by employers with employee involvement and workplace quality techniques than with any other area of HRM (Kochan and Dyer, 1993). Research on financial services suggests they have been no exception to this general trend, with considerable innovation occurring in this area (Snape *et al.*, 1993; Wilkinson, 1995a; Wilkinson *et al.*, 1997b). In our case study society, quality initiatives were developed in the late 1980s, ostensibly reflecting a growing recognition of the importance of the effective management of people as a source of competitive advantage (Watkins and Bryce, 1992). The visibility of employees to the customer and the nature of building societies as service organisations were also seen as significant. The need to search for new sources of competitive advantage is in turn a reflection of an increasingly competitive market.

The initiatives were seen, however, as being largely introduced as a form of impression management, with little strategic integration and proving largely ineffective. Many critics of developments in HRM and TQM have indeed emphasised the faddist and flavour-of-the-month nature of many of the innovations (Wilkinson *et al.*, 1992; Huczynski, 1993a, b; Marchington *et al.*, 1993a; Ramsay, 1996). Critics note the limited contribution of TQM to the success of organisations despite the many claims of its proponents. Indeed, as Hucyznski notes, customer perceptions rather than benefits may be the main aim – 'the success of the technique is irrelevant. Instead the company considers how a customer might view it if it is not seen using a technique. Thus a company may introduce a quality circle to signal to its customers that it is concerned with quality' (1993: 281).

While the launch of high-profile programmes is relatively easy to achieve (Storey, 1993), what is less clear, however, is the extent to which such initiatives can be sustained, developed and embedded into the day-to-day management style of BuSoc. In our case study this does seem not to have been achieved due to incoherence amongst the initiatives themselves. This in turn largely derives from a lack of strategic planning and an *ad hoc* approach to implementation. Although in this case study the quality initiatives were driven from the centre by the Business Development Unit, there was there no overall strategy.

Managerial relations are often seen as a key factor in explaining the failure of new initiatives (Marchington *et al.*, 1993a). At BuSoc, not only were branch managers unsupportive but at head office, the personnel department did not have much regard for the programme. It was described by the head of personnel as 'folksy and non-strategic', in that there was little evaluation in terms of the programme's contribution to more or better business. Furthermore, there was little attention paid to staff attitudes and there was no use of opinion surveys which the personnel specialists felt was an important omission, given the increasing pressure that was being felt at the branches as the organisation strove to keep costs under control.

From a staff perspective it seemed to be the latest initiative which would gradually fade away without any real explanation as the others did (briefing abandoned, performance pay under review, and so on). The different messages disseminated by the quality initiative and other organisation changes, such as restructuring, led to a situation where there was considerable 'indigestion' for those on the receiving end, and the management 'messages', rather than educating and informing, often generated uncertainty and even confusion amongst staff. Furthermore, the nature of building societies as highly bureaucratic, dominated by lengthy rules and procedures and with a conservative culture, meant that concepts such as 'employee empowerment' were limited by the organisational context.

One of the reasons staff reception was lukewarm was their rather jaundiced view of head office and any initiatives arising from there. Thus, their perception of the partnership programme was very much coloured by their previous experiences with other initiatives including EI schemes. Consequently, whatever the positive points of the initiative it was regarded as part of managers 'magic carpet' ride to a bigger and better job (Ahlstrand 1990: 229), part of the rite of 'impression management' (Barlow, 1989), whereby managers attempt to impress their superiors with their activities. This is often seen as the 'panacea conspiracy' practised by individuals who 'don't have the time, interest or awareness needed to learn their new craft, but they are anxious to produce immediately. What they are looking for, although they may profess to know better, are quick-fix solutions to dynamic complex problems' (J.C. Mayer, quoted in Huczynski, 1993a: 282). The context within which 'impression management' can thrive is also important; the political and economic climate over the last decade have provided employers with more room for manoeuvre and management is undoubtedly in the saddle. Also significant within the business arena has been the much talked about, and indeed talked up, ideas such as involvement and empowerment; this has meant that managers' ideas for introducing such initiatives were likely to fit in with senior management perceptions of what the competition is doing. Importantly, from the point of view of the champion, little technical knowledge is required and the champion is not dependent on putting together coalitions of managers to introduce its scheme, as might be the case, say, with an IT innovation. Initiatives such as TQM 'are relatively cheap to design, theoretically straightforward to introduce and the champion's effort can soon be rewarded in terms of its visibility (though probably not its impact)' (Marchington *et al.*, 1993a: 571). Furthermore, as Huczynski notes, 'the promotion of the latest management fad by managers has been used to help them gain company-wide visibility in the promotion stakes' (1993a: 213). Such an analysis suggests that though the initiative may have had little lasting impact on the organisation it may well have been successful in terms of the individuals who introduced it, insofar as it raises their profile. It would also imply that TQM is unlikely to be on the agenda for long as other managers are likely to introduce their own scheme, such as business process re-engineering, as a way of propelling them further up the hierarchy.

Though a great deal has been claimed by senior building society managers (for example, Murphy, 1988) and the management consultants involved (for example, Wynne, 1990) about the improvements that derive from the introduction of more participatory ways of managing, and despite the widespread appeal of these ideas to many practitioners, there are some doubts about whether there is any simple association between schemes of involvement such as TQM and commitment. TQM operates according to values that are essentially unitarist and individualistic in focus (Wilkinson *et al.*, 1991). Guest (1992a: 10) suggests that proponents of HRM assume that involving employees will lead to greater organisational commitment which in turn will lead to enhanced motivation and performance . On the basis of research from both the UK and the USA, however, he is dubious about the link between involvement and commitment, partly again because of the difficulties in measuring what is meant by commitment, and in assessing whether it is commitment to one's job, to work or to the organisation. Other studies (for example, Marchington, 1982: 66) also suggest that commitment is rarely given at anything more than the calculative level. Moreover, in our case, branches were under pressure to deliver in terms of sales, and it was clear that staff were under increasing strain. Staff did not seem taken in by 'propaganda and trinkets' (Hill, 1992). They seemed to have a high degree of customer awareness but saw themselves frustrated in their ability to 'deliver the goods' and there was a general feeling that head office did not understand this. Earlier initiatives such as profit sharing, while welcomed by staff, did not seem to be understood in terms of its formulae, and staff failed to see performance and reward links clearly. Furthermore, organisational change, such as the transformation of business into sales outlets, has fragmented work and the increased specialisation did not seem to have been welcomed by staff. With merger and redundancy, this has been a difficult context of change. With work pressure having increased and a projected fall in staff numbers, morale was understandably low. After some early enthusiasm, staff began to feel that the TQM initiative was seen as 'just for show'. The ability of staff to spend much time on the customer care initiative was heavily constrained. Branch managers themselves were indeed surprised that staff remained so keen. Perhaps the real question is why staff after their earlier experiences did, initially at least, appear receptive. Despite their past experiences it might be that when the programme was unveiled they were inclined to give management the benefit of the doubt, judging the initiative on face value as having some potential benefits. Once the programme had run up against its own limitations and it was apparent that it was ill thought out, and insufficiently resourced, then they lost faith and saw it as yet another false dawn, falling into the same pattern of failure as the other initiatives.

In the long term, as branch managers become more targeted and pressurised, they are less likely to develop a long-term view towards staff, and there is evidence of the erosion of the cosy paternalism. On our evidence we would suggest that quality initiatives had done little to improve relationships. Only 8 per cent of staff surveyed at BuSoc felt it was a 'good company to work for', although no-one felt that relations between management and the workforce were uncooperative. However, the latter relates more to staff relations within the branches rather than within the society as a whole. Indeed, 58 per cent of respondents felt that the various initiatives over the last five years had worsened things rather than improved them. The tendency for our sample to feel excluded from 'management' as they were more closely monitored and controlled is consistent with the results of Scase and Goffee (1989). They argue that middle managers have become less committed to their work in recent years, as career prospects have become more uncertain and managerial prerogatives have been questioned. Whilst Dobson and Stewart (1990) question the extent to which the more pessimistic views on the future of middle management are applicable to all managers and organisations, it is clear that it fits in this particular case. Branch managers felt that the pressures of new product management limited their autonomy by increasing the emphasis on staff training and administration and limiting the scope for business development work outside the office. There were also concerns in relation to career blockage and job insecurity. Managers felt increasingly isolated from the general head office management and hence were uncomfortable agents of change (see also Redman *et al.*, 1997).

Conclusion

Whilst the intensification of competition presents building societies with an incentive to develop quality initiatives, the uncertainty of the new environment means that the implementation of quality management is fraught with difficulty. Attempts by building societies to come to terms with a more competitive environment by adopting a more 'commercial' focus, with tighter control of performance and costs, can have a damaging effect on staff morale. This, in turn, may hinder attempts to build staff commitment through the vehicle of TQM. There is a danger, apparent in much of the prescriptive literature on TQM (as with HRM), of focusing almost exclusively on the initiatives of management and thereby seeing employees as essentially passive beings, whose attitudes are there to be moulded by management strategy in the pursuit of competitive advantage. The feasibility of a top-down approach to management has been challenged by many writers. This case illustrates that employees too may respond to changes in the competitive environment and the effective implementation of quality initiatives is more than simply a matter of management will. The paradox is that the competitive conditions which have produced a perceived need for TQM have also created conditions in which it is difficult to thrive or even survive.

CHAPTER 9

Re-imaging Customer Service: the Management of Quality in Food Retailing

Introduction

The management of quality is a key issue in UK food retailing, especially amongst three of the leading companies (J Sainsbury, Tesco and Safeway) at the so-called 'quality' end of the market. They compete with one another across a broad range, each striving for superior product quality, excellent customer service, and reasonable prices for the whole shopping basket. These goals are pursued through a mixture of mechanisms, such as tight controls on suppliers (both for quality standards and low prices), major investments in new technology (relating to food hygiene, stock and inventory control), and close attention to the management of staff (through management development programmes and a range of human resource policies). The emphasis is on creating a culture and environment in which front-line staff are motivated to want to deliver excellent customer service.

This is a far from easy task for managements in these companies, however, as they are confronted by a number of potential contradictions. Whilst, on the one hand, there are pressures to treat customers as individuals who find shopping a pleasant experience, there are also expectations that staff will conform to specification and follow routine instructions about how to interact with customers. Similarly, the front-line staff who represent the major point of contact with customers are amongst the lowest paid and most recently recruited employees in the industry (Tansik, 1990), often with little interest in or anticipation of long-term employment, and no reason to demonstrate high

142

levels of commitment to their company. Moreover, there are also aspects of the control systems used to monitor employees which are in stark contrast to the eulogies about the empowerment and autonomy that some of the TQM gurus assert is necessary for excellent customer service. For example, EPOS (electronic point of sales) technology and customer reports offer the opportunity for constant surveillance of employees. Significantly, the pressures to improve product quality and customer service – at the same time as reducing prices – have multiplied in recent years following the entry of some powerful European cost-cutters into the market.

Quality management in the industry takes a number of different forms. There are strict controls over suppliers, stringent regulations on health and safety, and the comprehensive use of technology to monitor sales and deliveries, as well as customer service. The use of 'full-blown' TQM, exemplified by the types of activities common in manufacturing, are unusual in retailing (Porter and Smith, 1993), although a strong customer-orientated priority is clearly evident in these organisations. For example, Porter and Smith (1993: 16) found that the six most important process improvement areas identified by senior managers related to customers, in particular their satisfaction and retention. Mintel (1995: 6) also noted this, suggesting that 'service and promoting customer loyalty will be the key issues in retail marketing for grocers in the short to medium term... Providing an enhanced level of service throughout all aspects of the store's operation and product offer will play a critical part in contributing to high levels of loyalty among core shoppers, as well as providing the grounds on which to attract new customers.' This was illustrated clearly with the introduction by Tesco and J Sainsbury of discount cards for regular shoppers, and the ensuing debate about how best to reinforce customer loyalty.

In a sense, all aspects of activity are geared up to enhancing the delivery of excellent customer service, so rather than attempt to analyse the complete range of quality initiatives, this case focuses explicitly on customer service and the means which the leading food retailers use to achieve this. It describes organisation structures and cultures, including mission statements, employee relations, and the ways in which managers are selected and developed. It examines the range of human resource policies designed to recruit and retain good staff, including selection criteria, induction programmes, communication and involvement. It also outlines the approaches used to train employees in customer care, as well as customer reports, 'mystery shoppers', and other surveillance and disciplinary techniques that are employed in the pursuit of excellent customer service. The case is a synthetic one, combining features of the leading companies in the market, and it is titled Superco for the purposes of this chapter. Before going on to outline the case, however, some background information is provided on the food retailing sector.

The changing context of food retailing

Food retailing is now one of the major industries in Britain and its market leaders rank amongst the largest in the country, both in financial and employment terms. The leading firms (J Sainsbury, Tesco and Argyll) are all placed firmly within the top 50 British companies in terms of market capitalisation. Much of their success has been built upon rapid advances in information technology, food hygiene, marketing, physical distribution and, of course, customer service. Some of the biggest employers in Britain now come from this sector as well, ranking alongside manufacturing companies such as Unilever and Cable and Wireless, albeit inflated by the large number of part-time staff who are employed at these companies.

It is an extremely competitive sector of the British economy, comprising not just the well-known leading superstores but also a mass of small (often family-owned) shops across the country. The market share held by the latter has been declining for many years, and the large multiples now account for about 80 per cent of all grocery sales in Britain (Mintel, 1995: 89). Indeed, during the early 1990s, the top four (J Sainsbury, Tesco, Asda and Safeway) held almost half of the market between them, a share which had grown dramatically over the previous decade (Clarke-Hill and Robinson, 1994). The market leaders all experienced substantial growth and healthy profits during the 1980s and early 1990s, in contrast to most other parts of British industry and indeed many other parts of retailing.

The last two decades have also seen an enormous growth in the number and size of stores, such that many of the newer stores occupy more than 25 000 square feet and employ more than a hundred staff, features which were unusual 20 years ago. A high proportion of the staff employed work part-time, the number of temporary staff increases dramatically at certain times of the year, and the workforce as a whole is relatively young (certainly compared with a well-established manufacturing or high technology company). As an example, Freathy and Sparks (1994: 509) compare the age structures of J Sainsbury and IBM (UK), finding that nearly half of the retailer's staff are under 30, and a quarter under 21. By contrast, about a quarter of IBM's employees are under 30 with hardly any under 21. A majority of the staff employed are women, the vast proportion of whom are on the lower grades, and the ratio of men to women increases the further one goes up the hierarchy – in common with most industries. The opening hours of these food retailers has increased substantially to the point where 75 or 80 hours per week (including 6 hours on Sundays) is now relatively common, and there has even been experimentation with 24-hour opening in some areas. Most of the leading companies also employ staff in the evening or at night (shelf-filling, warehousing, cleaning), and some occupations (for example, bakers) start work several hours before the shops are open to customers. The leading food retailers are now large employment units in their own right, employing more people than many factories and operating for more hours as well.

Wrigley (1994: 5–6) argues that during the late 1980s and early 90s the major food retailers found themselves on a treadmill of new store development programmes which had become the all-consuming engine of corporate growth. The mid-1990s has brought new pressures to bear in the industry, stimulated by the entry into Britain of large European-owned companies such as Aldi and Netto, who compete on the basis of low prices and few frills (Duke, 1994). There has been a knock-on effect, via the reintroduction of 'price wars' (last visited in the 1970s) to follow the 'store wars' of the 1980s (Wrigley, 1994). By the mid-1990s, however, it still seems that the challenge has had little impact on the shopping habits of people using the leading 'quality' food retailers, especially amongst the higher income groups (Schmidt *et al.*, 1994: 14–15). Indeed, Aldi and Netto have targeted the recession-hit and value-conscious industrial areas of the north-west and north of England, traditionally the heartland of Asda and Kwik Save.

The rate of increase in out-of-town new store development has slowed during the 1990s, and there has been a renewed interest in high street shops amongst the multiples, as well as an increasing tendency to shift capital abroad (see, for example, J Sainsbury's foray into the USA and Tesco's into mainland Europe). But the long promised 'saturation' of the UK food retailing market has not yet arrived, despite dire warnings since the 1980s. There is evidence of local saturation (Guy, 1994: 3), but the leading companies all recognise that there are still parts of the country without a large superstore in the vicinity. Duke (1994: 37–8) indicates why this may be the case; based on a survey of 847 women, three of the most important factors influencing store choice were convenience, closeness, and car parking facilities; quality and customer service typically figured much less highly in these assessments. Moreover, the most profitable stores are those that have opened recently (Wrigley, 1994: 6).

The management of quality in a large food retailer is therefore beset with tensions and contradictions. On the one hand, the overall market is relatively inelastic given our need for food, and the retailers at the top end of the market are able to retain the loyalty of middle-class families which have fared relatively well over the last decade. On the other hand, especially in urban areas for people with their own cars, there is a fair degree of choice in where to shop, and it is reckoned that customer service and store ambience plays a major part in such decisions. To keep down prices for customers, however, tight controls are maintained over raw materials from suppliers and the amount of money spent on staff wages. Of course, this highlights one of the dilemmas which confronts personnel managers in the stores, relating to the quantity and type of staff to be employed at any one time. There needs to be sufficient to deal with customers at the checkouts and around the store, but not too many to exceed the salaries budget for the week. In this context, recruiting, motivating and retaining the 'right' staff is deemed essential if market share and profitability are to be maintained through, *inter alia*, the provision of excellent customer service. The management of human resources therefore assumes a major importance for the food retailers which aim to compete at the top end of the market; in a sense, quality and HRM are inseparable. Unfortunately, much of the published material offers little critical analysis of human resource policies and practices, because most is written by academics whose specialist area of expertise is not in HRM (Sparks, 1987, 1992a; Freathy and Sparks, 1994) and who consequently address different problems and issues (Marchington, 1996).

Superco: good service at competitive prices

Organisation structure and culture

The company employs 75 000 staff across Britain, both at the headquarters in the south-east and in its 250 stores which are located around the country. Superco now has a national coverage, having expanded from its southern base, although there are still parts of the country where stores are less likely to be found. It is organised into regions and districts, with each district containing approximately 15 stores. The company also has a number of warehouses, each of which is located in a strategic position to ensure maximum speed of response for deliveries to individual stores. The vast bulk of products are held at these large warehouses, and deliveries are made to each store several times each day. It is company policy not to carry much in the way of stock, even of items with a longer shelf life.

The human resource function operates at four separate levels within the company (headquarters, region, district and store), and it is headed up by a main board director. This is seen to be important in ensuring the utility of the function to contribute specialist knowledge and expertise in the personnel area, but also to be aware of the links between business strategy and human resource management. Beneath the main board director are a number of other human resource directors, each of whom has responsibility for a particular part of the business. The members of this head office team are the architects behind the development of human resource policies which apply across the business as a whole; they also play a leading role in shaping the structure and culture of the company.

Superco has a recognition agreement with USDAW (the Union of Shop, Distributive and Allied Workers) solely for individual grievance and disciplinary cases or joint consultation. There is no provision for joint negotiations about pay and conditions. The agreement allows representation by the union if there is a 'substantial' membership at the store involved – although no figure is quoted for this. Once it is agreed that the union should have these rights at a store, members are allowed to nominate a shop steward from within the branch to represent them should the need arise. It is often difficult to find a willing recruit for the position of shop steward, and representing up to a hundred members is no easy task. Union membership across the company as a whole is less than 10 per cent of all staff, and union consciousness is low. A consultative committee structure also operates across the company at regional level, and to some extent fills some of the gaps left open by the lack of union traditions in the stores. These committees take an overview of issues that arise in the stores, and this enables management to detect if common problems are emerging. Staff are represented on these committees by full-time union officials and shop stewards, whilst management is represented by store, district and regional line managers plus representatives of the personnel function from region and head office.

Precise numbers in the management team at branch level are determined according to the size of the store, and whether or not it includes facilities such as a petrol station, cafe, and in-house bakery. Typically, however, each store is controlled by a branch manager, three deputy branch managers who oversee a particular aspect of store activity (for example, dry goods, fresh foods, customer services), and a personnel manager who works closely with the branch manager. It is at this level that the contribution of Personnel is most visible, since much of the activity tends to be of a tactical and fire-fighting nature – recruiting new staff, running induction programmes, dealing with absence and disciplinary problems, checking and updating staff records, ensuring the speedy dissemination of company information, and generally getting involved in the day-to-day activities of the store. Also, a number of departmental managers are responsible for areas such as the warehouse, bakery, and delicatessen.

Superco's mission statement demonstrates its commitment to market leadership through the provision of high-quality customer service, the importance of talented and motivated staff, working in partnerships with suppliers, participation in the local community, and of course support for the industry and rewards to shareholders. A copy of the mission statement is given to each new employee during the induction programme, and extra copies are available should anyone need one. The importance of this mission statement is made clear to staff by a statement from the chief executive in the booklet which introduces the company to them. In relation to employees, the ethos is one of 'resourceful humans', that is developing and involving staff to ensure that they possess the skills and abilities needed to achieve competitive advantage. Reference is made to training opportunities (both on and off the job), to welfare of staff, to their participation and involvement in teams, and to rewards and benefits at work. In brief, it states:

> We value our people. We will create an atmosphere in which our people can develop their talents and contribute as part of an energetic and enthusiastic team. We will invest in recruitment and training. We will reward them for achievement through the resourceful application of knowledge and skills.

The human resource team played a leading role in the introduction of TQM at board level and its dissemination within the entire organisation, and its message is central to this initiative. The aim is to create a climate where continuous improvement becomes 'the way we do things around here, not a programme with clearly identifiable end-objectives.' This new 'company direction' started at board level, then involved a cross-functional and cross-hierarchical section of staff (regional director and cleaner, for example) across the company, with the process facilitated by external consultants and the personnel directorate. Human resource values and ideas permeate all these documents, with reference to support for the role of local managers, employee motivation, and the importance of management processes not just outputs. At the same time, all activities have to be judged on how well they contribute to the preservation of high-quality customer service. Unlike some of the programmes which have focused solely on quality assurance and the achievement of BS5750/ISO9000, this is meant to be an overarching and ongoing process of cultural change which, over time, should become deeply embedded in the fabric of the organisation.

Management recruitment and development

Given the continuing growth in the size of Superco over the last decade, the recruitment and development of managers has been a key activity in the company, and considerable efforts have been made to ensure a steady supply of high-quality applicants who are motivated to achieve high levels of customer service. New managers are selected on the basis of specific competencies such as attitudes to customers, attention to detail, ability to cope with stress, and problem-solving abilities. Once appointed, each new recruit is allocated a mentor (typically a senior branch manager), and proceeds through a range of activities and courses, most of which relate to customer service. Regular appraisals and reports are used to assess each individual's progress during this period.

Managers are selected by one of two routes; first, the company has been increasing its stock of graduates from all disciplines, although the recent development of courses in retailing and allied subjects has led to a greater supply of applicants with special interests in the area. Irrespective of their background, however, all new graduates embark upon a development programme which combines a mix of standard and dedicated placements; for example, someone who was keen to join the personnel function would receive the standard broad grounding in the business as a whole plus more detailed exposure to the work of the personnel function. The period spent as a graduate trainee varies depending upon the progress of the individual, but typically this would last for 12 to 18 months. The second route into a management job is through Superco's internal promotion channels, whereby the company aims to develop (both on and off the job) individuals who express interest in career progression and are shown to have the capabilities in tests. The advantage of this route into management is that it reinforces the belief amongst staff that there is an open promotions policy, as well as tapping into a pool of highly competent labour which is already familiar with the company's commitment to excellent customer service. Through both routes, Superco is especially keen to provide opportunities for women who wish to advance.

At a higher level, the senior management development programme (SMDP) is designed to improve teamworking, ensure the cross-fertilisation of good ideas, enhance communications, and enable senior managers to perform to the full potential. These programmes consist of a series of modules over a one-year period interspersed with individual and group projects back at the workplace, and the principal subjects that are tackled include customer service, total quality management, managing change, and strategic planning. The SMDP is facilitated by the human resource team and delivered by external consultants as well as academics from leading management schools. The objective of the programme is simple: to ensure the preservation of high quality customer service by continuously improving the performance of all managers and staff.

Human resource policies

The importance of customer service is apparent at all stages of the employment process, starting with recruitment and finishing (in some cases) with disciplinary action and dismissal for failure to perform to a satisfactory level. The management of customer service, however, has a series of faces, which illustrate different meanings of the term. At its most obvious level, it can appear positive and benign, through opportunities for staff to develop further their careers and take pleasure in providing high quality service to customers. At a deeper level, it has a less employee-orientated face, evident in attempts to link explicitly the likelihood of continued employment security with customer satisfaction. Yet deeper, control by customers is less readily apparent through forms of surveillance and what is seen as the 'normal' enforcement of management prerogative. The impact of these on customer service is now examined.

Applicants for shop-floor jobs are evaluated in relation to their ability to provide excellent customer service under seven headings: physical make-up, including speech and appearance; attainments, for example technical knowledge; general intelligence and level of reasoning; special aptitudes, such as verbal expression and customer service; interests which are relevant to job success and evidence of team working; disposition, including ability to work under pressure and deal with customers; and domestic circumstances. A number of these are tested via situational questions, designed to assess how well applicants are able to cope with typical customer interactions and difficult service relationships. The importance of selecting the right kind of staff is crucial, given the potential for front-line staff to make a negative impression on customers and the massive costs of recruitment which are incurred due to high levels of labour turnover, especially during the first few months of employment. It is important to understand that labour turnover is typically in excess of 30 per cent per annum, and in some southern stores can be five times as high as this.

Much greater effort has been put into the whole selection process, and in some stores where it is difficult to retain staff special attempts have been made to attract older people to apply for jobs. Getting sufficient applicants has not been a problem in the northern stores, although ensuring that these people are satisfactory has been more difficult; now, store managers and their deputies complete a short, informal interview with potential applicants before the selection process is started in the hope that this will screen out weaker candidates. The selection process still relies heavily on interviews as opposed to the more sophisticated techniques which have become common in some manufacturing organisations for blue-collar employees.

As soon as the new staff member is appointed, induction training takes place under the auspices of a wide-ranging but carefully administered programme. Before taking up any duties, each new recruit is meant to spend several periods of time on basic induction, which is then followed by a further concentrated programme; indeed, the first 21 hours of a new recruit's time is charged to training. Over the next 12 weeks, more detailed training is undertaken on issues connected with customer care and department-specific matters such as correct procedures for meat preparation or baking. The formal induction programme is undertaken within the store by a team of trainers, who get the new recruits to complete a workbook containing a whole range of questions. This includes a number of forced-choice questions on customer relations and how to assess priorities at work, which are completed and then discussed with the staff trainer, as the following example demonstrates:

> It's a busy Friday evening. You have been told to fill an almost empty shelf of cereals, when all of a sudden you hear glass smashing as a customer drops a bottle of squash. What do you do?
>
> a) You carry on filling the shelves, meantime alerting customers to keep clear of the glass and the liquid on the floor. When you have finished you clear up the mess.
>
> b) You find a barricade and put it up in front of the breakage whilst you go to find something to clear it up with.
>
> c) You ask the customer to find a supervisor and report what has happened immediately.

New recruits also receive information about the company history (on which they are later questioned), health and safety, and more general rules and regulations. A company handbook details the key points of the employment package, as well as providing answers to the more typical questions asked by new employees. New starters also receive written information about the customer service campaign, and a series of brochures detailing the required standards of dress and hygiene. This is then supplemented by a set of videos presented by the trainers, and these messages are constantly reinforced throughout the individual's employment with the company. Departments are checked on a twice-daily basis to ensure that products are acceptable – that is, correctly labelled and priced, properly presented, and not past their sell-by date. On the checkouts, similar activities take place, and all employees are continually monitored for speed, accuracy, and relations with customers.

A unitarist philosophy is evident in much of the audio-visual material which is produced by Superco, with regular references to being 'vital members of the team', and to the ethos of all working together for the good of the company as a whole. For example, one of the induction videos encourages staff to 'buy into' the benefits offered by the company; if staff work hard, look smart, and maintain strict hygiene and service standards, it is suggested that Superco will be able to ensure that customers receive quality products and treatment, as well as value for money. The result of this is said to be secure employment for staff, profit sharing, good promotion prospects, and job satisfaction. The fact that staff can see relatively open lines of promotion into junior management positions also helps to reinforce the feeling that working together may represent a way forward for staff and the company alike.

On the other hand, this benign image of 'teamworking' and cooperation masks the tight controls that are exerted within the company, especially in the managerial hierarchy. First of all, there are strict formulae for the amount of labour which can be employed in any one period, although store managers are allowed some flexibility between full- and part-time employees according to their local needs. A commitment by the company to minimise queue lengths can fall foul of this strict formula if there is a sudden surge of activity at what is typically a quiet part of the day or week, or if there is a problem at one of the checkouts with a customer. Second, regional managers make spot visits to each of the stores on a regular but unscheduled basis, principally to check on store layouts, queue lengths, and general performance. These visits can be a cause of some consternation for managers, as their aim is to 'keep them on their toes', to make them constantly aware of the need for high quality service. In a similar vein, the use of 'mystery shoppers' and consumer reports are part of the arsenal of techniques that are used to ensure that staff maintain excellent levels of customer service at all times. Each of these has undertones of a low-trust management style.

Similarly, disciplinary standards are laid down precisely in the company rule book, and there are specific instructions about standards of cleanliness and dress. During induction, staff are required to answer a series of questions about hygiene, as well as understand Superco's dress policy relating to their uniforms and jewellery, standards of hair care, hands and nails. Departmental managers are required to take a firm line in relation to staff who violate these standards, and the list of offences for which disciplinary action is liable includes rudeness to customers, deliberate disregard of company rules, persistent work errors, and persistent lateness and absenteeism. Indeed, the desire to project a high quality image is central to much of the activity at the store. Behind the scenes, in the training room, a poster campaign emphasises the more instrumental reasons why employees should wish to deliver high-quality service: 'Satisfied customers who keep coming back again and again strengthen sales and jobs; CUSTOMERS make pay days possible!' Finally, video cameras are trained constantly on the sales area in an effort to deter pilferage by customers, and ensure that there is a record of events if the need arises for prosecution. At the same time, although this is not its purpose, the video cameras also act as an instrument of surveillance over staff who are aware that these recordings could be used against them as well as customers.

Pay rates and other terms and conditions of employment are determined by management each year. Whilst there is considerable reference to the external market and the amount which Superco can afford, it is also clear that the company is one of the top payers in the industry. Up until the late 1980s, a number of the larger firms were members of the Multiple Food Retailers' Employers Association (MFREA), and the rates negotiated there obviously had quite a strong influence over companies which were not members of the MFREA as well. Similarly, until its abolition in 1993, so did the pronouncements of the Wages Council for the industry because of its effect on the wages for the lowest paid employees in each company (Jackson *et al.*, 1992). The pay rates of leading rivals is a major factor in this exercise, and all the companies in this 'high-quality' segment of the market pay great attention to the deals which other firms have offered. All are keen to attract the best employees on the labour market, and certainly not pay less than their leading rivals. The profit-sharing scheme also plays a part here as well, because staff with more than two years consecutive service are eligible irrespective of the number of hours worked. About a third of those employed are members of the share scheme, and payouts for these staff can represent more than an additional month's salary each year. People who leave employment before the qualification date are not entitled to any profit-share payment.

Communications, involvement and customer care programmes

Having appointed (hopefully) the right type of staff, and introduced them to the key principles of customer service during induction, management makes use of employee involvement and customer care programmes to reinforce these values. A variety of techniques is used: written and verbal communications, videos, and customer care committees. Unlike many other large organisations, Superco has chosen not to introduce formal team briefing, preferring to rely on informal, face-to-face contact between managers and their staff on an *ad hoc* basis. This is justified by some senior management because of the nature of the product market environment: that is, continuous pressure from customers which requires immediate attention, allied to an employment policy which maintains strict controls on the total number of hours worked in any one store. Superco has not been prepared to offer additional payments for staff to attend team briefing sessions as overtime. Whilst more senior managers feel that staff are kept sufficiently informed, this feeling is not universally shared by staff who are dependent on local managers for the regular passage of information.

Although there is no formal machinery for regular face-to-face information-passing between managers and staff, written communications are comprehensive and highly polished. At each store, there is a system of noticeboards which assumes a key place within the framework of employee relations. These are placed prominently within the stores and are regularly updated. All employees walk past the board several times each day, on their way to and from the staff restaurant, and new items are highlighted, either on the board itself or on the door into the restaurant. A questionnaire survey of staff undertaken in two units indicated that the noticeboard was the most valued source of information in the store. The company also prides itself on the quality of its house journal, a newspaper which has been published ten times per annum since the late 1940s, and has won a string of awards from various bodies. It operates according to a set of written objectives which are broadly concerned with 'furthering good employee relations', 'improving the process of change' and 'conveying information accurately and effectively'. The journal was revamped towards the end of the 1980s, and now has the 'feel' of a Sunday newspaper colour supplement. It is 28 pages long and contains the usual mix of information about business items and social activities, although there is rather less of the former than is typical in house journals. All new store openings are featured in the newspaper, along with information about important events; for example, there is an annual report focusing on the company results, and there have been a number of feature articles on quality management and environmental affairs.

Training videos have formed a key part of Superco's campaign to highlight the importance of excellent customer service so as to maintain market share and profitability. The videos are shown by a staff trainer, with employees drawn from different parts of the store in order to minimise disruption to activities there. There is no attempt to use these sessions as a vehicle for team building, and it is rare for line managers to attend these meetings. The messages which are conveyed in these sessions tend to be simple and straightforward, varying in the degree to which they take a prescriptive line about the 'one best way' to serve customers. The image of the customer as all-powerful is central to these programmes, and once again the phraseology reflects unitarist assumptions. For example:

> Customer care is the Number One skill all Superco employees must have. Our future success will depend upon how well you apply this skill.

> Remember it is not what you are doing that is the most important thing, it is what the customer PERCEIVES you are doing.

> Make sure that you always say good morning, please, thank you, use the customer's name if known, always apologise if something is wrong or there is a delay, take customers to a display, always show concern.

Some of the more experienced staff in the stores found these customer care videos extremely simplistic, and actually became annoyed by them. They resented the way in which the message was put across, the patronising and condescending tone of the whole presentation, and the image that was conveyed by the stores in which the films were made; in these, the actors who were playing staff worked at a very leisurely pace, and had time to laugh and joke with the actors who were playing customers. On the other hand, senior management saw these devices as necessary in order to maintain the emphasis on quality customer service.

Customer service issues are also emphasised through the customer care committee operating at the store. This is a monthly meeting designed to allow a complete focus on quality improvement, with all non-managerial employees eligible for nomination to the committee, usually after some encouragement from the store management team. Committee members other than the store manager and personnel manager are allowed to vote for 'employee of the month', and scores are accumulated to enable the selection of 'employee of the year'. Cash prizes are awarded for each category, with a small £10 payment for the monthly prize and £500 for the major annual prize. The winner and her/his partner is invited to have dinner with the several members of the store management team. In general, employees at the store reacted favourably to this initiative and, despite the fact that a number of bogus entries were received in the first few months, the winners seemed satisfied with the accolade from their colleagues. Staff reported that the scheme made them feel 'more involved' in activities at the store, and the committees led to a number of improvements to the physical surroundings in the store; it should be noted, of course, that improvements to the shopping environment often also improve the *working* environment for staff as well.

Summary of TQM at Superco

The objectives of Superco are clearly aimed at the provision of high levels of customer service in its effort to retain existing shoppers and attract new ones. As the principal point of contact between customers and the company is through front-line staff, managing these employees to deliver quality service is critical. Human resource management at all stages of the employment relationship – recruitment and selection, induction, training and development, pay and appraisal, employee involvement – is therefore important.

With reference to Figure 4.3, the HR function at Superco made a contribution to the development of TQM both as a 'change agent' and a 'facilitator'. The head office team worked closely with senior managers in leading programmes of cultural change, both through the initiation of management development programmes and in setting the scene for board-level discussions about the HR contribution to customer service and competitive advantage. At store level, much of the personnel managers' and trainers' work was directed at coping with problems of recruitment and retention, of high levels of absenteeism and labour turnover, and of bringing customer service staff up to date with new products and processes. The influence of HR was also very apparent at the induction stage of the employment relationship as well. But, there are problems and tensions in the management of human resources, to some extent due to other pressures in the industry (for example, tight controls on wage costs, or the lack of suitable pools of labour) but also because of contradictions in the employment relationship more generally. This latter point is exemplified by the techniques of surveillance used by many of the large retailers.

Customer service from both sides of the checkout

Most studies that examine the issue of customer service have been from marketing or retailing specialists (Lewis, 1990, 1993). Sparks (1992b), for example, describes the policies of a sample of leading American companies and reproduces some of their literature on the importance of customer care. Reference is made to 'mystery shoppers', which have also been used by some British companies of course, and to statements made during induction and training programmes which specifically relate high levels of customer service to rewards and job security: 'The customer is crucial to your pay packet. If the company and staff don't deliver what the customer requires, then the future is going to be bleak' (Sparks, 1992b: 174). Moores (1990) summarises the activities of 23 American companies visited by a group of British executives, again making reference, *inter alia*, to mystery shoppers. Unfortunately, there is no analysis of the employment implications of these techniques, in particular for patterns of power, authority and conflict within retailing. The use of 'mystery shoppers' is seen somehow as 'neutral', as nothing more than a technique for *improving* customer service, in a way which overlooks the ramifications that this form of surveillance has for the balance of power in employee/management relations.

In contrast, there is a dearth of material on food retailing by students of human resource management and organisation behaviour, with the exception of studies on part-time working and labour market segmentation by Robinson (1990). In recent years, more HRM specialists have undertaken research in the area (see, for example, Ogbonna and Wilkinson, 1988, 1990; Gregory, 1991; Marchington and Harrison, 1991; Marchington, 1996) which has introduced different issues from those typically dealt with by the retailers. The way in which the concept of customer care is analysed by HRM specialists is radically different from that of the retailers. The major focus is on issues of power and authority, of imbalances in the employment relationship, and the subtle uses of customer power to obscure yet reinforce management prerogatives. Research is less likely to consider which policies and techniques managements might adopt to improve customer service, but instead to question whether such actions enable managements to maintain control over the employment relationship. Moreover, researchers are prone to examine how employees might adapt and bend rules in order to make their working lives tolerable, often in ways that are contrary to managerial and employer interests. In retailing, employee discontent rarely surfaces through collective industrial action, but through covert or individual acts of resistance or mere acquiescence (Mars, 1982; Marchington, 1992).

Interest in the area of customer service has been stimulated by the work of Hochschild (1983) on flight attendants in the USA. She argues that service workers, of which flight attendants are possibly an extreme example, are involved in the production of 'emotional work products', and are thus subjected to 'emotion management'. They engage in 'deep acting' which relies upon the commercialisation of human feeling, playing out a role which is designed to satisfy customers. According to Smith (1988: 146), this is potentially more deeply estranging than other forms of labour, in particular that based upon manual skills alone, and can lead to considerable stress at work and subsequently in the home. The highly visible environment in which work is undertaken adds to these pressures to 'perform' in line with management and customer expectations, and has clear implications for power relations.

These ideas have fuelled the research of a number of studies on retailing staff, typically linked with questions of customer service. For example, Ogbonna and Wilkinson (1988, 1990) assess the impact of corporate strategy and culture on human resource practices at the checkout, especially relations between employees and customers. They conclude that shop workers display little moral obligation to provide high levels of customer service, and suggest that any loyalty to the employer is principally instrumental in character. Their sample of quotes from checkout operators illustrates the 'performing' theme well: 'Putting on the smile'; 'I should have been an actress'; 'You have to differentiate between your home life and work… you forget your problems when you come to work' (Ogbonna and Wilkinson, 1990: 11). The emotional stress suffered by these workers is also apparent, with tales of employees bursting into tears after being confronted by an abusive customer, or customers 'moaning and groaning' whilst queuing for service. The notion of emotion management is spelled out well by one of their interviewees (1990: 12): 'We do get some very difficult customers… but customer service is something we pride ourselves on, so we have to learn to manage our feelings. When you get angry, you just go into the office and have a good swear at them and then come out smiling'. According to Weatherly and Tansik (1993: 5), customer-contact workers are regularly caught between the demands of management/organisational policy and the expectations of customers.

Fuller and Smith (1991) argue that service workers learn tacit skills to cope with this, varying their style and approach to deal with different customers. On the basis of interviews with managers and owners in a number of American firms, some of which were supermarkets, they conclude (1991: 4) that managers need to use techniques which 'simultaneously maintain their own control prerogatives but interfere as little as possible with employees' ability to exercise the amount of self-direction necessary to deliver quality service'. One way to achieve this is to make use of consumers' reports, through devices such as printed and telephone surveys, focus groups, and 'mystery shoppers'. They even report on one organisation where 'mystery shoppers' were 'wired up' so that all interactions with staff could be monitored (5–6), and a union official claimed that customer feedback had been used in supermarkets to initiate disciplinary action against employees (8). Fuller and Smith view customers as the 'formally designated accomplices (of management) in controlling workers'. Du Gay and Salaman (1992: 621) offer a less conspiratorial perspective, noting that some (paid) customers do feed back information about the quality of service provided by sales staff, and in a sense do aid the process of management through the use of 'new technologies of surveillance'.

Consumer feedback can help to *obscure* the real locus of managerial power, shifting some of the monitoring aspects of management activity onto an external party, in this case the customer. This can serve to legitimise management actions in a way which might well be unacceptable if it were not cloaked in the language of customer perceptions and competitive advantage. It is clear that 'mystery shoppers' represent the ultimate form of 'invisible' management control, leading them to draw parallels with Bentham's panopticon, recently repopularised by Foucault (1977) and others (Sewell and Wilkinson, 1992a,b). The panopticon ensures, *inter alia*, that 'surveillance is permanent in its effects, even if it is discontinuous in its action, that the perfection of power should tend to render its actual exercise unnecessary' (Foucault, 1977: 201). Power is both visible and unverifiable, in that sales staff know that they may be observed constantly but are unable to determine precisely when a 'mystery shopper' might be passing through the store. Because of this their actions are continuously constrained (Fuller and Smith, 1991: 11).

This type of low-trust control strategy (Fox, 1974) may also backfire as employees resent what is seen as a devious and underhand way in which to check up on them, and they experience role conflict and stress in trying to cope with multiple demands. Moreover, such approaches are fundamentally contradictory if employers are also seeking to develop more open management styles based upon the pursuit of enhanced employee commitment (Marchington, 1993). Categorisations provided by Shamir (1980) and Rafaelli (1989), which have been developed by Weatherly and Tansik (1993), are particularly apposite in this respect, and all three studies note that front-line staff develop strategies/tactics to maintain control of their encounters with customers. This includes a wide range of responses: *ignoring* customers by avoiding eye contact; *rejecting* customers by labelling them as pests and naggers; *reacting* to customer demands by arguing with them; *educating* customers by explaining company policy; *mindlessness*, by following pre-learned rituals, but without any commitment to them; *overacting*, by becoming absorbed with the role and in a sense playing games to make work tolerable (see also, Burawoy, 1979); *physical control*, through the provision of ropes to direct queues; *engaging* customers in the work process in order to keep them busy during the service encounter; and *rewarding* customers by ingratiating them and making them feel special (Rafaelli, 1989: 263–6; Weatherly and Tansik, 1993: 6–8). Clearly, many of these are unlikely to enhance customer perceptions of service quality, and may be used by employees who are alienated and frustrated by management actions.

Conclusion

Three points need to be reiterated as a conclusion to this chapter on quality management in food retailing. First, despite the fact that we have focused here on issues of customer service, this should not obscure the fact that quality management is also practised through other mechanisms as well, such as stringent controls on food hygiene or precise specifications for suppliers. Customer service is, however, central to the objectives of the leading 'high-quality' food retailers, and is seen as a key element in their search for customer loyalty and competitive advantage. Second, the interrelationship between customer service and HRM is readily apparent among the leading food retailers, especially because of the impact of front-line staff on sales. Recruiting, motivating and retaining the right staff is a crucial aspect of human resource policies in the leading companies, and this is heavily dependent on being able to attract and develop effective managers; thus, the emphasis on management recruitment and development, as well as internal promotion. Finally, there are major tensions between the so-called 'soft' and visible elements of HRM and TQM (involvement, development, and reward) and their 'harder' and less apparent counterparts (such as conformance, discipline and surveillance). This is particularly problematic in food retailing given the boundary-spanning role played by low status, non-professional staff, as well as the fact that employee *attitudes* play a major part in standards of work performance observed by customers. TQM therefore needs to be viewed from both sides of the checkout.

CHAPTER 10

Pay, Rewards and Recognition: Managing Quality in a Small Firm

Introduction

In this chapter we examine the case of a small firm – Richer Sounds – and the manner in which it seeks to manage its culture to create a customer-focused, quality-orientated organisation. In particular we examine the way it uses its payment system to support the desired quality culture. TQM writers stress the need to create a new corporate culture but are rather imprecise as to how this is to be achieved. As Seddon points out 'all the literature on TQM indicates that to be successful TQM requires a cultural change. That's usually where the literature stops' (1990: 81). For example a recent TQM text states that:

> A considerable thought needs to be given to facilitating and managing cultural change. Changing people's beliefs and attitudes is one of the most difficult tasks facing management, who must develop their own powers and skills of motivation and persuasion. (Dale and Cooper, 1992: 20).

As we have seen in Chapter 4, however, the literature on quality says more on *what* companies are trying to achieve in terms of employee commitment, than on *how* this is to be achieved. As far as this is addressed, the usual argument in the TQM literature is that employees are to be won over, not by compulsion but by leadership, communication, training and recognition (Oakland, 1993). This reflects an underlying assumption that employees are bound to derive satisfaction from involvement in continuous improvement and from doing a job well. Hill (1991a), however, claims that the proponents of TQM have understated the difficulties in getting staff at all levels in the organisation to 'buy in' to the ideals of TQM, and that they focus on too limited a range of change levers. Drawing on Schein (1985), he points out that mission statements and other statements of intent by managers are secondary mechanisms of change and what is required are the 'more coercive levers of persuasion available to top management by virtue of their command of organisational power, namely the deployment of organisational rewards and punishments' (Hill, 1991a: 557).

In this case, there is relatively little on the traditional formal and institutional mechanisms for TQM, but nonetheless it is clear that a TQM culture exists in Richer Sounds. To some extent this is due to company size but a great deal depends on the philosophy of the owner; on his whole approach to managing people at work, on his (almost) innocent and heartfelt commitment to empowerment, and on his obsession with excellent customer service. Richer Sounds is therefore different from each of the other cases we examine in this book, but its inclusion is important to demonstrate the range of ways in which TQM can be developed and sustained.

Remuneration and the management of culture

Much has been written on the subject of corporate culture in recent years. As Sackman notes, the topic of culture has entered the business world. 'This does not necessarily imply that the level of cultivation has increased in corporate life' (1991: 1). Business literature, in particular, has been packed with examples of programmes introduced by a wide range of organisations seeking to create a new corporate culture. Indeed, most major organisations, whether in the private or public sector, have introduced programmes of cultural change designed to break 'mind-sets', win 'hearts and minds', and change attitudes and values to be more supportive of strategic objectives. Part of the rationale for this is reflected in the view of Deal and Kennedy that 'a strong culture is a system of informal rules that spell out how people are to behave most of the time, it enables people to feel better about what they do, so they are more likely to work harder' (1982: 15). Furthermore, strong cultures can facilitate a measure of control without levels of bureaucracy.

A number of accounts of corporate culture programmes are now available (for example, Ogbonna and Wilkinson, 1988, 1990; Hopfl *et al.*, 1992; Storey, 1992). Most of these accounts have a common theme, in that organisations seem to be attempting to achieve similar goals: the creation of a new enterprise culture with the primacy of the customer (market) seen as central to the commercialisation of staff, even those staff without direct contact with external customers. The inspiration behind much of the interest is Peters and Waterman's best seller *In Search of Excellence*, which pointed out the lack of attention paid to managing cultures in the modern organisation and argued that strong corporate cultures were integral to business success. Others in the corporate culture school include Deal and Kennedy (1982), Pascale and Athos (1982), Ouchi (1981). All have been criticised for having a homogeneous view of culture based on senior management beliefs rather than reality (see, for example Anthony, 1990).

Despite the pessimistic tone of most academic work (Smirich, 1983; Ackroyd and Crowdy, 1990; Legge, 1994), it seems that organisations continue to seek cultural change through an array of initiatives, such as TQM, customer care and business process re-engineering, which show few signs of slackening. Furthermore, the TQM literature – by contrast with the social science literature – is tinged with optimism in relation to cultural change. From an HRM perspective, pay is seen as a key lever for change and indeed the 1980s and 90s witnessed an explosion of financial incentives such as performance related pay, bonuses and profit sharing, which were seen as key levers in the pursuit of cultural change (for example, Fowler, 1988; Mumford and Buley, 1988). The view, however, of most authorities on quality management is that financial incentives have little to contribute towards the implementation of TQM, and that they can in fact be counterproductive (Crosby, 1979; Deming, 1986; Drummond and Chell, 1992). As Oakland puts it:

> One approach that should definitely not be used… is a financial incentive – it does not form part of the TQM culture, and would defeat many of the objectives. Recognition and the chance to participate are the only incentives. (1993: 437)

Such a view can also be seen in the writings of Crosby and Deming, two of the leading US quality gurus. Crosby (1979) suggests that to reward an individual's commitment to quality with financial incentives is to risk demeaning them, by attaching a price tag to their efforts. He claims that recognition is the key, and recommends that organisations present quality awards and prizes, not necessarily of great financial value in themselves. Peer nomination for such awards is seen as a valuable way of emphasising their value in terms of recognition and motivation.

Deming (1986) goes even further, seeing the use of performance appraisal and management by objectives as one of the 'deadly diseases' of Western management. He characterises this approach as 'management by fear', claiming that individuals are forced to look for short-term, individual achievements in an attempt to meet their immediate appraisal objectives. Employees are discouraged from constructive criticism of their manager or of the system, and the emphasis is on avoiding risk. Perhaps most damning from the point of view of TQM is Deming's suggestion that it:

> leaves people bitter, crushed, bruised, battered, desolate, despondent, dejected, feeling inferior, some even depressed, unfit for work for weeks after receipt of rating,

unable to comprehend why they are inferior. It is unfair, as it ascribes to people in a group differences that they may be caused entirely by the system that they work in. (1986: 102)

and

Evaluation of performance, merit rating or annual review... it nourishes short-term performance, annihilates long term planning, builds fear, demolishes teamwork, nourishes rivalry and politics. (1986: 102)

In short, appraisals and incentive pay schemes which are linked to appraisal outcomes undermine the kind of cooperative, creative and committed behaviour necessary for a quality organisation. Some have suggested that performance-related pay may militate against the ideas of cooperation and teamwork espoused by TQM (Wilkinson *et al.*, 1992).

Some proponents of TQM, however, have seen the issue as one of choosing the appropriate type of incentive pay, rather than opposing such schemes *per se*. In a revised edition of his standard text on TQM, Oakland, for example, suggests that:

While it is desirable to introduce a TQM initiative or sustain an established one without direct financial incentives, it is possible to do so in the context of a pay structure with an incentive component, provided that the motivational impact of the incentive does not undermine the total quality aims. There would be, however, a major conflict between trying to create a total quality culture and trying to maintain a payment structure that was focused strongly on motivating individuals to maximise their output volume. (1993: 295).

Thus traditional output-based payment-by-results (PBR) systems are likely to contradict the aims of TQM by focusing employee attention on maximising output, subject to an external check on quality compliance. Quality becomes something for someone else to take responsibility for. However, it seems that other forms of incentive pay may after all be compatible with the successful implementation of TQM. Furthermore, Oakland goes on to suggest that:

There may even be opportunities to refocus incentives in ways that remove barriers to TQM and demonstrate practical commitment to the individual and organisational values implicit in a never-ending improvement. (1993: 296)

This is echoed in the guidelines to the US Baldrige awards for excellence in quality management, which suggest that performance reviews, compensation and rewards should all be restructured to support quality improvement (Hart and Schlesinger, 1991).

Furthermore, some employees may expect that they should receive increased pay in return for taking on greater responsibility for quality, and that they should share directly in the financial benefits of quality improvement (Drummond and Chell, 1992). Where this is not forthcoming, there may be a risk of employees becoming disillusioned with TQM. According to Ogbonna:

> The factors that are appraised and the favourable behaviours that are recognised and rewarded will provide a mental cue to employees in deciding what actions they should take. To encourage employees' dispositions towards a desired change in organisational culture, reward systems must be set in context: that is be matched with the desired culture. (1992/3: 4)

One US commentator has suggested that quality management programmes often 'run out of steam' three to five years on, as employees begin to lose interest in token rewards and praise amid a growing expectation that they are due a share of the financial benefits of their quality improvement efforts (T. Walker, 1992). It seems that praise and a pat on the back may go only so far in a society where cash has traditionally been regarded as the true measure of value. As Lawler suggests 'the value orientation in many countries says individuals and groups should be paid more when they perform better. When they are not paid more they tend to feel inequitably treated' (1992: 3). Thus a number of organisations seem to have linked pay and quality, both in the UK (Incomes Data Services, 1991) and in the USA (Sellers, 1990; Olian and Rynes, 1991: 312; Ross and Hatcher, 1992).

The literature on remuneration management also takes an optimistic view on the impact of financial incentives on quality. Whilst the standard accounts of output-based PBR tend to agree with Oakland that such systems carry a risk of undermining quality in a bid to maximise output (Incomes Data Services, 1991; Cannell and Wood, 1992), the remuneration literature is again consistent with Oakland in suggesting that other forms of financial incentive may avoid such a damaging effect. Cannell and Wood (1992: 108) argue that the impact of profit sharing on quality is likely to be neutral, whilst the impact of performance-related pay is likely to depend on the nature of the particular performance objectives. Thus, whilst many of the American quality gurus have spoken out very strongly against the use of financial incentives, this is not a unanimous view amongst the proponents of TQM. The literature on remuneration, whilst admitting that certain forms of financial incentive may undermine quality improvement, suggests that this is not necessarily true of all forms of financial incentive.

UK organisations are implementing QM initiatives side-by-side with formal appraisal systems and a range of financial incentives. The warnings of Deming and others on the incompatibility of appraisal and incentives on the one hand, and the TQM culture of continuous improvement on the other, seem not to have been heeded by most UK organisations. Snape *et al.* (1996) found no evidence to suggest that the use of formal appraisal and financial incentives necessarily undermines the successful implementation of TQM.

Indeed, there was some evidence that such practices are positively correlated with greater success.

Managing a quality culture in the small firm

Small firms may offer a better opportunity to manage culture than large firms,where sub-cultures and departmental barriers are more likely to hinder the development of a managed corporate culture. The literature on small firms, however, tends to present two ideal type pictures. First, the 'small is beautiful' scenario, where small firms facilitate close and harmonious working relationships. This was seen in the Bolton report, (1971), which suggested that small firms provide a better working environment. Thus communication was easier, there was greater flexibility and conflict was very low. A second view is that small firms are dictatorially run, with employees having little involvement in decisions and suffering poor working conditions (Rainnie, 1989). Both views have been questioned. As Curran argues, 'small firms do offer more varied work roles and greater opportunities for close face to face relations in a flexible social setting with less of the bureaucracy of the larger enterprises. But these conditions also offer greater opportunities for inter-personal conflicts' (quoted by Roberts *et al.*, 1992: 242). In reality small firms are diverse in terms of management style and in many other aspects of their operation (Ritchie, 1993). It is generally true to say, however, that few small businesses place a high priority on the management of human resources. The evidence suggests that small firms do not have highly formalised business strategies and 'informal routinisation' plays a large part in the day-to-day running of the firm (Scott *et al.*, 1989). Strategy is 'crafted' rather than 'designed' (Mintzberg, 1978) and this is particularly so in relation to managing staff and human resources.

The view that cooperation rather than conflict is the norm and that management need to examine HR issues only when there are problems, rather than make contingent plans, stems partly from the unitary view of most small firm employers. Thus order is seen as the norm and management prerogative is seen as a right and not to be challenged. Given that many owners define the small firm as their own creation, it is perhaps not surprising that everybody else's views of what is best for the firm should be seen as subordinate to their own (Scott *et al.*, 1989).

Informality, then, characterises employment relations in small companies. Small workplaces often have little in the way of formal control systems, and communication strategies are usually non-existent. This is justified by the owner on the grounds that the small workplace facilitates communication and that the 'family atmosphere' of the small firm builds high trust. Other policies are often similarly minimalist (Ritchie, 1993). Recruitment is through networks of family and employee friends, training and development is limited, and remuneration is also subject to management prerogative. According to Scott *et al.* (1989), the interpenetration of personal and industrial relations is a key feature of relationships in small firms. Indeed, they argue that affective ties and other networks function to obscure the employment relationship by gaining the goodwill and commitment of some of the workers whilst exerting pressure in an indirect way upon others (*op cit.*: 47); or, as Roberts *et al.* put it:

> Relations are not of the impersonal 'structured' type characteristic of many large firms. But neither are they merely a collection of individual interpersonal relationships involving a loosely structured distribution of power, as in ties of friendship. Rather the characteristic feature of small firms is the overlap between personal and employee relations. (1992: 243)

In the remainder of this chapter, we present a case study of a relatively small firm which is attempting to sustain a quality-orientated culture. The case illustrates many of the themes raised above about the potential role of remuneration and also about the particular features of small firms.

The company: Richer Sounds

The company

Richer Sounds is a hi-fi separates retailer in the UK, a small firm characterised by a small market share, personalised management and owner control. It has 15 branches (in some 11 cities), a warehouse and a head office. It employs over a 100 full-time staff, with a handful of part-time workers. The company is an unlisted plc owned by Julian Richer, a self-made entrepreneur. The hi-fi market has two elements: one comprises the package of complete music systems which are dominated by the retail chains, both department stores and general electrical retailers. The second is the more specialised hi-fi separates where consumers mix and match hi-fi components from various manufacturers. In the latter market product knowledge is high and the market offers a niche to small retailers such as Richer Sounds (Drummond and Ensor, 1991).

The company's success comes from high stock turnover combined with low overheads. It sells discounted, often discontinued end-of-line, products in small shops (average size under 200 square feet) in secondary (non-high street) locations. During the recession it has bucked the market trend, with profits (before tax) doubling in the period 1992–3 and sales reaching a high of £18 million. Richer Sounds has overcome the unwillingness of some major companies to deal with them and the company is in the *Guinness Book of Records* for having the highest sales value per square foot of any major retailer in the world, as well as the highest sales per employee.

Company philosophy – a quality customer service

As in many small firms, the owner–manager exerts a strong influence and there is a considerable hagiography about Richer Sounds. The official story is disseminated in much of the company literature. According to this literature, at the age of 14 he bought and sold second-hand turntables to make money, and he was also involved in buying and selling candles during the energy crisis. Richer opened his first shop in 1978 with £20 000 borrowed from a photographic retailer who regarded him as a 'whizz kid'. In 1985, as profits mounted, Richer bought out his percentage of the business.

A quality customer service is seen as the driving philosophy behind the organisation. Officially, this is stated as 'providing second-to-none service and value for money for our customers'. More simply, the idea is that excellent customer service is not a 'sell at all costs' philosophy. Employees are encouraged to help the customer to buy rather than go for the 'hard sell'. The small shops are also seen to facilitate a more informal and friendly atmosphere. Given the specialised nature of the products, staff need a high degree of product knowledge.

The owner argues that the basic principles underpinning Richer Sounds are quality products (branded names, and so on), value for money and customer service, although branches do not provide demonstrations in busy hours and the company claims that the 'nearest you get to installation is an instruction book'. The owner points out that whilst the first two can be controlled by head office, customer service is very much in the hands of the ordinary branch employee, and therefore this needs to be given particular attention. Judging from the company's own internal staff attitude survey, the customer service message seems to have come through clearly. Thus 100 per cent of staff agreed with the proposition that 'customers are number one at Richer Sounds'.

There is a distinct American flavour of the type promulgated by Peters and Waterman's book *In Search of Excellence*, and seen in companies in the UK like the restaurant chain 'Thank God it's Fridays' (TGI Fridays). Indeed, Julian Richer claims that the book changed his life. The organisation chart is presented in inverted form, with the customer at the top, followed by sales staff (called colleagues) and middle management, and ending with the top management, to reflect the importance of customers and ordinary staff members. However, there is no question concerning who is in charge of the company. Richer himself says he 'leads from the front' and that the firm is a 'benevolent dictatorship'. Like Macdonalds or Euro-Disney, induction is intense; staff are imbued with the ethos, history, standards and values of the organisation and 'communications, marketing and training become one' (Storey and Sisson, 1993: 11).

The emphasis is very much on 'fun' for customers (and also for staff). Customers are invited to bring their pets to help them choose their purchase. Those buying a hi-fi when it is raining receive a free umbrella, and scratch cards with free gifts are distributed. Even the warnings to shoplifters are done with humour – 'Free ride in a police car for shoplifters only'.

The company has a freephone 24-hour-a-day customer problem line, with a board director who has responsibility for handling customer complaints. A 'we're listening' suggestion card scheme provides the opportunity for those who do not buy to make comments, and this is then sent directly to the chairman. Sales colleagues are expected to make a number of customer telephone calls each week, aimed in particular at older customers and first time buyers, to ensure that they are satisfied with the purchased items.

Management style

Like most small firms, Richer Sounds is characterised by personalised management with informality and close relations in contrast to the bureaucratic relations of large firms (Roberts *et al.*, 1992). For a small firm, however, the company has quite a sophisticated range of personnel policies and practices. This can be seen in the induction booklet which includes details of the company philosophy, the organisational chart, company history, contract, blank suggestion slips, an A–Z of hi-fi terms, a health booklet and a 50-page staff training manual. The basic management style has been described as 'fun but caring'. Influences include both the American management gurus Peters and Waterman, as well as the UK retailer Marks and Spencer. The latter influence derives from the chairman's parents, who worked there, and finds expression in paternalist attitudes. For example 20 per cent of profits are directed either to profit share (15 per cent), to charity (4 per cent), or to a hardship fund (1 per cent). Staff benefits include life insurance and a subsidised medical scheme. This paternalism is also reflected in the staff induction pack, which includes advice on health. There is also an attempt to create a 'family' feeling, with a bonus of £100 for staff introducing new employees to the company. Clearly this word-of-mouth recommendation can help facilitate an integrated workforce and existing social relationships can exert pressure on the new recruit. Staff are also provided with the chairman's home phone number. The company provides subsidised outings three times a year for staff and training sessions take place twice yearly at the chairman's country home in York. Holiday homes in Eastbourne and Scarborough are made available free to staff (a benefit which the Inland Revenue costs at £30 a day, on which the company pays tax). This is not done for altruistic reasons. As Richer himself has noted 'if you are good to your people, it saves enormous recruitment and training costs; they are happier, which is so much the better for the customers'. He points out that stock shrinkage is half that in the industry as a whole (see Wilkinson *et al.*, 1996: 266–74).

Staff turnover is very low, although there is what the organisation calls a 'high infant mortality rate' – that is people do leave because they are unable to adapt to the culture (the so-called induction crisis). The company has a policy of only promoting internally, except for expert specialists such as in marketing. Many of the staff are young hi-fi enthusiasts who enjoy working in the 'informal' environment (the informality is, of course, a carefully managed one), and dealing with other hi-fi enthusiasts. If 'love of product' (Peters and Waterman, 1982: 76) is a result of a successfully managed culture, then an organisation recruiting staff already interested in the product have a head start.

TABLE 10.1   HR approach at Richer

Employee entry channels	through personal contacts of employees
Work structure	formalised but high involvement
Task performance	rulebound but high involvement
Reward systems	formalised but dynamic
Working culture	management created
Retention and development	high initial turnover

Source: Adapted from Ritchie (1993).

Pay is above average for the industry. Sales assistants earn a basic rate of around £10 000 but commission, profit share and the customer service bonus raises this to around £15 000. Profit share alone has worked out at around £1300 for each sales colleague in recent years.

Staff wear name badges to encourage greater individual responsibility. Staff who perform above and beyond the call of duty (ABCD in Richerspeak) receive gold aeroplanes as a recognition of their high achievement. Wooden spoons are given to staff for acts of amazing stupidity. On a more serious level, the company computes a customer service index for each member of staff. Individuals are assessed monthly on a range of indicators and results are related to payment (see below).

In small firms, the frequency of personal contact has led managers to see more formalised channels as unnecessary, but the potential isolation of branches from head office in Richer Sounds has led to communications being regarded as something which must be managed. A weekly video is produced with details of company performance. The company also has a highly successful suggestion scheme, which won the UK Association of Suggestion Schemes prize for the highest number of suggestions per staff – 1500 from 70 staff in 1991. Staff are rewarded with up to £180 for each suggestion, with the best two (not necessarily those which say the most) each quarter receiving a day trip on the Orient Express. To facilitate suggestions, there is a monthly £5 drink allowance so employees can go out as a group to discuss possible ideas. Many of the ideas are hard to quantify in terms of bottom-line impact (for example, a bell provided for disabled shoppers), but the scheme is seen in the broader context of building morale and team spirit. All suggestions are seen and replied to by the chairman.

As well as incentives based on the individual there are also team/group incentives to encourage quality. For example, a competition is held between all the branches and departments. This is the Richer Way League which is run on the basis of customer service and profit but not sales, and provides a prize of the use of a Bentley car for a week. 'We measure different aspects of performance to give everyone an equal chance.' The winners share the car between them. So a branch of four colleagues each get the Bentley for a week. Peer group pressure is central to this operation and the small branch size with no more than a handful of employees brings out the visibility of staff actions.

Surprisingly for a small organisation and its emphasis on informality, the company's staff satisfaction is monitored via an annual attitude survey. A recent survey (with an 80 per cent response rate) found that 95 per cent of respondents claimed they enjoyed the job, 88 per cent saying that they believed payment reflected the job they did and 99 per cent saying it was fun. It is also interesting to note that 95 per cent felt that they worked 'very much as a team' in their store/department.

The array of incentives and innovations is quite wide and it is the management philosophy to develop these continually in a bid to maintain the sense of involvement and fun.

Pay and customer satisfaction

A customer service index (CSI) is used to assess individual employees on a range of indicators: how quickly they answer the phone, the number of customer complaints, quality of overall service, positive and negative comments from questionnaires, and punctuality. Points are added and subtracted each month and are reflected in a cash bonus paid with salary. Again, peer group pressure is seen as critical. CSI results are fed to managers on each individual's performance and are then published and distributed internally. Clearly, staff who have performed poorly are under pressure to improve their performance or leave the organisation.

The company believes in linking customer satisfaction and pay (see Chapter 4). Each purchase receipt includes a freepost questionnaire, inviting the customer to assess the level of service provided by the salesperson, who is identified by payroll number on the form (see Appendix 1). Individual's bonuses are related to this feedback. Thus if a customer ticks 'excellent' the sales colleagues receives an extra £3, if 'poor' a deduction of £3 takes place (see Table 10.2). These are totalled up at the end of each month and a bonus paid. The company is at pains to point out that any deductions are far outweighed by the bonuses. Indeed, it is unlikely that anyone with a stream of negative feedback would actually retain their job at Richer Sounds. Questionnaires are mailed direct to the chairman and the company claims a 30 per cent response rate.

It must not be forgotten, however, that commission is still part of the remuneration package and counts for more in monetary terms than the cash bonuses. Thus it is important to see that the customer service questionnaire acts more as a corrective to the sales-orientated commission payments than as a direct incentive itself. In other words, the key in this area is less that cash bonuses act as an incentive than the possibility of negative assessments of service and deductions, and, more importantly, disciplinary action as a result of pushing sales. As Willmott observes in relation to corporate culture programmes 'campaigns to strengthen corporate culture are frequently tied to presentations that stress the strategic importance of employees taking their responsibilities seriously for the performance of the organisation and by implication their own job security and career prospects' (1993: 522).

TABLE 10.2 Pay and customer service

Bonus to staff (£)	How would you describe the overall level of service you received?	Analysis June 1993
3	Excellent	71%
0	Good	28%
−1	Mediocre	0.75%
−3	Poor	0.5%

Conclusions

There are a number of issues arising from this case. First, it is interesting to note that the company did not have a formal quality initiative such as a TQM programme, although the quality philosophy certainly pervaded the organisation, particularly in terms of the importance of the customer and the overall corporate mission. 'Quality' was reinforced through a wide range of vehicles at the company, including the training, reward and recognition schemes as well as being widely communicated from the top. The dangers of constructing a new layer of TQM bureacracy – by prescribing procedures to be followed and behaviours to be displayed – as a way of reducing the existing bureacracy is, of course, rather ironic. Given that many firms are criticised, both in the UK and US, for focusing on the new TQM procedures rather than outcomes (for example, the criticisms of the Baldrige award in the USA made by businessmen and indeed some of the quality gurus such as Crosby and Deming – Garvin, 1991) it might be that much can be learnt from Richer Sounds in this regard. Clearly, there are dangers of rules taking on a life of thier own and people paying lip service rather than abiding by the spirit of what they are intended to do.

Second, the company we have examined is a small firm. Unlike many small firms, however, the company has a clear HR strategy which is coherent and fits well in terms of its links with corporate strategy. It is also important to appreciate that Richer Sound's success owes much to innovative marketing and purchasing strategies: the management of HR and corporate culture is a contributory factor but not the sole explanation for corporate achievement. Like many small firms the charismatic leader holds centre stage and there is much of the small firm ethos – staff recommend friends as potential staff and paternalism pervades the company – which facilitates the creation of an integrated workforce. There is of course another side to the paternalism and this family ethos. For example, the practice of recruiting friends recommended by existing workers implicates relationships beyond the employment relationship. As Scott *et al.* note, 'it can provide an effective network through which pressure can be exerted by the owner/manager on individuals without directly implicating the power inequalities inherent in the employment relationship' (1989: 47). Thus workers can 'have a word with their mates' to warn or counsel them on their attitude or performance, which is facilitated at Richer Sounds by the very small and visible working environment. Indeed, while Richer Sounds is a small firm, its retailing business means that, unlike many small firms, control of the labour process cannot be achieved through the close proximity of the owner/manager (see Scott *et al.*, 1989). Consequently, such control is via a number of formal mechanisms, for example pay, the creation of a corporate culture which emphasises customer orientation and quality, and the creation of an environment in which peer group pressures ensure that employees comply with the desired behaviour.

The company utilises a wide range of methods to encourage this preferred behaviour. In terms of Oliver's (1990) model (see Chapter 4), there is both explicitness in terms of direct individual responsibility via the customer questionnaire with the individual salesperson identified by a payroll number, and publicity both through that mechanism and also in terms of a whole range of techniques designed to enhance peer group pressure. The company is continually revising its methods so as to keep initiatives fresh and interesting to employees, which in turn is seen to produce higher performance. Watson (1986) coined the term, 'the paradox of consequences' by which he meant that all personnel procedures contained the seeds of their own destruction; by this he argued that once a pattern had been established, it inevitably resulted in people or groups becoming entrenched and consequently inflexible. Thus any new procedures or initiatives, such as systems to reward TQM, inevitably take on a life of their own and become internally contradictory. There is therefore a need continually to change procedures to avoid this happening (see Huczynski, 1993: 292). Thus at Richer Sounds management wish to keep things moving to avoid entrenchment as staff 'work out' the system and then undermine its objectives. No doubt staff's 'natural enthusiasm' as hi-fi fanatics fits well with the corporate culture that management wish to create. Thus the company is not faced by reluctant employees: employees seem to have an intrinsic interest in their work and the company seeks to harness this to achieve corporate goals. As Willmott observes in relation to corporate culture programmes, 'self direction is commended but, crucially, its scope and course is *dictated* and directed by the construction of employee commitment to core corporate values' (1993: 254). The company does have certain advantages even before it seeks to 'manage' its employees. Being a 'fun' employer, however, does not mean easy work for staff. On the contrary, staff acknowledge the hard work *and* the pressure, and both the company and staff agree this is not a culture to everyone's liking. Beneath the fun and gimmicks is a tough managerial style with little time for people who are unable to perform in this environment.

Pay and other incentives (both individual and team-based) are used to underpin the development of quality and particularly service quality. However, we must recognise that pay was not seen as a stand-alone issue. Quality improvement and customer satisfaction were addressed through a broad range of measures, of which pay was only one part of a broader recognition strategy, and perhaps a subsidiary one at that. A distinctive management style, and the cultivation of a sense of employee involvement and fun were also contributing factors. The role of pay was to highlight the key quality improvement goals and it was not seen simply as an attempt to 'buy' commitment to quality.

Finally, it is important to appreciate that what seems to work well for Richer Sounds may not translate easily elsewhere. The Richer style is based to a large extent on keeping things moving; to this end, new initiatives are introduced continuously. The workforce is relatively young and enthusiastic about the product. In these circumstances the 'sense of fun' carefully cultivated by Richer may be easier to sustain than elsewhere. Furthermore, as a relatively young organisation, it clearly lacks the 'before and after' transformation found in many accounts of culture change programmes. Moreover, it is also important to see that the context of good corporate performance plays a key part in explaining the positive attributes of staff. The story of Richer Sounds has been one of growth and expansion, and future competitive prospects also seem optimistic. Thus management can maintain their friendly entrepreneurial style and the iron glove does not need to appear except in relation to those individuals who do not perform; even these 'exits' are seen more as the fate of people unable to 'fit in to the culture' rather than the punitive actions of a harsh management. In other words a 'feel good' factor was undoubtedly operating. A different environmental context will present a greater test of the way the organisation is currently managed. It may also indicate if employees' commitment is conditional and calculative, dependent on the organisation being profitable and providing good wages and job security.

The case illustrates how there is no single path to quality. Indeed, the TQM approach, as reflected in the Baldrige award, has been criticised for being too bound up with procedures and processes, and not concerned enough with outcomes. At Richer Sounds the company does utilise traditional control mechanisms but also seeks to embed them in everyday management style through its pervasive message of customer service and quality.

Appendix 10.1   Customer questionnaire

Please help us to give you 100% satisfaction

Dear Customer

In a serious attempt to improve our service to you we'd be extremely grateful if you'd spend a couple of minutes filling in this short questionnaire.

Our aim is to give you the very best service because by doing so, we hope you'll recommend us to others and be a customer for life.

Please help us by giving your frank answers to a few simple questions because it is only by listening to what you say we can improve our standards.

If the service you received was good then I'd *like* to hear about it; if it has not been up to scratch in any way I *need* to hear about it.

I will be seeing all your replies and comments so please *do* tell me what you think.

Thank you for your help.

Julian Richer,
Founder

1. Was the sales assistant who served you friendly?

   Excellent ☐   Good ☐   Mediocre ☐   Poor ☐

   If you required technical information and the sales assistant was not familiar with your question, was he/she helpful in obtaining it?

   Excellent ☐   Good ☐   Mediocre ☐   Poor ☐   N/A ☐

   Was the sales assistant who served you too pushy?

   Yes ☐   No ☐

   How would you describe the overall level of service?

   Excellent ☐   Good ☐   Mediocre ☐   Poor ☐

   Would you recommend us to others?

   Yes ☐   Maybe ☐   No ☐

2. If you have tried to get through to us on the phone have you experienced difficulties?

   Yes ☐   No ☐   Haven't tried ☐

3. Branch visited: _____

4. How old are you?

   Under 18 ☐   18–30 ☐   31–40 ☐   41+ ☐

5. Do you have any comments or suggestions to improve the service you received, or any complaints or grievances however small? (Your comments would be particularly appreciated in the areas you rated mediocre or poor.)

   _____

   _____

   _____

   _____

   _____

   Please continue on another sheet if necessary.

CHAPTER 11

Conclusions: Whither TQM?

Why TQM?

The evidence suggests that in the private sector, TQM is usually implemented in response to perceived competition, and represents an attempt to win and sustain competitive advantage. This is associated with a growing awareness of the importance of staff, be this front-line staff in a customer services environment or manufacturing employees in a highly competitive market where quality, delivery on time and cost competitiveness are crucial. There has been an element of learning by example in the spread of TQM; in its adoption by Western manufacturers learning from their Japanese competitors and in its subsequent take-up in the services sector.

At British Steel, TQM was adopted with both 'hard' and 'soft' objectives in mind. Improvements in yields, product conformance, delivery reliability, costs and stock levels were amongst the former, sought in response to intense competition and increasingly demanding customers. Management also looked to TQM to foster employee involvement and a less autocratic management style. Management recognised that the autocratic approach, which they had seen as an asset during the restructuring of the early 1980s, was now ill-matched to the competitive requirements of the business. In this case, TQM was seen as being necessary to build employee trust and commitment to continuous improvement, following an era of restructuring and job losses, which had achieved considerable short-term gains in terms of cost reduction, and productivity improvement.

In BuSoc, the quality management initiatives reflected a growing awareness of the importance of people to competitive advantage, again in the context of growing competition. Similarly, in the other two private service sector case studies (Superco and Richer Sounds), the aim was primarily to foster continuous improvement in customer service. Other areas, such as product mix and supplier costs, were also important, but service quality was seen by management as a more sustainable basis for competitive advantage, given that purchasing and marketing strategies may be relatively easy for competitors to copy.

The public sector represents the high water mark for the spread of TQM. Here, the pressures to adopt such initiatives are part of a move towards instituting 'market' disciplines into previously bureaucratic or professional service-led organisations, thus addressing many of the criticisms previously levelled at the public services as being inefficient, wasteful and unresponsive to user needs. In our case study of Modern Metro, a metropolitan local authority, the quality management initiatives date from the mid-1980s, when a customer service programme was initiated in advance of more recent pressures by central government. As a Conservative controlled authority, Modern Metro anticipated what was to come from central government, and the approach adopted was strongly influenced by the new right agenda, with a clear 'consumerist' perspective.

The TQM challenge

TQM can be seen as a major and long-term challenge for organisations, with far-reaching implications for management style and organisational culture. It involves an attempt to become customer-driven, with the identification of a chain of internal customers involving all employees in the satisfaction of customer requirements. It thus attempts to move away from bureaucratic and specialist functional views of organisations, and instead emphasises cooperative teamworking and the involvement of employees to pursue continuous improvement.

In most of our cases, developments in quality management involved attempts to shift towards a more open management style, with the empowerment of lower-level staff. As we have seen, at British Steel the aim was to move away from adversarial industrial relations and the aggressive management style of the past in an attempt to move beyond compliance and win employee commitment to continuous improvement. At BuSoc, the aim was to move to a more decentralised structure and to go beyond compliance to administrative rules by encouraging greater personal initiatives and flexibility. This represented a major challenge for the organisation, characterised in the past by a hierarchical, rule-bound bureaucratic structure, with an emphasis on risk avoidance and compliance, and in the event the quality management initiatives met with limited success. Perhaps the most profound challenge appears in the public sector. Here TQM challenges the professional provider-led culture of many public services, ostensibly attempting a shift in the balance of power towards the consumer, with management in many cases seeking to legitimise its actions by reference to the customer or the market. However, attempts to push through such change cannot be taken for granted. The pursuit of 'quality' can be a double-edged sword for management with the potential for employees and their representatives to point out the contradictions of organisational practice. For example, employees may argue that limitations on resources inhibit them from doing a quality job. As Hill (1995: 50) has argued, workers are not 'cultural dopes' and are unlikely to be taken in by rhetoric alone, endorsing TQM only when they are convinced management mean what they say. In this light it is interesting to observe that the TUC has introduced the Quality Work Assured servicemark, which it is issuing to public services that demonstrate their commitment to 'quality staff, providing a quality service in a quality work environment' (TUC, 1992).

TQM and HRM

In this book, we have been particularly concerned with the organisational and HRM implications of quality management initiatives. Given the need for organisational and attitudinal change, people–management issues emerge as central to the implementation of TQM. Indeed, one US study suggests that the main benefits of TQM lie in the 'soft' aspects which the successful implementation of TQM may foster, such as an open organisational culture and employee empowerment, rather than being the direct consequence of particular quality management procedures or techniques (Powell, 1995).

In Chapter 4 we argued that whilst HR issues are central to effective TQM, the TQM literature has provided little guidance in this area, beyond simply stating the need for leadership, education and employee recognition. Deming's work in particular is dismissive of performance management approaches to improvement (for example, performance appraisal and management by objectives). He suggests that we should avoid 'blaming the individual', and instead look to changes in the work system as the means to achieve continuous improvement. However, we questioned whether there was necessarily a choice to be made between these two approaches, and suggested that performance management and a work-systems focus may not necessarily be mutually exclusive. In this vein, a review of the literature on organisational culture suggested that HR policies and practices, job design, management style and the work context in general may all be important in effective change management.

Both British Steel and Richer Sounds utilise pay incentives in the context of a broader quality management strategy. British Steel link the local bonus scheme with delivery to time targets, whilst Richer Sounds adopt a range of incentives linked to service quality, at both the individual and group level. In neither case did management see a contradiction between a performance management approach (pay incentives) and continuous improvement. British Steel managers felt that the bonus was useful in focusing employee attention on the key quality indicators, although the bonus was introduced some time after the launch of TQM, and only once the quality indicator had been sufficiently refined to be acceptable to the trade unions. Management were at pains to point out that there was no question of 'buying' commitment to continuous improvement, the incentive was simply a way of sharing some of the benefits with the workforce. In both companies, the incentives were only one part, and perhaps a subsidiary part, of management's overall approach to quality management. Our view is that any attempt to 'drive' continuous improvement through pay incentives is likely to fail without the necessary organisational changes mentioned above, but that incentives may help to maintain interest and demonstrate management's continuing commitment some years after the initial implementation of TQM.

The centrality of HRM to effective quality management is brought out very clearly in the Superco case study. Front-line staff are critical to customer service and sales, and recruitment, retention and motivation move to centre stage. In the case study, recruitment and selection, induction, training and development, and staff communications were all used to underpin the quality of customer service. This included a strong emphasis on developing managers with the appropriate skills to ensure high-quality customer service. There are tensions in the approach of the food retailers, however, and these are illustrated in the case study. First, there is the question of the appropriate degree of prescription in the customer service training. Many of the more experienced SuperCo front-line staff found the training over-simplistic and even patronising, with a tendency to present too positive an image of the store and with a condescending tone in the prescriptions offered. This may be simply a question of pitching the training material at an appropriate level, itself a difficult task given the diversity of the workforce in terms of age and experience. It may, however, echo a more fundamental tension in the HRM literature between the call for empowerment and individual innovation on the one hand and the requirement for conformance to tight behavioural specifications on the other. While some writers have seen TQM as 'likely to institutionalize participation on a permanent basis' (Hill, 1991a: 541), or empowering (Grant *et al.*, 1994), others have argued that TQM enhances managerial surveillance and control of rank and file employees (Delbridge *et al.*, 1992). A more pragmatic line has been taken by others who have argued that TQM does extend opportunities for participation, albeit mainly in relation to task-based issues (Wilkinson *et al.*, 1992; Rees, 1995). It has also been suggested that while TQM may not involve a major redistribution of power, it ought not to be simply dismissed as trivial and insignificant (Wilkinson *et al.*, 1997b). As Pfeffer suggests, one should be careful to:

> compare programs not to some ideal but to the situation that would exist in their absence. In other words, just because a program doesn't solve every problem or move the organisation all the way, particularly initially to where it wants and needs to be does not mean that it is a failure. A program fails when it produces either no

sustained change or else change that is dysfunctional and ineffective. Some remediation of problems in managing the employment relations is certainly better than none at all. (1994: 206)

Second, the experience of food retailers highlights the unitarist perspective implicit in TQM and the contradictions which this entails. This is seen most clearly in the use of 'mystery shopper'-type surveillance techniques which, whilst a powerful tool for management to impose prescribed norms of customer care behaviour, nevertheless represent a low-trust strategy which risks alienating workers and undermining their genuine commitment to service quality and continuous improvement. This underlines the potential contradiction in approaches which seek to combine elements of the control and commitment strategies to HRM (Walton, 1985), and suggests the need to evaluate quality management from an employee perspective.

The implicit unitarism of TQM means that the customer-defined goals of continuous improvement are asserted as beyond question and the language of labour-management conflict is replaced by that of inter-firm competitive conflict in the market. 'Us' now means our firm; 'them' are our market competitors. On this reading, TQM takes on ideological, even manipulative, overtones, providing strong legitimation for management prerogatives and rendering employee dissent illegitimate. Not surprisingly trade unions may be suspicious of TQM.

In our case studies however, there was little sign of explicit union resistance to quality management, although at British Steel the bonus had to be negotiated with the union, which meant that quality targets could be incorporated only once a clear and reliable measurement system had been established. Also, the term 'Total Quality Performance' had been used in place of 'Total Quality Management', apparently to avoid upsetting the unions with an overly managerialist overtone. In none of our other cases were unions an issue in the implementation of quality management. This may reflect the low level of unionisation of the cases but it is possibly a reflection of the general situation with union influence over management initiatives much reduced since the 1970s.

Does TQM work?

The survey evidence presented in Chapter 5 suggests that quality is often seen as an important contributor to competitive success, but that TQM itself is often difficult to implement successfully. TQM seems often to fail quite early on and the overall findings on its impact are mixed. There is some evidence to suggest that TQM can make a significant contribution to organisational success where it has been fully implemented. Given this uneven pattern, it is important to explore those factors which may impair successful implementation, and our own UK study provided some insights here. Key difficulties encountered in the implementation of TQM included resource limitations, cost constraints, an emphasis on short-term goals, the impact of recession on staff morale, difficulties in the measurement of quality and lack of commitment within the organisation, including top management.

This unevenness was also reflected in our case studies. British Steel claimed success for their TQP programme, attributable in large part to their adoption of a strategic approach linked to competitive strategy and to sustained management commitment, even in the face of a severe recession in the early 1990s. BuSoc, however, was less successful. Here, the quality management initiatives were more *ad hoc* and lacked strategic integration, being seen by branch managers in particular as the latest in a succession of short-term (and indeed short-lived) initiatives. Whilst staff were initially receptive to the quality management initiatives, their enthusiasm soon waned as the award scheme was seen as inequitable and TQM came to be viewed as yet another of a long line of head office initiatives. This is not to say that management must implement TQM and then leave well alone. Consistency and integration are vital, but so is the demonstration of sustained management commitment. Thus, Richer Sounds maintained staff interest by constantly updating its recognition strategy, thus avoiding Watson's (1986) 'paradox of consequences', whereby HR practices left unchanged for long periods may eventually lead to entrenched attitudes and behaviour. The aim is to maintain the momentum and consistently to reaffirm management's commitment to quality and service in the context of a consistent strategy and set of objectives.

Does TQM have universal applicability?

As we have seen, quality management techniques have their origins in the manufacturing sector. However, given that TQM is ultimately about building an organisation-wide commitment to continuous improvement in quality, widely defined to include not only product conformance but also customer service standards, delivery times and so on, it appears also to be relevant to services. Thus, by the mid-1980s, TQM was spreading into most sectors of the economy, and by the end of the decade into the public services. But to what extent is TQM really transferable into services?

The survey evidence examined in Chapter 5 confirms the spread of quality management. By the early 1990s, the use of quality management techniques was still more widespread in manufacturing than in services, but the latter seemed to be catching up. Our case studies in retailing, financial services and local government suggest that quality management strikes a chord with management in these sectors, given the growing pressure to meet customer/client needs more effectively. As we saw in Chapter 3, however, the particular characteristics of services – their intangibility, inseparability, heterogeneity and perishability –

raise a number of issues which differentiate services from manufacturing. In services, the front-line employee is often effectively indistinguishable from the product itself and, in this sense, even relatively junior staff may already be 'empowered' with a level of discretion higher than that found in manufacturing. At Welsh Water, for example, district inspectors are now provided with a cheque book so as to pay compensation to customers immediately rather than waiting for a payment to be issued from the finance department.

The task facing quality management here is to build and maintain employee commitment to meeting customer needs, if necessary by further empowering front-line staff so that they can meet customer requirements more effectively. Not surprisingly, the services sector has tended to focus much more on the customer service aspects of quality, with a strong emphasis on customer care training for front-line staff. However, there are real difficulties in specifying conformance standards for the service encounter, and many customer care programmes seem to have fallen into the trap of offering prescribed behaviour pattern to trainees, which may be seen by staff as patronising and may fail to address the real issue of building commitment and responsiveness to customer needs. This is especially problematic with more complex services, and designers of customer care programmes would do well to think very carefully about the precise nature of the service before adopting programmes 'off the shelf'.

In the public sector, the contrasts with private sector manufacturing are even more marked. Public services are often highly complex, involving considerable professional judgement and discretion. Aside from the difficulties in defining and measuring performance standards, there is the additional issue of the traditional professional autonomy. As we saw in Chapter 6, professional groups may become a focus for resistance to change and resent what they see as 'interference' from management. Private sector management techniques, including those of quality management, risk being seen as 'anti-caring' by certain professional groups, so that the difficulties in winning commitment may be considerable. On top of all this, quality management has become politicised. Whilst politicians of all persuasions seem to be taking on elements of the 'quality' message, there are political differences in the form which this takes (as shown by our distinction between the 'New Right', 'New Left' and 'New Managerialist' views in Chapter 6). In the eyes of many, certain aspects of quality management, and particularly the language of 'markets' and 'customers', have been strongly associated with compulsory competitive tendering and the Conservative's public sector reforms, which are seen as having had more to do with cost control than service quality. This again increases the possibility of resistance from employees, unions and others.

Perhaps even more fundamental is the difficulty in defining who exactly the 'customer' is for such complex public services as planning, economic development and even law and order and social services. The notion of the well-informed, assertive, sovereign customer may simply be inappropriate for many public services. The 'New Right' approach, as reflected in our Modern Metro case study, uses the language and techniques of the private sector, but the 'New Left', whilst accepting the need to empower the users of public services, is more likely to focus on the rights of citizens, the need for public participation and worker involvement. Thus, although there is widespread recognition of the need to improve the quality of public services, 'quality' is itself a 'contested concept' in the public sector.

Overall, quality management and TQM in particular, when viewed as a management philosophy rather than a collection of specific techniques, seem to have something to offer in sectors other than manufacturing, provided that it is implemented in a customised fashion, recognising the distinctive features of the services being provided. Even in the public sector, whilst there is controversy over the extent to which the 'market' allegory is applicable, notions of service quality and continuous improvement have found support across the political spectrum. In our view, the success or failure of quality management initiatives may have more to do with organisation-specific factors, particularly the extent to which initiatives are implemented in a strategic manner with continuing management commitment, than with sectoral factors.

Quality and transformational change: beyond TQM?

Quality management has a strong association with transformational change and quality programmes are often introduced as part of a wider change initiative. Thus, Deming's book *Out of the Crisis* aims at 'the transformation of the style of American management' (1986: ix). The term 'transformation' is increasingly being applied to business strategy, management style, and work organisation. When applied to the latter, it is often linked to notions such as 'the high commitment organisation' (Lawler, 1986); the 'HRM organisation' (Sisson, 1994); the 'high performance work organisation' (Brown, Reich and Stern, 1993); the 'excellent company' (Peters and Waterman, 1982), the 'best practice' organisation (Dertouzos *et al.*, 1989; Shadur *et al.*, 1994), and the 'world class company' (Anderson, 1994). There are many prescriptions on the nature of the 'transformation' required, and a considerable literature has emerged advising managers on how to achieve it.

According to Tuckman the 'central feature of TQM is the idea of culture change grafted onto earlier quality management theory and practices' (1994: 730), and TQM is often a key ingredient in workplace transformation (for example, Lawler *et al.*, 1992; Osterman, 1994). Ford, and Deming's role in its turnaround, are often used to exemplify the importance of transformational culture change as a key element of TQM (Pascale, 1991). With slipping market share and sales, Ford was losing over $1000 on every car sold and Deming's advice as a consultant was sought. According to a senior Ford executive:

I distinctly remember some of Dr Deming's first visits. We wanted to talk about quality, improvement tools, and which programs work. He wanted to talk to us about management, cultural change, and senior managers' vision for the company.(Betti quoted in General Accounting Office, 1990: 15).

Why is there such a strong association between TQM and transformational change? For many companies, TQM was adopted in a period of crisis, as in the Ford example above. It could thus be characterised as 'lifeboat' management, where an increasingly desperate management looks to TQM to deliver a major cultural reorientation and thus to ensure survival. Such periods of crisis are particularly amenable to large scale or transformational change (Schein, 1985). Crisis reduces resistance, sharpens the case for change and elicits extra effort. Often the cost of not changing is perceived as the disposal of businesses, plant closures, downsizing, and job losses.

Some writers, however, have questioned whether TQM is compatible with all forms of large scale organisational change, such as the rapid, radical 'slash and burn' change management which seems to be the current corporate order of the day. Indeed, some writers argue that TQM, with its emphasis on continuous incremental improvement, is unreconcilable with the requirement for radical strategic change that faces many companies (Grant *et al.*, 1994). For some, the emphasis of TQM is on stability and gradual improvement, and thus it may be more suitable for already successful companies wishing to maintain and steadily improve their market positions. It is interesting that British Steel implemented TQM *after* the large scale restructuring and job losses of the early 1980s, and saw it as an attempt to build on the initial corporate turnaround success in the longer term. TQM might even be a barrier to the change required by radical business restructuring, because its incremental nature may be associated with 'comfortable' changes, a little better than last year, rather than with more demanding levels of performance.

Indeed, TQM has come under attack from those offering new panaceas. In particular, business process re-engineering (BPR) proponents have criticised quality initiatives for working within established structures and territories rather than transforming them:

Quality programs work within the framework of a company's existing processes and seek to enhance them by means of what the Japanese call *kaizen*, or continuous incremental improvement. The aim is to do what we already do, only to do it better. Quality improvement seeks steady incremental improvement to process performance. Re-engineering, as we have seen, seeks break-throughs, not by enhancing existing processes, but by discarding them and replacing them with entirely new ones. Re-engineering involves, as well, a different approach to change management from that needed by quality programs. (Hammer and Champy, 1993: 49)

In many respects, the ideas seem to be a familiar echo of many of the ideas of TQM. In particular they have emphasised developing cross-functional approaches to the design and delivery of goods and services. They argue that organisations should 'be broken apart and rebuilt as a process orientated business... where everyone regards working in cross functional teams as the norm... and where everyone knows that the key goal is to produce a service or product that the marketplace perceives to be best' (Johanssen *et al.*, 1993: 7).

It is obvious why such an approach may seem attractive at a time of recession and increasing pressure from shareholders to produce quick results. Indeed, it could be said that TQM in its fullest sense went against the grain for many British firms in its emphasis on cultural transformation, teamwork, new management styles, a degree of bottom-up participation, and a long-term approach. Conversely BPR might be seen as more attractive to senior managers, as it emphasises large projects headed by senior managers producing fast results.

However, the BPR critique is to a large extent based upon a misunderstanding. TQM (in theory at least) is about improving processes both incremental and transformational. The former may in fact often lead to the latter. According to Greene (1995) the 1963 document from Matsushita Electrical Company which won the Deming Prize for best quality, indeed provides evidence of large-scale processing re-engineering within TQM. It is fair to say that many initiatives under the banner of TQM have, in practice, focused more on incremental change as they have been based at shop-floor level, where the more limited scope of jobs and discretion mean it is unlikely for radical change to take place. At higher levels of the organisation, where cross-functional management teams may work, it is more likely to produce change on a larger scale. As Hill (1995) has pointed out, the commonly made distinction between efficiency and effectiveness applies to TQM's dual focus in that it is about doing existing things right but also doing right things. Of course, the reasons why such approaches have less often been taken relates to the difficulties of bringing together managers from different departments and functions, the realities of organisational power and so on.

But, given this, it is by no means apparent why the BPR recipe will work any better than TQM. Indeed, it is interesting to note growing disillusionment with BPR which has itself been criticized for being implemented too narrowly (that is, within functions), for lacking effective leadership from the top and for not being integrated with the wider changes taking place within the organisation (Hall *et al.*, 1993). It could be argued that process re-engineering is less likely to succeed outside TQM because it utilises similar methods and processes but on an *ad hoc* basis, without the training, experience and organisational infrastructure of TQM. Furthermore organisational resistance is more likely in the absence of a TQM culture where planned quality change is seen as the norm (Hill and Wilkinson, 1995: 18–19).

Yet another new approach is the so-called 'stretch management' being applied in US companies such as Boeing (to drive down costs) and 3M (to improve product innovation). Stretch management involves setting demanding objectives for the organisation – the so-called 'stretch' targets. Accounts, reminiscent of TQM's early days, chronicle its success in achieving major performance improvements in areas such as return of investment, product innovation, productivity, capital utilisation (Tully, 1994). A good example is provided by Alcoa, the world's largest aluminium company. Following the appointment of a new chief executive, a large-scale TQM programme was initiated in 1987 and by many standards proved highly successful (Kolesar, 1993). By 1991, however, a new strategy emerged due to the chief executive officer's frustration with the slow pace of TQM. The new strategy demanded intense and focused commitment to 'quantum-leap' rather than continuous improvement management.

Given its recent introduction it is perhaps to early to write off 'stretch management', but its sustainability, when compared to TQM which it purports to replace, must be open to question. Even TQM is not without its stresses and strains for both managers and employees, and critics see it as a form of 'management by stress' (Parker and Slaughter, 1993). However, the potential for early burnout under a regime of stretch management seems unimaginable in comparison. Indeed, the early reports show an especially high casualty rate amongst middle managers, with reports of between a third and a half of managers being unable to cope (Tully, 1994).

TQM: a management flavour of the month?

Amidst all the euphoria about TQM, and latterly about BPR and stretch management, it is not surprising that some writers have warned about the dangers of adopting 'flavour of the month' solutions (Huczynski, 1993a, b; Watson, 1994). Thus TQM is derided as yesterday's solution, no longer on the menu at the consultants cafe (Oliver, 1993). This can be seen as part of the general cycle of fads (Gill and Whittle, 1992; Ramsay, 1996), whereby recipes go through a fairly predictable cycle, from infatuation to disillusionment (Caulkin, 1993; *Economist*, 1994) and having run out of steam, new ones take their place. This fits the world weary view of many observers and academics who claim to have seen it all before (Wilkinson, 1995b: 202–3). The accusation is that innovations such as TQM, BPR, stretch management, as well as management by objectives and organisational development before them, are enticingly presented by consultants to a receptive managerial audience which, driven by panic in the face of emerging competitive threats and/or declining organisational fortunes, is anxious to secure a 'quick fix' solution to its problems. The rapid succession of new ideas in the 1980s and 90s is cited as evidence of an intensification of such a tendency (Pascale, 1991).

Whilst there must be something in the argument that managers are seeking quick and easy solutions to their ever-growing problems, there is an alternative perspective within which to view the so-called 'management fads'. As we saw in the introductory chapter, one analysis suggests that there has been a fundamental restructuring of the competitive environment in recent years, even amounting to a questioning of the mass production and bureaucratic paradigms. The environment is seen to require greater flexibility and customer responsiveness, and staff are expected to show greater commitment, flexibility and concern for quality than hitherto. On this view, it is no coincidence that most of the 'fads' of the 1980s and 90s reflect these common themes, and we may be seeing the development of different approaches to the implementation of the same organisational transformation.

For example, Hammer and Champy, the self-proclaimed originators of BPR, argue that their ideas complement TQM. As they put it:

> Re-engineering and TQM are neither identical nor in conflict; they are complementary. While they share a focus on customers and processes, there are also important differences between them. Re-engineering gets a company where it needs to be fast; TQM moves a company in the same direction, but more slowly. Re-engineering is about dramatic, radical change; TQM involves incremental adjustment. Both have their place. TQM should be used to keep a company's processes tuned up between the periodic process replacements that only re-engineering can accomplish. (1994: 219)

We would question the suggestion that TQM is simply about keeping processes 'tuned up'; the focus on cultural changes, employee empowerment and the development of employee commitment are a refreshing corrective to the exclusively top-down emphasis of many management innovations, BPR included. Indeed, some more recent studies have suggested that the radical approach to BPR is being revised in a more pragmatic fashion (Davenport, 1994). Thus commentators are increasingly questioning the distinctiveness of revisionist BPR and TQM (Valentine and Knights, 1997). For our present purposes, however, the point is simply that the new management ideas need not necessarily be seen as being competitive, save in terms of bookshop shelf space and consultant's fees! Furthermore, there is an alternative interpretation of the reduction in the 'headline hype' concerning TQM organisations. One line of argument suggests that TQM practices have become 'normalised' – part of the normal process of conducting business. Thus an increased emphasis on the customer, a move to flatter organisations with greater cross-functional working, metrics such as cost of quality, and increased employee involvement have become embedded in the fabric of some organisations. Thus, it is not surprising that the high profile of TQM has faded. This can be seen as a sign of success rather than of failure (Greene, 1993). From a practitioner's point of view, labels are not important; what works can be absorbed and the other elements discarded. As Cole suggests 'the best firms learn the most valuable elements in each successive "quality fad" and incorporate each of them into their efforts to bring about the necessary organisational transformation' (1993: 9). Initiatives become domesticated, reflecting the demands and pressures of the organisation and its environment (Wilkinson, 1995b: 202–3). Thus, while the high tide of the TQM movement may have receded, this does not mean that its impact has been negligible or insignificant: it has left its mark on British management.

This is perhaps to end on too optimistic a note. Much of the research evidence suggests that there has been a large gap between the espousal of TQM and what has actually been implemented (Kolesar, 1995). In theory TQM offers or seems to offer, a number of things to improve organisational performance. The theory of TQM emphasises the importance of the workforce and is critical of a purely financial orientation to the organisation, its measures of success and the management of its staff. Gabor's (1990) account of Deming's ideas provides the example of a paint process developed at Ford in 1958 to deal with the rust problem. However, the finance department argued that as rusting occurred outside the warranty period, taking steps to prevent it was not a worthwhile investment to make. Arguably the rise of 'Quality' at Ford has provided the manufacturing section with a tool to take on such a mentality.

Thus, while in theory TQM promises teamwork, empowerment (of a limited kind), customer focus and problem prevention, in reality these ideas are rarely achieved; the concepts are often re-interpreted by managers who are reluctant to give up power and are driven by short-term considerations. The result is often a bastardized form of TQM which, far from offering a route away from Taylorism and the dominance of the finance function (Pfeffer, 1994: 206–20), is in fact coloured by these very forces. Accordingly, TQM is too often implicated within existing ideologies and cultures rather than being used to transform them. In practice, therefore, Partial Quality Management is characteristic of the broader experience of TQM in the UK, and as such its potential benefits have not yet been realised; indeed, given some of our findings, they may never be achieved.

References

Ackroyd, S. and Crowdy, P. (1990) Can culture be managed? Working with 'raw material': the case of the English slaughterman, *Personnel Review*, **19**(5): 3–13.

Adams, R.J. (1988) 'The old industrial relations' and corporate competitiveness: a Canadian case, *Employee Relations*, **10**(2): 3–7.

Adler, P.S. (1993) Time-and-motion regained, *Harvard Business Review*, January/February: 97–108.

Ahlstrand, B. C. (1990) *The Quest for Productivity: A Case Study of Fawley After Flanders*, Cambridge: Cambridge University Press.

Andersen Consulting (1993) *The Lean Enterprise Benchmarking Project Report*, London: Andersen Consulting.

Andersen Consulting (1994) *The Second Lean Enterprise Report*, London: Andersen Consulting.

Anon. (1989) Making people the difference at Abbey National, *Transition*, August: 11–13.

Anthony, P. (1990) The paradox of the management of culture, or 'he who leads is lost', *Personnel Review*, 19(4): 3–8.

Arthur, J. B. (1992) The link between business strategy and industrial relations systems in American Steel Minimills, *Industrial and Labor Relations Review*, **45**(3): 488–506.

Atkinson, J. and Meager, N. (1986) *Changing Working Patterns: How Companies Achieve Flexibility to Match New Needs*, London: National Economic Development Office.

Atkinson, P. (1990) *Creating Cultural Change: The Key to Successful Total Quality Management*, Bedford: IFS.

Aubrey, C. and Felkins, P. (1988) *Teamwork: Involving People in Quality and Productivity Improvements*, Milwaukee, WI: ASQC, Quality Press.

Avis, B. (1990) British Steel: a case of decentralization of collective bargaining, *Human Resource Management Journal*, **1**(1): 90–9.

Bain, T. (1992) *Banking the Furnace. Restructuring of the Steel Industry in Eight Counties*, Michigan, US: Upjohn Institute for Employment Research.

Ball, J. and Proctor, D. (1994) Zero-accident approach at British Steel, Teesside Works, *Total Quality Management*, **5**(3): 97–104.

Balmer, J. and Wilkinson, A. (1991) Building societies: change, strategy and corporate identity, *Journal of General Management*, **17**(2): 20–32.

Bamber, G. (1984) Relations between British Steel and its employees, especially its managerial employees, *Employee Relations*, **6**(1): 3–11.

Bank, J. (1992) *The Essence of Total Quality Management*, Hemel Hempstead: Prentice Hall.

Barlow, G. (1989) Deficiencies and the perpetuation of power; latent functions in management appraisal, *Journal of Management Studies*, **26**(5): 499–517.

Beaumont, P. B. (1992) The US human resource management literature: a review, in Salaman, G. (1992) *op. cit.*

Belohav, J. (1993) Quality, strategy and competitiveness, *California Management Review*, **35**(3): 55–67.

Bennington, J. and Taylor, M. (1992) The renewal of quality in the political process, in Sanderson, I. (ed.) *Management of Quality in Local Government*, Harlow: Longman, pp. 164–86.

Berry, L. L., Zeithaml, V. A. and Parasuraman, A. (1985) Quality counts in services too, *Business Horizons*, May/June: 44–52.

Berry, L. L., Zeithaml, V. A. and Parasuraman, A. (1989) Five imperatives for improving service quality, *Sloan Management Review*, **31**: 89–91.

Binney, G. (1992) *Making Quality Work – Lessons from Europe's Leading Companies*, London: Economist Intelligence Unit.

Birat, J. P. (1987) Manufacture of flat products for the 21st century, *Iron and Steelmaking*, **14**(2): 84–92.

Blackburn, R. and Rosen, B. (1993) Total quality and human resources management: lessons from Baldrige award winning companies, *Academy of Management Executive*, **7**(3): 49–66.

Block, P. (1993) *Stewardship: Choosing Service Over Self-Interest*. San Francisco, CA: Berrett-Kochler.

Blyton, P. (1992) Steel: a classic case of industrial relations change in Britain, *Journal of Management Studies*, **29**: 635–50.

Boje, D.A. (1993) Editorial: post TQM, *Journal of Organisational Change Management*, **6**(4): 4–8.

Bolton Report (1971) Report to the Commission of Inquiry on Small Firms, (chaired by J.E. Bolton) Cmnd 4811. London: HMSO.

Bosner, C. F. (1992) Total quality education, *Public Administration Review*, **52**(5): 504–12.

Boulding, W., Kalra, A., Staelin, R. and Zeithaml, V. A. (1993) A dynamic process model of service quality: from expectations to behavioural intentions, *Journal of Marketing*, **57**, February: 7–27.

Bowen, D. E. and Lawler, E. E. (1992) Total quality-oriented human resources management, *Organizational Dynamics*, **20**(4): 29–41.

Boxall, P. (1992) Strategic human resource management: beginnings of a new theoretical sophistication?, *Human Resource Management Journal*, **2**(3): 60–79.

Brockman, J. (1992) Total quality management: the USA and UK compared, *Public Money and Management*, October–December: 6–9.

Brown, C., Reich, M. and Stern, D. (1993) Becoming a high performance work organi-sation: the role of security, employee involvement and training, *International Journal of Human Resource Management*, **4**(2): 247–75.

Burawoy, M. (1979) *Manufacturing Consent*, Chicago: University of Chicago Press.

Burns, T. and Stalker, G. (1961) *The Management of Innovation*, London: Tavistock.

Butler, A. J. (1992) Developing quality assurance in police services, *Public Money and Management*, January–March: 23–7.

Butler, D. (1991) Steel's big chill, *Management Today*, April, 50–3.

Buzzell, R. and Gale, B. (1987) *The PIMS Principles: Linking Strategy to Performance*, New York: Free Press.

Campbell, J. (1992) *Steel News*, February, (14):1.

Cannell, M. and Wood, S. (1992) *Incentive Pay*, London: IOM.

Cappelli, P. and Rogovsky, N. (1994) New work systems and skill requirements, *International Labour Relations Review*, **133**(2): 205–20.

Carlzon, J. (1987) *Moments of Truth*, Cambridge, MA: Bellinger.

Caudron, S. (1993) Change keeps TQM programs thriving, *Personnel Journal*, October: 104–9.

Caulkin, S. (1993) Leaner, faster, cheaper, *Observer*, 3 October.

Clarke, F. (1992) Quality and service in the public service, *Public Finance and Accountancy*, October: 23–5.

Clarke-Hill, C. and Robinson, T. (1994) Argyll Group plc., in McGoldrick, P. (ed.) *Cases in Retail Management*, London: Longman, pp. 86–105.

Clinton, R. J., Williamson, S. and Bethke, A. L. (1994) Implementing total quality management: the role of human resource management, *Advanced Management Journal*, **59**(2): 10–16.

Cole, R. (1979) *Work, Mobility and Participation*, Berkeley, CA: University of California Press.

Cole, R. (1993) Introduction, special issue total quality management, *Californian Management Review*, **35**(3): 7–11.

Collard, R. (1989) *Total Quality Success Through People*, London: Institute of Personnel Management.

Collard, R. and Dale, B. (1989) Quality circles, in Sisson, K. (ed.) *Personnel Management in Britain*, Oxford: Blackwell, pp. 356–77.

Coyle Shapiro, J. (1995) The impact of a TQM intervention on teamwork: a longitudinal assessment, *Employee Relations*, **17**(3): 63–74.

Cronin, J. J. and Taylor, S. A. (1994) SERVPERF versus SERVQUAL: reconciling performance-based and perception-minus-expectations measurement of service quality, *Journal of Marketing*, **58**, January: 125–31.

Cronshaw, M., Davis, E. and Kay, J. (1994) On being stuck in the middle or good food costs less at Sainsbury's, *British Journal of Management*, **5**: 19–32.

Crosby, P.B. (1979) *Quality is Free: The Art of Making Quality Certain*, New York: Mentor.

Crozier, M. (1964) *The Bureaucratic Phenomenon*, London: Tavistock.

Cruise O'Brien, R. (1995) Employee involvement in performance improvement: a consideration of tacit knowledge, commitment and trust, *Employee Relations*, **17**(3): 110–20.

Cruise O'Brien, R. and Voss, C. (1992) *In Search of Quality*, London Business School Working Paper.

Crump, T. (1992) *The Japanese Numbers Game: Numbers in Modern Japan.* London: Routledge.

Dale, B. (1984) Quality circles in UK manufacturing industry: a state of the art survey, Occasional Paper no. 8402, Manchester School of Management, UMIST.

Dale, B. (1994a) A framework for quality improvement in public sector organizations: a study in Hong Kong, *Public Money and Management,* **14**(2): 55–64.

Dale, B. (1994b) (ed.) *Managing Quality,* 2nd edn, Hemel Hempstead: Prentice Hall.

Dale, B. and Cooper, C. (1992) *Total Quality and Human Resources: An Executive Guide,* Oxford: Blackwell.

Dale, B. G. and Plunkett, J. J. (1990) *Managing Quality,* 1st edn, Herts.: Philip Allan.

Dale, B., van der Wiele, T., Timmers, J. G., Williams, R. and Bertsch, B. (1993) Communal education, *Training for Quality,* **1**(1): 24–8.

Daniel, S. and Reitsberger, W. (1991) Linking quality strategy with management control systems: empirical evidence from Japanese industry, *Accounting, Organisations and Society,* **6**(7): 601–15.

Davenport, T. (1994) Saving IT's soul: human-centred information management, *Harvard Business Review,* March–April: 119–31.

Davies, K. and Hinton, P. (1993) Managing quality in local government and the health service, *Public Money and Management,* January–March: 51–4.

Dawson, P. (1994) *Organizational Change: A Processual Approach,* London: Chapman.

Dawson, P. and Palmer, G. (eds) (1994) *Total Quality Management: Breaking the Myth,* Melbourne: Longman Cheshire.

Dawson, P. and Webb, J. (1989) New production arrangements: the totally flexible cage?, *Work, Employment and Society,* **3**(2): 221–38.

Deal, T. and Kennedy, A. (1992) *Corporate Cultures,* Reading, MA: Addison-Wesley.

Dean, J. and Bowen, D. (1994) Management theory and total quality: improving research and practice through theory development, *Academy of Management Review,* **19**(3): 392–418.

Deblieux, M. (1991) Performance reviews support the quest for quality, *HR Focus,* November: 3–4.

Delbridge, R., Turnbull, P. and Wilkinson, B. (1992) Pushing back the frontiers: management control and work intensification under JIT/TQM factory regimes, *New Technology, Work and Employment,* **7**(2): 97–106.

Deloitte and Touche (1992) *Winning in Global Markets: Surveys of US and Japanese Manufacturing,* New York: Deloitte and Touche Manufacturing Consulting Services.

Deming, W.E. (1982) *Quality, Productivity and Competitive Position,* Centre of Advanced Engineering Study, Cambridge, MA: MIT.

Deming, W.E. (1986) *Out of the Crisis,* Cambridge: Cambridge University Press.

Dertouzos, M., Solow, R, and Lester, R. (1989) *Made in America.* New York: Harper Perennial.

Devanna, M. A., Fombrun, C. J. and Tichy, N. M. (1984) A framework for strategic human resource management, in Fombrun, C. J., Tichy, N. M. and Devanna, M. A. (eds) *Strategic Human Resource Management,* New York: John Wiley & Sons.

Dickson, M. (1991) How Nucor is stealing a march on the big mills, *Financial Times,* 29 May: 12.

Dobson, J. (1981) IR in British Steel: a test of flexibility under stress, *Personnel Management,* September: 48–51.

Docherty, C. (1983) *Steel and Steelworkers: The Sons of Vulcan.* London: Heinemann.

Donaldson, L. (1994) On their best mettle, *Personnel Today*, 22 February: 35.

Donnelly, M., Wiseniewski, M., Dalrymple, J. F. and Curry, A, C. (1995) Measuring service quality in local government: the SERVQUAL Approach, *International Journal of Public Sector Management*, **8**(7): 15–20.

Dopson, S. and Stewart, R. (1990) What is happening to middle management?, *British Journal of Management*, 1(1): 3–16.

Drummond, G. and Ensor, J. (1991) Richer Sounds, European Case Clearing House, Bedford: Cranfield Institute of Technology.

Drummond, H. (1992) *The Quality Movement: What Total Quality Management is Really All About!*, London: Kogan Page.

Drummond, H. and Chell, E. (1992) Should organizations pay for quality?, *Personnel Review*, **21**(4): 3–11.

Du Gay, P. and Salaman, G. (1992) The Cult(ure) of the Customer, *Journal of Management Studies*, **29**(5): 615–33.

Duke, R. (1994) European new entry into UK grocery retailing, *International Journal of Retail and Distribution Management*, **21**(1): 35–9.

Easton, G. (1993) A Baldrige examiner's view of US total quality management, *California Management Review*, **35**(3): 32–54.

Economist (1994) Re-engineering reviewed, 2 July.

Edgett, S. and Parkinson, S. T. (1993) Marketing for service industries: a review, *Service Industries Journal*, **13**(3): 19–39.

Elcock, H. (1993) Local government, in Farnham, D. and Horton, S. (eds) *Managing the New Public Services*. Basingstoke: Macmillan, pp. 150–71.

Ennew, C. and Wright, M. (1990) Building societies in transition: strategy in a new market environment, *Managerial Finance*, **16**(5): 14–24.

Ernst and Young/American Quality Foundation (1992) *International Quality Study: Topline Findings*, New York: Ernst and Young.

Eureka, W. and Ryan, E. (1988) *The Customer Driven Company: Managerial Prospectus on QFD*. American Supplier Institute.

Evans, J. and Lindsay, W. (1993) *The Management and Control of Quality*, Minneapolis: West Publishing.

Feigenbaum, A. V. (1951) *Total Quality Control*, New York: McGraw-Hill.

Feigenbaum, A. V. (1983) *Total Quality Control*, 3rd edn, New York: McGraw-Hill.

Ferner, A. and Colling, T. (1991) Privatization, regulation and industrial relations, *British Journal of Industrial Relations*, **29**(3): 391–409.

Fernie, S., Metcalf, D. and Woodland, S. (1994a) Does HRM boost employee–management relations? Paper presented at BUIRA conference.

Fernie, S., Metcalf, D. and Woodland, S. (1994b) What has HRM achieved in the workplace?, *Economic Policy Institute Economic Report*, **8**(3): May.

Fletcher, C. (1993) *Appraisal: Routes to Improved Performance*, London: Institute of Personnel Management.

Flood, R.L. (1992) *Beyond TQM*, Chichester: John Wiley & Sons.

Foucault, M. (1977) *Discipline and Punish; the Birth of the Prison*, London: Allen Lane.

Fowler, A. (1988) New directions in perfomance pay, *Personnel Management*, November: 30–4.

Fowler, A. (1993) How to use quality management in personnel, *Personnel Management*, October: 29–30.

Fox, A. (1974) *Beyond Contract; Work, Trust and Power Relations,* London: Faber & Faber.

Franz, H.W. (1991) Quality strategies and workforce strategies in the open iron and steel industry, in Blyton, P. and Morris, J. *A Flexible Future? Prospects for Employment and Organization.* Berlin: Walter de Gruyter.

Freathy, P. and Sparks, L. (1994) Contemporary developments in employee relations in food retailing, *The Service Industries Journal,* **14**(4): 499–514.

Fuller, L. and Smith, V. (1991) Consumers' reports: management by customers in a changing economy, *Work, Employment and Society,* **5**(1): 1–16.

Gabor, A. (1990) *The Man Who Invented Quality,* Harmondsworth: Penguin.

Garvin, D. (1988) *Managing Quality,* New York: Free Press.

Garvin, D. (1991) How the Baldrige Award really works, *Harvard Business Review,* November/December: 80–93, and *Debate* January/February 1992: 126–47.

Gaster, L (1992) Quality in service delivery: competition for resources or more effective use of resources?, *Local Government Policy Making,* **19**(1): 55–64.

Geary, J. F. (1993) Total quality management: a new form of labour management in Great Britain?, in Ambrosini, M. and Saba, L. (ed.) *Participation and Involvement in Great Britain,* Milan: Franco Anglei.

General Accounting Office (1990) *Quality Management: Scoping Study,* Washington: United States General Accounting Office.

Giles, E. and Williams, R. (1991) Can the personnel department survive quality management?, *Personnel Management,* April: 28–33.

Gill, J. and Whittle, S. (1992) Management by panacea: accounting for transience, *Journal of Management Studies,* **30**(2): 281–95.

Glover, J. (1993) Achieving the organizational change necessary for successful TQM, *International Journal of Quality and Reliability Management,* **10**(6): 47–64.

Goldstein, S. (1988) Organisational dualism and quality circles, *Academy of Management Review,* **10**(3): 504–17.

Grant, R. M., Shani, R. and Krishnan, R. (1994) TQM's challenge to management theory and practice, *Sloan Management Review,* Winter: 25–35.

Green Bits (1995) Commitment to the environment, *Green Bits,* Summer (20): 14–15.

Greene, R. (1993) *Global Quality,* Milwaukee, MI: ASQC, Quality Press.

Greene, R. (1995) *Emergent Re-Engineering: From Design to Emergent Forms of Work,* New York: Addison Wesley.

Gregory, A. (1991) Patterns of working hours in large scale grocery retailing in Britain and France: convergence after 1992?, *Work, Employment and Society,* **5**(4): 497–514.

Griffin, R. (1988) Consequences of quality circles in an industrial setting, *Academy of Management Journal,* **31**: 338–58.

Gronroos, C. (1983) *Strategic Management and Marketing in the Service Sector,* Cambridge, MA: Marketing Science Institute.

Guest, D. (1987) Human resource management and industrial relations, *Journal of Management Studies,* **24**(5): 503–21.

Guest, D. (1989) Human resource management and its implications for industrial relations, in Storey, J. (ed.) *op. cit.:* 41–55.

Guest, D. (1992a) Human resource management in the UK, in Towers, B. (ed.) *A Handbook of Human Resource Management,* Oxford: Blackwell, pp. 3–26.

Guest, D. (1992b) Employee commitment and control, in Hartley, J. and Stephenson, G. (eds) *Employment Relations,* Oxford: Blackwell, pp. 111–35.

Guy, C. (1994) Grocery store saturation: has it arrived yet?, *International Journal of Retail and Distribution Management*, **22** (1): 3–11.

Hackman, R. and Wageman, R. (1995) Total quality management: empirical, conceptual and practical issues, *Administrative Science Quarterly*, **40**, June: 317–42.

Hall, G., Rosenthal, J. and Wade, J. (1993) How to make re-engineering really work, *Harvard Business Review*, November/December: 119–31.

Hammer, M. and Champy, J. (1993) *Re-engineering the Corporation*, London: Nicholas Brearley.

Hammer, M. and Champy, J. (1994) *Re-engineering the Corporation: A Manifesto for a Business Revolution*, New York: Harper Business.

Hammons, C. and Maddux, G. (1990) Total quality management in the public sector, *Management Decision*, **28**(4): 15–19.

Harkin, G. (1994) Some thoughts on competition, *Local Government Management*, **1**(9): 10–11.

Hart, C. and Bogan, C. (1992) *The Baldrige: What it is, How it's Won, and How to Use it to Improve Quality in Your Company*, New York: McGraw-Hill.

Hart, C. and Schlesinger, L. (1991) Total quality management and the human resource professional: applying the Baldrige Framework to human resources, *Human Resource Management*, **30**(4): 433–54.

Hartley, J., Kelly, J. and Nicholson, N. (1983) *Steel Strike,* London: Batsford.

Hasell, N. (1994) Britain's most admired companies, *Management Today*, December: 40–9.

Heery, E. (1993) Industrial relations and the customer, *Industrial Relations Journal*, **24**(4): 284–95.

Heller, R. (1995) British Steel rolls ahead, *Management Today*, June: 40–9.

Hiam, A. (1993) *Does Quality Work? A Review of Relevant Studies,* New York: The Conference Board.

Hill, S. (1991a) Why quality circles failed but total quality might succeed, *British Journal of Industrial Relations*, **29**(4): 541–69.

Hill, S. (1991b) How do you manage a flexible firm? The total quality model, *Work, Employment and Society*, **5**(3): 397–415.

Hill, S. (1992) People and quality, in Bradley, K. (ed.) *Human Resource Management: People and Performance*, Aldershot: Dartmouth.

Hill, S. (1995) From quality circles to total quality management, in Wilkinson, A. and Willmott, H. (eds) *op. cit.*: 33–53.

Hill, S. and Wilkinson, A. (1995) In search of TQM, *Employee Relations*, **17**(3): 8–25.

Hochschild, A. (1983) *The Managed Heart: The Commercialisation of Human Feeling,* California: University of California Press.

Hopfl, H., Smith, S. and Spence, S. (1992) Values and valuations: corporate culture and job cuts, *Personnel Review*, **21**(1): 24–38.

Huczynski, A. (1993a) *Management Gurus*, London: Macmillan.

Huczynski, A. (1993b) Explaining the succession of management fads, *International Journal of Human Resource Management*, **4**: 443–63.

Iles, P. (1993) Achieving strategic coherence through competence based management and organisation development, *Personnel Review*, **22**(6): 63–80.

Imai, M. (1986) *Kaizen, The Key to Japan's Competitive Success,* London: McGraw-Hill.

Incomes Data Services (1991) Bonus Schemes Part II. Incomes Data Service Study no. 492, October.

Incomes Data Services (1994) *Quality in Practice*. Incomes Data Service Study no. 563, October.

Industrial Relations Review and Report (1991) *The State of Selection*, 24 May.

Industrial Relations Review and Report (1993) Employee involvement: the current state of play, *IRS Employment Trends*, 545(October): 3–11.

Industrial Relations Service (1990) Decentralised bargaining at British Steel, *IRS Employment Trends*, **474**: 11–15.

Industrial Relations Service (1994) Total quality in local government, Braintree District Council, *IRS Employment Trends*, **563:** 13–16.

Ingham, H. and Wong, P. (1994) Corporate control in the UK building society sector: an examination of failed mergers, *Services Industries Journal*, **14**(3): 352–68.

Institute of Personnel Management (1993) *Quality: People Management Matters*, London: Institute of Personnel Management.

Ishikawa, K. (1985) *What is Total Quality Control? The Japanese Way*, Englewood Cliffs, NJ: Prentice Hall.

Jackson, M., Leopold, J. and Tuck, K. (1992) Decentralisation of collective bargaining; the case of the retail food industry, *Human Resource Management Journal*, **2**(2): 29–45.

James, G. (1991) *Quality of Working Life and Total Quality Management*, Work Research Unit Occasional Paper No 50, November.

Jamieson, P. and Proctor, D. (1990) Total quality is no accident, *Health and Safety Practitioner*, August: 25–9.

Jenkins, S., Noon, M. and Martinez-Lucio, M. (1995) Negotiating quality: the case of TQM in Royal Mail, *Employee Relations*, **17**(3): 87–98.

Johannsson, H., McHugh, P., Pendlebury, A. and Wheeler, W. (1993) *Business Process Re-Engineering*, London: John Wiley & Sons.

Johnson, G. and Scholes, K. (1993) *Exploring Corporate Strategy: Texts and Cases*, 3rd edn, London: Prentice Hall.

Juran, J. M. (1951) *Quality Control Handbook*, New York: McGraw-Hill.

Juran, J. M. (1964) *Managerial Breakthrough*, New York: McGraw-Hill.

Juran, J. M. (1974) Basic concepts, in Juran, J. M., Gryna, F. M. and Bingham, R. S. (eds) *Quality Control Handbook*, 3rd edn, London: McGraw-Hill.

Juran, J. M. (1989) *Juran on Leadership for Quality*, New York: Free Press.

Juran, J.M. (1993) Made in the USA: a renaissance of quality, *Harvard Business Review*, July/August: 42–50.

Kano, N. (1993) A perspective on quality activities in American firms, *California Management Review*, **35**(3): 12–31.

Kanter, R. M. (1989) *When Giants Learn to Dance*, New York: Simon & Schuster.

Kanter, R. M. (1992) The future of bureaucracy and hierarchy in organizational theory: a report from the field, in Bourdieu, P. and Coleman, J. (eds) *Social Theory for a Changing Society*, Boulder: Westview Press, pp. 63–87.

Kearney, A. T. in association with *TQM magazine* (1992) *Total Quality: Time to Take Off The Rose Tinted Spectacles*, a report, Kempston: IFS Publications.

Kelliher, C. and McKenna, S. (1988) The employment implications of government policy: a case study of public sector catering, *Employee Relations*, **10**(2): 8–13.

Kelly, J. (1983) Management strategy and the reform of collective bargaining: cases from the British Steel Corporation, *British Journal of Industrial Relations*, **22**(2): 135–53.

Kessler, I. (1995) Reward systems in J. Storey (ed.) *Human Resource Management: A Critical Text*, London: Routledge.

Kirkpatrick, I. and Martinez-Lucio, M. (1995) *The Politics of Quality: the Management of Change in the Public Sector*, London: Routledge.

Knutton, P. (1994) A model approach to self-assessment, *Works Management*, December: 12–16.

Kochan, T. and Dyer, L. (1993) Managing transformational change: the role of human resource professionals, *International Journal of Human Resource Management*, **4**: 569–90.

Kohn, A. (1993) Why incentive plans cannot work, *Harvard Business Review*, September/October: 54–63.

Kolesar, P. (1993) Vision, values and milestones. Paul O'Neill starts Total Quality at Alcoa, *Californian Management Review*, **35**(3): 133–65.

Kolesar, P. (1995) Partial quality management: an essay, *Production and Operations Management*, **4**(3): 195–200.

Kordupleski, R. E., Rust, R. T. and Zarhorik, A. J. (1993) Why improving quality doesn't improve quality (or whatever happened to marketing), *California Management Review*, **35**(3): 82–95.

Krause, T. and Finley, R.M. (1993) Safety and continuous improvement. Two sides of the same coin, *The Health and Safety Practitioner*, September 19–22.

Lawler, E.E. III (1986) *High-involvement Management*, San Fransisco: Jossey-Bass.

Lawler, E.E. III (1992) *Pay Systems that Support Quality*, Centre for Effective Organisations: University of Southern California.

Lawler, E. E. III (1993) Debate, *Harvard Business Review*, May/June: 32.

Lawler, E. E. III, Mohrman, S., Albers, S. and Ledford, J. Jr (1992) *Employee Involvement and Total Quality Management: Practice and Results in Fortune 1000 Companies*, San Francisco: Jossey-Bass.

Legge, K. (1994) *Human Resource Management: Rhetorics and Realities*, London: Macmillan.

Levitt, T. (1960) Marketing myopia, *Harvard Business Review*, **38**(3): 45–56.

Lewis, B. (ed.) (1990) Customer service and service quality, special issue of *Marketing Intelligence and Planning*, **8**(6).

Lewis, B. (1993) Service quality measurement, *Marketing Intelligence and Planning*, **11**(4): 4–12.

Lillrank, P. and Kano, N. (1989) *Continuous Improvement: Quality Control Circles in Japanese Industry*, Ann Arbor, MI: Centre for Japanese Studies, University of Michigan.

McArdle, L., Rowlinson, M., Proctor, S. *et al.* (1995a) Employee empowerment or the enhancement of exploitation, in Wilkinson, A. and Willmott, H. (eds) *op. cit.*: 156–72.

McGoldrick, P. and Greenland, S. (1992) Competition between banks and building societies in the retailing of financial services, *British Journal of Management*, September **3**(3): 169–79.

McKinlay, A. and Starkey, K. (1992) Competitive strategies and organizational change, in Salaman, G. *op. cit.*

Macey, R. and Wells, D. (1987) New legislation accelerates change in building society culture, *Management Accounting*, July/August: 34–6.

Madu, C. N. and Kuei, C. (1993) Introducing strategic quality management, *Long Range Planning*, **26**(6): 121–31.

Main, J. (1994) *The Quality Wars: The Triumphs and Defeats of American Business*, New York: Free Press.

Malloch, H (1991) Strategic management and the decision to subcontract, in Blyton, P. and Morris, J. (eds) *A Flexible Future? Prospects for Employment and Organization*, Berlin: Walter de Gruyter.

Marchington, M. (1982) *Managing Industrial Relations*, Maidenhead: McGraw-Hill.

Marchington, M. (1992) Managing labour relations in a competitive environment, in Sturdy, A., Knights, D. and Willmott, H. (eds) *Skill and Consent in the Labour Process*, London: Routledge, pp. 149–84.

Marchington, M. (1993) Close to the customer: employee relations in food retailing, in Legge, K., Clegg, C. and Gowler, D. (eds) *Case Studies in Organisation Behaviour and Human Resource Management*, London: Paul Chapman, pp. 234–43.

Marchington, M. (1995) Fairy tales and magic wands: new employment practices in perspective, *Employee Relations*, **17**(1): 51–66.

Marchington, M. (1996) Shopping down different aisles: a review of the literature on HRM in food retailing, *Journal of Retailing and Consumer Services*, **3**(1): 21–32.

Marchington, M. and Harrison, E. (1991) Customers, competitors and choice: employee relations in food retailing, *Industrial Relations Journal*, **22**(4): 286–300.

Marchington M., Wilkinson, A. and Dale, B. (1993b) Quality and the human resource dimension: the case study section, *Quality, People Management Matters*: London: Institute of Personnel Management: 23–64.

Marchington, M., Goodman, J., Wilkinson, A. and Ackers, P. (1992) New Developments in Employee Involvement, Employment Department Research Paper No. 2.

Marchington, M., Wilkinson, A., Ackers, P. and Goodman, J. (1993a) The influence of managerial relations on waves of employee involvement, *British Journal of Industrial Relations*, **31**(4): 553–76.

Mars, G. (1982) *Cheats at Work*, Harmondsworth: Penguin.

Meyerson, D. and Martin, J. (1987) Cultural change: an integration of three different views, *Journal of Management Studies*, **24**(6): 623–47.

Miller, C. (1992) TQM value criticised in new report, *American Marketing Association Journal*, 9 November: 16.

Millward, N., Stevens, N., Smart, D. and Hawes, W. (1992) *Workplace Industrial Relations in Transition*. Dartmouth: Aldershot.

Mintel Retail Intelligence (1995) *Food Retailing*, London: Mintel Intelligence Group.

Mintzberg, H. (1978) Crafting strategy, *Harvard Business Review*, **65**(4): 65–75.

Mohrman, S., Tenkasi, R., Lawler, E. E. III and Ledford J. Jnr (1995) Total quality management: practices and outcomes in the largest USA firms, *Employee Relations*, **17**(3): 26–41.

Moores, B. (1990) The service excellence experience, *Marketing Intelligence and Planning*, **8**(6): 18–24.

Morgan, C. and Murgatroyd, S. (1994) *Total Quality Management in the Public Sector*, Buckingham: Open University Press.

Morgan, J. and Everett, T. (1991) Introducing quality management in the NHS, *International Journal of Healthcare and Quality Assurance*, **3**(5): 23–36.

Morris, J., Blyton, P., Bacon, N. and Franz, H-W. (1992) Beyond survival: the implementation of new forms of work organization in the UK and German steel industries, *International Journal of Human Resource Management*, 3: 307–29.

Mumford, J. and Buley, T. (1988) Rewarding behavioural skills as part of performance. *Personnel Management*, December: 33–7.

Munro, R. (1995) Governing the new province of quality: autonomy and accountability, in Wilkinson, A. and Willmott, H. (eds) *op. cit.* 1995a: 127–55.

Murphy, T. (1988) Changing corporate culture, *Industrial Participation*, Summer: 3–8.

Nellis, J. and Litt, H. (1990) *The Challenge of Change in Building Societies: A Survey of Branch Managers' Views*, Cranfield: Cranfield Press.

Niven, D. and commentators (1993) When times get tough what happens to TQM?, *Harvard Business Review*, May/June: 20–37.

Oakland, J.S. (1989) *Total Quality Management*, London: Butterworth-Heinemann.

Oakland, J. S. (1993) *Total Quality Management: The Route to Improving Performance*, 2nd edn, London: Butterworth–Heinemann.

Ogbonna, E. (1992/93) Managing organisational culture: fantasy or reality?, *Human Resource Management Journal*, 3(2): 42–54.

Ogbonna, E. and Wilkinson, B. (1988) Corporate strategy and corporate culture: the management of change in the UK supermarket industry, *Personnel Review*, 17(6): 10–14.

Ogbonna, E. and Wilkinson, B. (1990) Corporate strategy and corporate culture: the view from the checkout, *Personnel Review*, 19(4): 9–15.

Olian, J. and Rynes, S. (1991) Making total quality work: aligning organisational processes, performance measures and stakeholders, *Human Resource Management*, 30(3): 303–33.

Oliver, J. (1993) Shocking to the core, *Management Today*, August: 18–23.

Oliver, N. (1990) Employee commitment and total quality control, *International Journal of Quality and Reliability Management*, 7(1): 21–9.

Oliver, N., Delbridge, R. and Lowe, J. (1996) Lean production practices: international comparisons in the auto components industry, *British Journal of Management*, 7: 529–44.

Oliver, N., Delbridge, R., Jones, D. and Lowe, J. (1994) World class manufacturing: further evidence in the lean production debate. *British Journal of Management*, 5: 53–63.

Osterman, P. (1994) How common is workplace transformation and who adopts it?, *Industrial and Labour Relations Review*, 47(2): 173–88.

Oswald, S., Scott, C. and Woerner, W. (1991) Strategic management of human resources: the American Steel and Wire Company, *Business Horizons*, May–June: 77–82.

Ouchi, W. (1981) *Theory Z. How American Business Can Meet The Japanese Challenge*, Reading, MA: Addison Wesley.

Overman, S. (1994) No-frills HR at Nucor, *Human Resource Magazine*, July: 56–60.

Paddon, M. (1992) Quality in an enabling context, in Sanderson, I. (ed.) *op. cit.*: 66–92.

Painter, J. (1991) Compulsory competitive tendering; the first round, *Public Administration*, 69: 191–210.

Parasuraman, A., Zeithaml, V. A. and Berry, L. L. (1985) A conceptual model of service quality and its implications for further research, *Journal of Marketing*, 49: 41–50.

Parker, M. and Slaughter, J. (1993) Should the labour movement buy TQM?, *Journal of Organisational Change Management*, 6(4): 43–56.

Pascale, R. (1991) *Managing on the Edge*, Harmondsworth: Penguin.

Pascale, R. and Athos, A. (1982) *The Art of Japanese Management*, London: Allan Lane.

Pendleton, A. (1995) The emergence and use of quality in British Rail, in Kirkpatrick, I. and Martinez-Lucio, M. (eds) *op. cit.*, pp. 213–32.

Peters, T. (1989) *Thriving on Chaos*, London: Pan.

Peters, T. and Waterman, R. (1982) *In Search of Excellence*. Harper & Row: New York.

Pettigrew, A. M. (1985) *The Awakening Giant. Continuity and Change at ICI*. Oxford: Blackwell.

Pfeffer, J. (1994) *Competitive Advantage Through People*, New York: Free Press.

Pfeffer, N. and Coote, A. (1991) *Is Quality Good for You?* London: Institute of Public Policy Research.

Phillips, L., Chang, D. and Buzzell, R. (1983) Product quality, cost position and business performance: a test of some key hypotheses, *Journal of Marketing*, **47**: 26–43.

Pickard, J. (1992) TQM in the public sector, *Personnel Management Plus*, **3**(8): 20–1.

Piore, M. J. and Sabel, C. (1984) *The Second Industrial Divide*, New York: Basic Books.

Pollitt, C. (1990) Doing business in the temple? Managers and quality assurance in the public services, *Public Administration*, **68**: 435–52.

Pollitt, C. (1993) *Managerialism and the Public Services*, Blackwell: Oxford.

Porter, M. (1980) *Competitive Strategy*, New York: Free Press.

Porter, M. (1985) *Competitive Advantage*, New York: Free Press.

Porter, L. and Smith, G. (1993) Total quality management in the UK retail sector, *International Journal of Retail and Distribution Management*, **21**(4): 13–19.

Powell, T.C. (1995) Total quality management as competitive advantage: a review and empirical study, *Strategic Management Journal*, **16**(1): 15–37.

Preece, D. and Wood, D. (1995) Quality management: who is using the sums and for what purpose? *Human Resource Management Journal*, **5**(3): 41–55.

Price, M. and Eva Chen, E. (1993) TQM in a small high technology firm, *California Management Review*, **35**(3): 96–117.

Procter, D. (1990) If you can spare them – I don't want them, *Total Quality Management*, **1**(2): 269–74.

Procter, D. (1992) Training for total quality: British Steel shows the way, in Hand, M. and Plowman, B. *Quality Management Handbook*, London: Butterworth-Heinemann.

Procter, D., Young, M. and Howlett, V. (1990) Training for total quality performance: the experience of British Steel, *Total Quality Management*, **1**(3): 319–26.

Purcell, J. (1989) The impact of corporate strategy on human resource management, in Storey, J. (ed.) *New Perspectives on Human Resource Management*, London: Routledge.

Purcell, J. and Ahlstrand, B (1994) *Human Resource Management in the Multi-divisional Company*, Oxford: Oxford University Press.

Rafaelli, A. (1989) When cashiers meet customers: an analysis of the role of supermarket cashiers, *Academy of Management Journal*, **32**(2): 245–73.

Raffio, T. (1992) Quality and the Delta Dental Plan of Massachusetts, *Sloan Management Review*, **34**(1): 101–10.

Rainnie, S. (1989) *Industrial Relations in Small Firms*, London: Routledge.

Rajan, A. (1987) *Services – the Second Industrial Revolution: Business and Jobs Outlook in the UK Growth Industries*, London: Butterworth.

Ramsay, H. (1996) Managing sceptically: a critique of organisational fashion, in Clegg, S. and Palmer, G. (eds) *The Politics of Management Knowledge*, London: Sage, pp. 155–72.

Redman, T. and Snape, E. (1992) Upward and onward: can staff appraise their managers?, *Personnel Review*, 21(7): 32–46.

Redman, T., Snape, E. and Wilkinson, A. (1996) The long haul: sustaining TQM at British Steel Teesside works, *International Journal of Manpower*, 17(2): 34–51.

Redman T., Wilkinson, A. and Snape, E. (1997) Stuck in the middle? Managers in a Building Society, *Work, Employment and Society*, 11(1): 101–14.

Rees, C. (1995) Quality management and HRM in the service industry: some case study evidence, *Employee Relations* 17(3): 99–109.

Reeves, C. and Bednar, D. (1994) Defining quality: alternatives and implications, *Academy of Management Review*, 19(3): 419–45.

Regan, W. (1963) The service revolution, *Journal of Marketing*, 27(3): 247–53.

Reichheld, F. F. and Sasser, W. E. (1990) Zero defections: quality comes to services, *Harvard Business Review*, September/October: 105–11.

Ritchie, J. (1993) Strategies for human resource management: challenges in smaller and entrepreneurial organizations in Harrison, R. (ed.) *Human Resource Management*, New York: Addison-Wesley.

Roberts, I., Sawbridge, D. and Bamber, G. (1992) Employee relations in small firms, in Towers, B. (ed.) *A Handbook of Industrial Relations Practice*, London: Kogan Page.

Robinson, O. (1990) Employment policies in the service sector: training in retail distribution, *Service Industries Journal*, 10(2): 284–305.

Robinson, O. (1993) Employment in services: perspectives on part–time employment growth in North America, *Service Industries Journal*, 10(2): 284–305.

Ross, T. and Hatcher, L. (1992) Gainsharing drives quality improvement. *Personnel Journal*, November: 81–9.

Sabel, C. (1992) Moebius-strip organizations and open labour markets, in Bourdieu, P. and Coleman, J. (eds) *Social Theory for a Changing Society*, Boulder: Westview Press, pp. 23–54.

Sackman, S. (1991) *Cultural Knowledge in Organizations: Exploring the Collective Mind*, California: Sage.

Salaman, G. (ed.) (1992) *Human Resource Strategies*, London: Sage.

Sanderson, I. (ed.) (1992a) *Management of Quality in Local Government*, Harlow: Longman.

Sanderson, I. (1992b) Introduction: the context of quality in local government, in Sanderson (ed.) *op. cit.*: 1–15.

Sanderson, I. (1992c) Defining quality in local government, in Sanderson (ed.) *op. cit.*: 16–41.

Scase, R. and Goffee, R. (1989) *Reluctant Managers*, London: Unwin.

Schein, E. H. (1985) *Organisational Culture and Leadership: A Dynamic View*, San Francisco: Jossey-Bass.

Schilit, W. (1994) The case against quality, *Business Horizons*, November/December: 27–34.

Schmidt, R., Segal, R. and Cartwright, C. (1994) Two-stop shopping or polarisation; whither UK grocery shopping?, *International Journal of Retail and Distribution Management*, 22(1): 12–19.

Schneider, B. (1980) The service organisation: climate is crucial, *Organisational Dynamics*, **8**, Autumn: 52–65.

Schneider, B. and Bowen, D. (1993) The service organisation: human resources management is crucial, *Organisational Dynamics*, **21**, Spring: 39–52.

Scholey, R. (1991) *British Steel and the Environment*, pamphlet, London: British Steel.

Schonberger, R. (1986) *World Class Manufacturing*, New York: Free Press.

Schonberger, R. (1990) *Building a Chain of Customers*, London: Hutchinson.

Schuler, R. S. and Harris, D. (1992) *Managing Quality: The Primer for Middle Managers*, New York: Addison-Wesley.

Schuler, R. S. and Jackson, S. E. (1987) Linking competitive strategies with human resource management practices, *Academy of Management Executive*, **1**(3): 207–19.

Scott, M., Roberts, I., Holroyd, G. and Sawbridge, D. (1989) Management and industrial relations in small firms, Employment Department Research Paper No. 70.

Seddon, J. (1990) A successful attitude, *TQM Magazine*, January: 181–4.

Sellers, P. (1990) What customers really want, *Fortune*, 4 June: 62–70.

Sensenbrenner, J. (1991) Quality comes to city hall, *Harvard Business Review*, March/April: 64–75.

Sewell, G. and Wilkinson, B. (1992a) Empowerment or emasculation?: shopfloor surveillance in a total quality organization, in Blyton, P. and Turnbull, P. (eds) *Reassessing Human Resource Management*, London: Sage, pp. 97–115.

Sewell, G. and Wilkinson, B. (1992b) Someone to watch over me: surveillance, discipline and the just-in-time labour process, *Sociology*, **26**(2): 271–90.

Shadur, M., Rodwell, J., Simmons, D. and Bamber, G. (1994) International best practice, quality management and high performance: inferences from the Australian automotive sector, *International Journal of Human Resource Management*, **5**(3): 603–31.

Shamir, B. (1980) Between service and servility: role conflict in subordinate service roles, *Human Relations*, **33**(6): 741–56.

Shewart, W.A. (1931) *Economic Control of Quality of Manufactured Products*, New York: Van Nostrand.

Siehl, C. and Bowen, D. E. (1991) The role and rites of integration in service delivery, *International Journal of Service Industry Management*, **2**(1): 15–34.

Simmons, D., Shadur, M. and Preston, A. (1995) Integrating TQM and HRM, *Employee Relations*, **17**(3): 75–86.

Sisson, K. (ed.) (1994) *Personnel Management in Britain*, 2nd edn, Oxford: Blackwell.

Skelcher, C. (1992) Improving the quality of local public services, *Service Industries Journal*, **12**(4): 463–77.

Smirich, L. (1983) Concepts of culture and organizational analysis, *Administrative Science Quarterly*, **28**(3): 203–20.

Smith, A. (1993) Leeds and N&P call off merger proposal, *Financial Times*, 27 October: 1.

Smith, D. (1986) Organisational culture and management development in building societies, *Personnel Review*, **15**(3): 15–19.

Smith, S. (1988) How much change at the store? The impact of new technologies and labour processes on managers and staff in retail distribution, in Knights, D. and Willmott, H. (eds) *New Technology and the Labour Process*, London: Macmillan, pp. 143–62.

Snape, E., Redman, T. and Bamber, G. J. (1994) *Managing Managers: Strategies and Techniques for Human Resource Management*, Oxford: Blackwell.

Snape, E., Redman, T. and Wilkinson, A. (1993) Human resource management in building societies: making the transformation, *Human Resource Management Journal,* **3**(3): 43–60.

Snape, E., Wilkinson, A. and Redman, T. (1996) Cashing in on quality? Pay incentives and the quality culture, *Human Resource Management Journal,* **6**(4): 5–17.

Snape, E., Wilkinson, A., Marchington, M. and Redman, T. (1995) Managing human resources for TQM: possibilities and pitfalls, *Employee Relations,* **17**(3): 42–51.

Sonnenfeld, J. A., Peiperl, N. A. and Kotter, J. P. (1992) Strategic determinants of managerial labour markets, in Salaman, G. *op. cit.*

Sparks, L. (1987) Employment in retailing: trends and issues, in Johnson, G. (ed.) *Business Strategy in Retailing,* Chichester: John Wiley and Sons, pp. 239–55.

Sparks, L. (1992a) Restructuring retail employment, *International Journal of Retail and Distribution Management,* **20**(3): 12–19.

Sparks, L. (1992b) Customer service in retailing: the next leap forward?, *The Service Industries Journal,* **12**(2): 165–84.

Speed, R. (1990) Building societies: new strategies for a competitive era, *Service Industries Journal,* **10**(1): 110–23.

Steingard, D. S. and Fitzgibbons, D. E. (1993) A postmodern deconstruction of total quality management, *Journal of Organizational Change Management,* **6**(5): 27–42.

Stevens, M. (1992) Workplace Industrial Relations Survey (Computer File) ESRC Data Archive.

Stewart, J. (1988) *Understanding the Management of Local Government,* Harlow: Longman.

Stewart, J. and Clarke, M. (1987) The public service orientation; issues and dilemmas, *Public Administration,* **65**: 161–77.

Storey, J. (ed.) (1989) *New Perspectives on Human Resource Management,* London: Routledge.

Storey, J. (1992) *Developments in the Management of Human Resources,* Oxford: Blackwell.

Storey, J. (1993) The take-up of human resource management by mainstream companies: key lessons from research, *International Journal of Human Resource Management,* **4**: 529–53.

Storey, J. and Fenwick, N. (1990) The changing face of employment management in local government, *Journal of General Management,* **16**(1): 14–30.

Storey, J. and Sisson, K. (1993) *Managing Human Resources and Industrial Relations,* Buckingham: Open University Press.

Swiss, J. E. (1992) Adapting total quality management to government, *Public Administration Review,* **52**(4): 356–62.

Tansik, D. (1990) Managing human resource issues for high-contact service personnel, in Bowen, D., Chase, R. and Cummings, T. (eds) *Service Management Effectiveness,* San Francisco: Jossey-Bass, pp. 152–76.

Teas, R. K. (1993) Expectations, performance evaluation and consumers perceptions of quality!, *Journal of Marketing,* **57**, October: 18–34.

Terry, F. R. (1994) Editorial, *Public Money and Management,* **14**(2): 3–4.

Thompson, W. (1992a) Local experience of managing quality, in Sanderson, I. (ed.) *op. cit.*: 187–213.

Thwaites, D. (1989) The impact of environmental change on the evolution of the UK building society industry, *The Service Industries Journal,* **9**(1): 40–60.

Thwaites, D. and Edgett, S. (1991) Aspects of innovation in a turbulent market environment: empirical evidence from UK building societies, *The Service Industries Journal,* **11**(3): 346–61.

Thwaites, D. and Lynch, J. (1992) Adoption of the marketing concept in UK building societies, *The Service Industries Journal,* **12**(4): 437–62.

Trades Union Congress (1992) *The Quality Challenge: Quality in Public Services,* London: TUC.

Tuckman, A. (1994) The yellow brick road: total quality management and the restructuring of organisational culture, *Organisation Studies,* **15**()5: 727–51.

Tuckman, A. (1995) Ideology, quality and TQM, in Wilkinson, A. and Willmott, H. (eds) *op. cit.,* pp. 54–81.

Tully, S. (1994) Stretch targets, *Fortune,* 14 November: 83–90.

UBS Phillips and Drew (1991) Building Societies Research: The Major Players, UBS Phillips and Drew Global Research Group, July.

Upham, M. (1980) The British Steel Corporation: retrospect and prospect, *Industrial Relations Journal,* **11**(3): 5–21.

Upham, M. (1990) Passages on the path to privatisation: the experience of British Steel, *Industrial Relations Journal,* **21**(3): 87–97.

Valentine, R. and Knights, D. (1997) TQM and BPR – can you spot the difference? *Personnel Review.* Forthcoming.

Van de Vliet, A. (1994) The Brent conversion, *Management Today,* March: 34–38.

Vogel, C. (1979) *Japan as Number One: Lessons For America,* Cambridge, MA: Harvard University Press.

Waldegrave, W. (1993) Charter packaging, *Local Government Management,* **1**(6): 10–11.

Waldman, D. (1994) The contributions of total quality management to a theory of work performance, *Academy of Management Review,* **19**(3): 510–36.

Walsh, K. (1990) Managing quality in the public sector, *Management Education and Development,* **21**(5): 394–400

Walsh, K. (1991) Quality and public services, *Public Administration,* **69**: 503–14.

Walsh, K. (1995) Quality through markets; the new public service management, in Wilkinson, A. and Willmott, H. (eds) *op. cit.* 1995a: 82–104.

Walker, J. W. (1992) *Human Resource Strategy,* New York: McGraw-Hill International.

Walker, R. (1992) Rank Xerox – management revolution, *Long Range Planning,* **25**(1): 9–21.

Walker, T. (1992) Creating quality improvement that lasts, *National Productivity Review,* Autumn, 473–8.

Walton, R. E. (1985) From control to commitment in the workplace, *Harvard Business Review,* **63**, March/April: 77–84.

Ward, D. (1993) Untitled, *Steel News,* 6 March: 63.

Waters, R. (1993) The unions step on board, *Financial Times,* 27 October: 14.

Watkins, J. and Bryce, V. (1992) HORATIO: *A Survey of Human Resources Ratios in the Retail Financial Services Sector,* Bristol: Bristol University/KPMG Management Consulting.

Watson, T. (1986) *Management, Organisation and Employment Strategy,* London: Routledge & Kegan Paul.

Watson, T. J. (1994) Management 'flavours of the month': their role in managers' lives, *International Journal of Human Resource Management*, **5**(4): 893–909.

Weatherly, K. and Tansik, D. (1993) Tactics used by customer-contact workers: effects of role stress, boundary spanning and control, *Industrial Journal of Service Industry Management*, **4**(3): 4–17.

Webb, J. (1995) Quality management and the management of quality, in Wilkinson, A. and Willmott, H. (eds) *op. cit.*1995a: 105–26.

Webb, J. (1996) Vocabularies of motive and the 'new' management, *Work, Employment and Society*, **10**(2): 251–71.

Wilkinson, A. (1992) The other side of quality: soft issues and the human resource dimension, *Total Quality Management*, **3**(3): 323–9.

Wilkinson, A. (1994) Managing human resources for quality, in Dale, B. G. (ed.) *Managing Quality*, 2nd edn, Hemel Hempstead: Prentice Hall, pp. 273–91.

Wilkinson, A (1995a) Towards HRM? A case study from banking, *Research and Practice in Human Resource Management*, **3**(1): 97–116.

Wilkinson, A. (1995b) Re-examining quality management, *Review of Employment Topics*, **3**(1): 187–211.

Wilkinson, A. (1996) Three roads to quality: variations in total quality management, in Storey, J. (ed.) *Blackwell Cases in Human Resource and Change Management*, Oxford: Blackwell: 173–89.

Wilkinson, A. and Ackers, P. (1995) When two cultures meet: new industrial relations at Japanco, *International Journal of Human Resource Management*, **6**(4): 849–71.

Wilkinson, A. and Willmott, H. (eds) (1995a) *Making Quality Critical: Studies in Organizational Change*, London: Routledge.

Wilkinson, A. and Willmott, H. (1995b) Total quality – asking critical questions, *Academy of Management Review*, **20**(4): 789–91.

Wilkinson, A. and Witcher, B. (1991) Fitness for use: barriers to full TQM in the UK, *Management Decision*, **29**(8): 44–9.

Wilkinson, A. and Marchington, M. (1994) TQM – instant pudding for the personnel function?, *Human Resource Management Journal*, **5**(1): 33–49.

Wilkinson, A., Allen, P. and Snape, E. (1991) TQM and the management of labour, *Employee Relations*, **13**(1): 24–31.

Wilkinson, A., Godfrey, G. and Marchington, M. (1997b) Bouquets, brickbats and blinkers: total quality management and employee involvement, *Organization Studies*.

Wilkinson, A., Marchington, M. and Dale, B. (1994a) Manufacturing more effective TQM, *Research and Practice in Human Resource Management*, **2**(1): 69–88.

Wilkinson, A., Redman, T. and Snape, E. (1993) *Quality and the Manager: An IM Report*, Corby: Institute of Management.

Wilkinson, A., Redman, T. and Snape, E. (1994b) The problems with quality management: the views of managers, *Total Quality Management*, **5**(6): 397–404.

Wilkinson, A., Redman, T. and Snape, E. (1995) New patterns of quality management in the UK, *Quality Management Journal*, **2**(2): 37–51.

Wilkinson, A., Redman, T. and Snape, E. (1996) Payment for customer service? in Storey, J. (ed.) *Blackwell Cases in Human Resource and Change Management*, Oxford: Blackwell, pp. 266–74.

Wilkinson, A., Redman, T. and Snape, E. (1997a) Employee involvement in the financial services sector: problems and pitfalls, *Journal of Retailing and Consumer Services*. Forthcoming.

Wilkinson, A., Marchington, M., Goodman, J. and Ackers, P. (1992) Total quality management and employee involvement, *Human Resource Management Journal*, **2**(4): 1–20.

Williams, A. L. (1993) Teesside Works – Total Quality Performance, unpublished MBA dissertation, University of Teesside.

Williams, A., Dobson, P. and Walters, M. (1991) *Changing Cultures*, 1st edn, London: Institute of Personnel Management.

Williams, A., Dobson, P. and Walters, M. (1993) *Changing Culture: New Organizational Approaches*, 2nd edn, London: Institute of Personnel Management.

Willmott, H. (1993) Strength is ignorance: slavery is freedom: managing cultures in modern organizations, *Journal of Management Studies*, **30**(4): 515–22.

Willmott, H. C. (1994) Business process reengineering and human resource management, *Personnel Review*, **23**(3): 34–6.

Wilson, D. (1992) *A Strategy for Change*, London: Routledge.

Witcher, B. (1993) *The adoption of total quality management in Scotland*. Centre for Quality and Organisational Change, Durham: Durham University Business School.

Witcher, B. (1995) The changing scale of total quality management, *Quality Management Journal*, Summer: 9–29.

Witcher, B. and Whyte, J. (1992) The adoption of total quality management in Northern England, Durham University Business School Occasional Paper Series.

Womack, J. P., Jones, D. T. and Roos, D. (1990) *The Machine that Changed the World*, New York: Macmillan.

Wood, M. (1994) Statistical methods for monitoring service processes, *International Journal of Service Industry Management*, **5**(4): 53–68.

Wood, S. and Peccei, R. (1995) Does total quality management make a difference to employee attitudes?, *Employee Relations*, **17**(3): 52–62.

Wrigley, N. (1994) After the store wars: towards a new era of competition in UK food retailing, *Journal of Retailing and Consumer Services*, **1**(1): 5–20.

Wynne, B. (1990) Leadership and excellence, *Management Decision*, **28**(1): 15–19.

Young, K. (1993) All change now, *Local Government Management*, **1**(6): 28–31.

Zairi, M., Letza, S. and Oakland, J. (1994) Does TQM impact on bottom line results?, *TQM Magazine*, **6**(1): 38–43.

Zellweger, M. (1993) Total Quality Management at British Steel Plc General Steels Teesside Works: Getting the Balance Right, unpublished MBA dissertation, University of Teesside.

Zeithaml, V., Parasuraman, A. and Berry, L. (1990) *Delivering Service Quality*, New York: The Free Press.

Index

A

Ackers, P. 34
Ackroyd, S. 162
Adams, R.J. 112
adult and community education
    (ACE) in Modern Metro case study
    101–3, 105–6
Ahlstrand, B.C. 57, 139
Aldi 145
Anderson Consulting 64, 183
Anthony, P. 162
appraisal in HRM cycle 42–3, 44
Argyll 144
Arthur, J.B. 38
Asda 144, 145
A.T. Kearney survey 65, 66
Athos, A. 23, 162
Atkinson, J. 118
Atkinson, P. 5
Aubrey, C. 4
Avis, B. 112

B

Bain, T. 112
Baldridge awards 163
Ball, J. 116
Bamber, G. 112
Bank, J. 6, 106
Barlow, G. 139
Beaumont, P.B. 38
Bedfordshire County Council 53
Bednar, D. 7, 8
Belohlav, J. 5

Bennington, J. 90, 91, 93–4
Berry, L.L. 28
Betti 184
Binney, G. 2, 4, 68
Birat, J.P. 110
Blackburn, R. 122
Blyton, P. 112
Bogan, C. 11
Boje, D.A. 9
Bolton report (1971) 165
Bosner, C.F. 30
Boston Consulting Group 38
Boulding, W. 28
Bowen, D. 9–10, 11, 27, 41, 43, 44–5, 52,
    54
Boxall, P. 38
Bradford study of TQM 65, 68–9
Brent Council 30
British Institute of Management 70
British Quality Association (BQM) 11
British Quality Foundation 30
British Rail 31
British Steel
    cyclical nature of business 110–11
    HRM in 112
    restructuring 109–10
    success of 109
    see also Teesside Works
Brockman, J. 30
Brown, C. 183
Bryce, V. 138
building societies
    case study see BuSoc

competition for 126–7
  interest cartel in 125–6
  and 'new' building societies 127
Building Societies Act (1986) 126
Building Societies Association (BSA) 125
Buley, T. 162
Burawoy, M. 158
Burns, T. 16
business process re-engineering (BPR)
  184–5, 187
BuSoc case study 128–37
  diversification 128
  employee involvement initiative
    131–7, 176, 177
    commercialisation 132–3
    employee reports 132–3
    information and consultation
      131–2
    joint consultation and negotiation
      council 131
    national minimum service
      standards 135
    paying for performance 133
    quality culture, creating 133–7
    team briefings 132
  HRM issues in 130
  management style 129
  managers, status of 129–30
  personnel managers in 130
  sales, emphasis on 129
  staffing policy 128–9
Butler, A.J. 30
Butler, D. 110
Buzzell, R. 62–3

C
Campbell, J. 111
Cannell, M. 164
Cappelli, P. 38, 50
Carlzon, J. 100
Caudron, S. 11
Caulkin, S. 186
Centre for Effective Organization study
  78
Champy, J. 184, 187
change agents in personnel departments
  53, 54, 55
Chartermarks 92
Chell, E. 44, 51, 162, 164
Chief Executive Officers in TQM study
  (USA) 78
Ciba-Geigy 68

Citizen's Charter 92, 95
citizenship and quality management in
  local government 105
Clarke, F. 29
Clarke, M. 94
Clarke-Hill, C. 144
Clinton, R.J. 54
Club Med 68
Cole, R. 21, 118
Collard, R. 23, 120
Colling, T. 51
communications
  in Superco case study 152–4
  in TQP at Teesside Works (British
    Steel) 121
compensation policies in HRM 40
competitive advantage 4, 176
  and quality 60
competitive success and quality 61
compulsory competitive tendering
  (CCT)
  in local government 91
  in Modern Metro case study 95
Conference Board study 77
Conservative government 90
continuous improvement 11, 13
contracting-out in local government 91,
  92
Cooper, C. 3, 34, 160
Coote, A. 6
costs and quality 63–4
Cronin, J.J. 28
Cronshaw, M. 63
Crosby, P.B. 3, 9, 10, 12, 14, 19, 48, 162
Crowdy, P. 162
Crozier, M. 16
Cruise O'Brien, R. 2, 3, 66
Crump, T. 20
customer care programmes
  in Modern Metro case study 96–7
  in Superco case study 152–4
Customer First Programme (Modern
  Metro) 96–7
customer focus/orientation 11, 12–13
customer satisfaction 34
  in food retailing 155–8
  feedback on 157–8
  in Richer Sounds case study 170–1
customer service index in Richer Sounds
  case study 170–1

D

Dale, B. 3, 5, 10, 23, 25, 30, 34, 114, 160
Davenport, T. 187
Davies, K. 30
Dawson, P. 6, 50, 51, 88
Deal, T. 161–2
Dean, J. 9–10, 11
Deblieux, M. 41
Delbridge, R. 50, 55, 179
Deloitte and Touche 5
Deming, W.E. 3, 10, 12, 18–19, 21–3,
    42–4, 46, 48–9, 162, 183
Dertouzos, M. 183
Devanna, M.A. 41
development in HRM cycle 42, 43–4
Dickson, M. 110
direct labour organisations (DLO) in
    local government 91
Dobson, J. 112
Docherty, C. 112
Donaldson, L. 114
Donnelly, M. 29
Dopson, S. 141
Drummond, G. 166
Drummond, H. 6, 44, 51, 162, 164, 166
Du Gay, P. 157
Duke, R. 145
Durham University Business School
    study of TQM 65, 67
Dyer, L. 138

E

Economist Intelligence Unit study 65, 68
Edgett, S. 27
education
    in Modern Metro case study 101–3,
        105–6
    in TQP at Teesside Works (British
        Steel) 113–14
Elcock, H. 90, 92
emotion management 156–7
employee involvement
    in BuSoc case study 131–7
        commercialisation 132–3
        employee reports 132–3
        information and consultation
            131–2
        joint consultation and negotiation
            council in 131
        national minimum service
            standards 135
        paying for performance 133

quality culture, creating 133–7
        team briefings 132
    in Superco case study 152–4
    in TQM 49–50
employee relations 48–52
employees
    attitudes in TQP at Teesside Works
        (British Steel) 120–3
    commitment of 34–5
        model of 47–8
        to quality management 81–2, 83
        in service industry 182
        in TQP at Teesside Works (British
            Steel) 121
        and work context 47–8
    in food retailing
        contradictory demands on 157, 179
        customers as agents of management
            157–8
        emotion management by 156–7
    turnover
        in Richer Sounds case study 168–9
        in Superco case study 150
    voice policies in HRM 40
employment assurances in HRM 40
Ennew, C. 126
Ensor, J. 166
environmental issues at Teesside Works
    (British Steel) 116–17
Ernst and Young 79
Eureka, W. 5
European Foundation for Quality
    Management 26, 122
Evans, J. 6, 11
Everett, T. 30
explicitness in model of employee
    commitment 47, 48

F

facilitator in personnel departments 53,
    55
failure mode, effect and criticality
    analysis (FMECA) 15
Federal Express 68
Federal Quality Institute 30
Feigenbaum, A.V. 8, 12, 17, 19
Felkins, P. 4
Fenwick, N. 90
Ferner, A. 51
Finance Act (1988) 133
financial incentives and performance
    162–3

financial services 125–41
Finley, R.M. 115
'fitness for use' concept 3, 10
Fitzgibbons, D.E. 11
Fletcher, C. 43
flexible specialisation 38
flight attendants 156
Flood, R.L. 30
Florida Light and Power Company 21
food retailing 142–59
    case study *see* Superco case study
    changing context of 144–6
    discount cards in 143
    growth in stores 144
    out-of-town developments 145
    quality management in 145–6
    staffing 144–5
Ford Motor Co. 183–4
Foucault, M. 157
Fowler, A. 56, 162
France: productivity in 64
Franz, H.W. 111, 112
Freathy, P. 144, 146
Fuller, L. 157–8

G
Gabor, A. 188
Gale, B. 62–3
Garvin, D. 7, 18, 19
Gaster, L. 30, 31
Geary, J.F. 49
General Accounting Office study 77–8
Giles, E. 56
Gill, J. 186
Glover, J. 34, 43
GMB union 95
Goffee, R. 141
Goldstein, S. 24
Grant, R.M. 13, 184
Green Bits 117
Greene, R. 185, 187
Greenland, S. 126
Gregory, A. 156
Griffin, R. 24
Gronoos, C. 28
Grundfos 68
Guest, D. 38, 51, 128, 131, 140
Guy, C. 145

H
Hackman, R. 7, 10, 80
Hall, G. 185

Hammer, M. 184, 187
Hammons, C. 30
Harkin, G. 91
Harris, D. 35, 45
Harrison, E. 156
Hart, C. 11, 163
Hartley, J. 112
Hasell, N. 109
Hatcher, L. 164
health and safety at Teesside Works
    (British Steel) 115–16
Heery, E. 51
Heller, R. 109
Hiam, A. 77
hidden persuaders in personnel
    departments 53, 54–5
Hill, S. 12–13, 15–16, 23–4, 34–5, 122,
    140, 161, 178–9, 185
Hinton, P. 30
Hitachi 21
Hochschild, A. 156
Home Care Service in Modern Metro
    case study 100–1
Hopfl, H. 161
Huczynski, A. 138, 139, 173, 186
human resource management 35
    cycle of 41–2
    strategic 37–41
    in Superco case study 149–52
    and TQM 3–4, 178–80
    workforce strategies 39–40

I
IBM 64, 144
ICL Product Distribution 68
Ilford Ltd 54
Imai, M. 13
improvement tools 14
Incomes Data Services 164
Industrial Relations Services 30, 31
Institute of Management study 65, 70–7
    quality management
        changes in 71, 72
        effects of 73, 76
        extent of 70–1
        implementing 71–5
        measurement of 73, 74
        success of 73, 75
    sample 70
Institute of Personnel and Development
    (IPD) 57
Institute of Personnel Management 52, 57

Institute of Quality Assurance 26
Institute of Training and Development
    (ITD) 57
internal contractor in personnel
    departments 53–4, 55
internal customer 3, 34
International Quality study of TQM
    79–80
Ishikawa, K. 2, 3, 12, 21, 22, 48

J
Jackson, M. 152
Jackson, S.E. 38
James, G. 47
Jamieson, P. 116
Japan
    productivity in 64
    TQM in 20–2
Japanese Engineering Standards 21
Japanese Management Association
    (JMA) 21
job design in HRM 39
    and employee commitment 47–8
Johanssen, H. 185
Johnson, G. 109
Juran, J. 3, 8, 10, 12, 14–15, 18, 20–2, 34
just-in-time (JIT) 25–6

K
Kano, N. 2, 13, 20–1
Kearney, A.T. 4
Keisler 47
Kelliher, C. 92
Kelly, J. 112
Kennedy, A. 161–2
Kessler, I. 45
Kirkpatrick, I. 6, 31
Knights, D. 187
Knutton, P. 9
Kochan, T. 138
Kolesar, P. 188
Komatsu 21
Kordupleski, R.E. 9
Krause, T. 115
Kuei, C. 5
Kwik Save 145

L
Labour Party 93
labour-management relations in HRM
    40
Lawler, E.E. 41, 43–5, 50, 52, 54, 183

lean production 38, 63–4
Legge, K. 162
Levitt, T. 16
Lewis, B. 155
life skills courses in Modern Metro case
    study 98, 101
Lillrank, P. 2, 13, 20–1
Lindsay, W. 6, 11
local government 88–108
    changing nature of 89–90
    competing models of quality in 91–4
        New Left 93
        New Managerialism 93–4
        New Right 91–2, 105, 183
    Modern Metro case study *see* Modern
    Metro
    quality management, alternative
        models of 104–7
        professionalism in 106–7
        tensions between 104–5
Lockheed Corporation 23
London Business School study 65, 66–7

M
Macey, R. 126
Maddux, G. 30
Madu, C.N. 5
Major, John 91
Malloch, H. 118
management
    commitment to quality management
        81–2, 83
    and culture of quality 35
    and employee commitment 34–5
    and organisational culture 36–7
        in HRM 39–40
    for radical change, and TQM 184
    and remuneration 161–5
    style
        in Richer Sounds case study
            168–70
        in TQP at Teesside Works (British
            Steel) 121
        in Superco case study 147
    recruitment 148–9
Marchington, M. 35, 51–2, 89, 130,
    138–40, 146, 156, 158
Mars, G. 156
Martin, J. 36
Martin Company 19
Martinez-Lucio, M. 6, 31
Matsushita Electrical Company 185

Mayer, J.C. 139
McGoldrick, P. 126
McKenna, S. 92
McKinlay, A. 38
Meager, N. 118
measurement systems 14
Meyerson, D. 36
Miles 38
Miller, C. 4
Millward, N. 57
Mintel Retail Intelligence 143, 144
Mintzberg, H. 165
Modern Metro case study 94–104
    adult and community education
        101–3
    Home Care Service in 100–1
    quality assurance in EHTS 98–9
    quality management in 96–8
        in EHTS 99
    quality service teams 97, 100–1
    structure and policies 94–5
Mohrman, S. 78
Moores, B. 155
Morgan, C. 88, 105–7
Morgan, J. 30
Morris, J. 112
Multiple Food Retailers' Employers
    Association (MFREA) 152
Mumford, J. 162
Murgatroyd, S. 88, 105–7

N

National Society of Quality Circles 23
Netto 145
New Left model of quality in local
    government 93
New Managerialism model of quality in
    local government 93–4
New Public Management 92
New Right model of quality in local
    government 91–2, 105, 183
Nissan Motors UK 68
North-eastern US study 78–9

O

Oakland, J.S. 1–2, 5–6, 12–13, 15, 34–5,
    50, 120, 160, 162–4
Ogbonna, E. 36, 156–7, 161, 164
Olian, J. 164
Oliver, J. 186
Oliver, N. 47, 64, 172
organisational culture in TQM 14, 36–7

Osterman, P. 183
Oswald, S. 112
Ouchi, W. 23, 162
Overman, S. 110, 112

P

Paddon, M. 91–3
Painter, J. 92
Palmer, G. 6
Parasuraman, A. 8, 28
Parker, M. 186
Parkinson, S.T. 27
Pascale, R. 8, 16, 23, 162, 183, 186
payment-by-results (PBR) and
    performance 163–4
Pendleton, A. 31
performance
    expectations in HRM 39
    management of
        in HRM cycle 42–4
        and rewards 162–3
        and TQM 45–6
personnel departments 52–8
    assessment of 57–8
    as change agents 53, 54, 55
    as facilitator 53, 55
    future of 56–7
    as hidden persuaders 53, 54–5
    as internal contractor 53–4, 55
    operational role of 52–3
    profile of 52–3
    strategic role of 52–3
Peterborough Priority Services 54
Peters, T. 1, 8, 16, 28, 100, 161, 167–9, 183
Pfeffer, J. 179, 188
Pfeffer, N. 6
Phillips, L. 63
Pickard, J. 30, 31
Piore, M.J. 1, 38
'plan do check action' concept 10
Plunkett, J.J. 10
Pollitt, C. 29, 31, 88, 107–8
Porter, M. 2, 4, 38, 143
Powell, T.C. 11, 78–9, 80, 124, 178
private markets in local government 91
private service sector in local government
    105–6
process orientation 13
Procter, D. 113–14, 116
Profit Impact Market Strategy Associates
    (PIMS) 61–3

public sector
  quasi-markets in 29–30
  TQM in 29–32, 177, 182–3
Public Services Privatisation Research
  Unit 92
publicity in model of employee
  commitment 47, 48
Purcell, J. 38, 57

Q
quality
  and competitive advantage 60
  and competitive success 61
  and costs 63–4
  defined 7–9
  TQM *see* total quality management
quality assurance in Modern Metro case
  study 98–9, 106
  in ACE 102–3
quality circles 21, 23–4, 25
quality control 10–11
Quality Control Research Group (Japan)
  21
quality customer service in Richer
  Sounds case study 167–8
quality function deployment (QFD) 15
quality improvement teams in TQP at
  Teesside Works (British Steel) 114–15
quality initiatives in BuSoc case study
  133–7
quality management 177
  in BuSoc case study 138–41
    criticisms of 138–9
    staff reaction to 139–40
  difficulties with 81–6
    bureaucracy of 85–6
    commitment 81–2
    company reorganisation 84
    recession 83
    resources for 82, 83
    seen as fad 84–5
    short-term attitudes 82–3
  in food retailing 145–6
  Institute of Management *see under*
  Institute of Management Study
  in local government 91
    alternative models 104–7
    professionalism in 106–7
    tensions between 104–5
  in Modern Metro case study 96–8
    in EHTS 99

and rewards 164
and transformational change 183–6
quality of working life (QWL) 10
quality service teams in Modern Metro
  case study 97, 100–1
quasi-markets in public sector 29–30

R
radical change management and TQM
  184
Rafaelli, A. 158
Raffio, T. 11
Rainie, S. 165
Rajan, A. 126
Ramsay, H. 138, 186
Redman, T. 43, 123, 141
Rees, C. 179
Reeves, C. 7, 8
Regan, W. 26
Reich, M. 183
Reichheld, F.F. 26
relative perceived quality 61–2
remuneration and rewards
  in corporate culture 161–5
  in HRM cycle 42, 44–5
  and performance appraisal 162–3
  in Richer Sounds case study 169,
  170–1
return on investment (RoI) and quality
  61, 62
return on sales (RoS) and quality 61–2
revocability in model of employee
  commitment 47, 48
Richer Sounds case study 166–71
  employee turnover 168–9
  human resource approach 169
  management style 168–70
  quality customer service in 167–8, 176
  remuneration 169, 170–1, 178
  success of 166
'right first time' concept 3, 10
Ritchie, J. 165
Roberts, I. 165, 166, 168
Robinson, O. 156
Robinson, T. 144
Rogovsky, N. 38, 50
Rolls Royce 23
Rosen, B. 122
Ross, T. 164
Ryan, E. 5
Rynes, S. 164

S

Sabel, C. 1, 38
Sackman, S. 161
Safeway 142, 144
Sainsburys 142, 143, 144, 145
Salaman, G. 157
Salancik 47
Sanderson, I. 29, 88, 89, 92, 93, 106
Sasser, W.E. 26
Scase, R. 141
Schein, E. 36, 37, 161, 184
Schilit, W. 77
Schlesinger, L. 163
Schmidt, R. 145
Schneider, B. 27, 28
Scholes, K. 109
Scholey, R. 116
Schonberger, R. 26
Schuler, R.S. 35, 38, 45
Scott, M. 165, 172
Seddon, J. 160
selection in HRM cycle 42
Sellers, P. 164
senior management development
    programme (SMDP)
    in Modern Metro case study 97–8, 101
    in Superco case study 149
Sensenbrenner, J. 31
services
    heterogeneity of 27–8
    inseparability of 27
    intangibility of 27
    perishability of 28
    TQM in 26–9, 181–2
        measurement of 28–9
Sewell, G. 50, 157
Shadur, M. 183
Shamir, B. 158
Shewart, W.A. 18–19
Siehl, C. 27
Sisson, K. 38, 167, 183
Skelcher, C. 91
Slaughter, J. 186
small firms 160–75
    case study *see* Richer Sounds
    informality in 165
    quality culture in 165–6
Smirich, L. 162
Smith, D. 126–7
Smith, G. 143
Smith, S. 156
Smith, V. 157–8

Snape, E. 34, 41, 42, 43, 119, 123, 127,
    138, 164
Snow 38
Sonnenfeld, J.A. 38
Spain: productivity in 64
Sparks, L. 144, 146, 155
Speed, R. 126–7
Stalker, G. 16
Starkey, K. 38
statistical process control (SPC) 21
Steingard, D.S. 11
Stern, D. 183
Stewart, J. 88, 94
Stewart, R. 141
Storey, J. 38, 42, 52, 58, 90, 138, 161, 167
strategic purchasing in TQP at Teesside
    Works (British Steel) 118
stretch management 186
Superco case study 146–55
    communications in 152–4
    conditions of employment 152
    customer care programmes 152–4,
        176
    employee involvement 152–4, 179
    human resource policies 149–52
    labour turnover 150
    management in 147
        recruitment 148–9
    organisation structure 146–8
    training 150–1, 153
    union membership 146–7
supervisors: commitment to quality
    management 81–2
supplier management at Teesside Works
    (British Steel) 117–19
Swiss, J.E. 30

T

Tansik, D. 142, 157–8
Taylor, M. 90, 91, 93–4
Taylor, S.A. 28
teamwork 11
Teas, R.K. 28
Teesside Works (British Steel) 109–24
    competitive strategy of 111
    investment 110
    products 110
    restructuring 109–10
    total quality performance (TQP) at
        111–15, 180, 181
        efficiency in 117
        employee attitudes 120–3, 177

environment in 116–17
evaluation of 115–23
hard objectives of 111–12, 176
health and safety in 115–16
pay incentives 178
quality improvement teams 114–15
soft objectives of 112, 176
supplier management 117–19
training in 113–14
zero accident initiative in 116
Terry, F.R. 31
Tesco 142, 143, 144, 145
Thompson, W. 93
total quality management
applicability of 181–3
in British Steel *see* Teesside Works
(British Steel)
built in 3
challenges for 177–8
company-wide quality 24–6
defined 2–3
development and principles 9–14
effectiveness of 180–1
evaluation of 65–80
UK studies 65–77
US studies 77–80
future of 32–3
hard aspects of 14–15
as innovation 2
and organisational change 34–59
origins 17–20
and performance management 45–6
soft aspects of 15
as transformational change 183–6
in western firms 22–32
total quality performance (TQP) at
Teesside Works (British Steel) *see*
Teesside Works
Toyota Motor Company 21, 63
trade unions
commitment to quality management
81–2
at Teesside Works (British Steel) 180
and TQM 51
Trades Union Congress 31, 51, 178
training
in Superco case study 150–1, 153
in TQP at Teesside Works (British
Steel) 113–14
Tuckman, A. 21, 22–3, 24, 91
Tully, S. 186

U
UBS Phillips and Drew 127
Union of Japanese Scientists and
Engineers (JUSE) 21, 22
Union of Shop, Distributive and Allied
Workers (USDAW) 146
UNISON 95
United Kingdom
A.T. Kearney survey 65, 66
Bradford study 65, 68–9
Durham University Business School
study 65, 67
Economist Intelligence Unit study 65,
68
Institute of Management study 65,
70–7
London Business School study 65,
66–7
TQM evaluation studies 65–77
United States
Centre for Effective Organization
study 78
Conference Board study 77
General Accounting Office study 77–8
International Quality study 79–80
North-eastern US study 78–9
productivity in 64
TQM evaluation studies 77–80
Upham, M. 112

V
Valentine, R. 187
Van de Vliet, A. 30
Vogel, C. 23
volition in model of employee
commitment 47, 48
Voss, C. 2, 3, 66

W
Wageman, R. 7, 10, 80
Waldman, D. 46
Walker, J.W. 37–8
Walker, T. 44, 164
Walsh, K. 29, 30, 31, 32, 91, 92, 104–5
Walton, R.E. 38, 48, 180
Ward, D. 111
Waterman, R. 1, 8, 28, 161, 167–9, 183
Waters, R. 112
Watkins, J. 138
Watson, T. 128, 172, 181
Weatherly, K. 157–8
Webb, J. 6, 50, 88

Wells, D. 126
Whittle, S. 186
Whyte, J. 2, 67
Wilkinson, A. 1–4, 6, 10–13, 16, 20, 70, 81, 179, 185–6, 188
    on financial services 127, 130, 134, 138, 140
    on food retailing 156–7
    on HRM 34–5, 49, 51–2
    on local government 88
    on small firms 161, 163, 168
    on Teesside Works (British Steel) 120, 122–3
Wilkinson, B. 50, 157
Williams, A. 36, 111
Williams, R. 56
Willmott, H. 6, 10, 11, 20, 171, 173
Witcher, B. 2, 6, 67
Womack, J.P. 1, 38, 63

Wood, M. 3
Wood, S. 164
Workplace Industrial Relations Survey (WIRS) 57, 61
Wright, M. 126
Wrigley, N. 145
Wynne, B. 126, 140

Y
Young, K. 91

Z
Zairi, M. 68–9
Zeithaml, V. 28
Zellweger, M. 111, 117
zero accident initiative in in TQP at Teesside Works (British Steel) 116
'zero defects' concept 10, 19, 26